D1282306

Form and Meaning in the Novels of John Fowles

Form and Meaning in the Novels of John Fowles

by
Susana Onega

U·M·I Research Press

Ann Arbor / London

Copyright © 1989
Susana Onega Jaén
All rights reserved

Produced and distributed by
UMI Research Press
an imprint of
University Microfilms Inc.
Ann Arbor, Michigan 48106

Library of Congress Cataloging in Publication Data

Onega Jaen, Susana.
Form and meaning in the novels of John Fowles / by Susana
Onega.
    p. cm—(Challenging the literary canon)
    Bibliography: p.
    Includes index.
    ISBN 0-8357-1949-9 (alk. paper)
    1. Title. II. Series.
PR6056.085Z794   1989
823'.914—dc19   89-4700
                                                      CIP

British Library CIP data is available.

To Francisco, Jorge, and Alberto

The poet is a light and winged and holy thing, and there is no invention in him until he has been inspired and is out of his senses, and reason is no longer in him: no man, while he retains that faculty, has the oracular gift of poetry.

(Plato, *Ion* 15)

Contents

Preface

I gratefully acknowledge the receipt of a traveling grant from the Comité Conjunto Hispano Norteamericano, which helped me travel to the United States in 1986 in order to gather material for this book.

I should like to thank the British Council for financing the coming of John Fowles to the 10th A.E.D.E.A.N. Conference in Zaragoza, thus allowing me to get to know the writer personally and to interview him.

The following individuals helped me in various ways: Prof. J. Hillis Miller read the manuscript and encouraged me to publish it. Edward D. Ruiz provided information from Yale University Library.

My thanks are also due to the staff of the Department of English and German Philology of the University of Zaragoza, especially to Tim Bozman, who read the manuscript and helped me make true his motto *finis coronat opus,* to Francisco Collado, who shared his specialist knowledge of myth criticism with me, to the other specialists of English Literature, and to my students for lively discussion and support.

Finally, my thanks are due to the editors of the *Revista Canaria de Estudios Ingleses* for their kind permission to reprint in the third chapter of this book aspects of my article "Form and Meaning in *The French Lieutenant's Woman.*"

Introduction

In the Preface to *The Contemporary English Novel,* Malcolm Bradbury and David Palmer synthesize the situation of post-war English fiction, rejecting the widely held view of that moment that the "writing of this period (was) a late, lowered and unambitious phase in the long history of the English novel" (p. 7). According to Bradbury and Palmer, the explanation for this current belief was a consequence of two major factors: firstly, the tendency to see post-war English fiction in the shadow of Modernist writing, and secondly, the fact that the most influential critics writing in the 1960s were American, and they mention three main general surveys of post-war English fiction: Frederick R. Karl's *A Reader's Guide to the Contemporary English Novel* (1959), James Gindin's *Post-War British Fiction: New Accents and Attitudes* (1962), and Rubin Rabinowitz's *The Reaction against Experiment in the English Novel: 1950–1960* (1967).

As the title of Rabinovitz's book suggests, these American critics tended to assume "the isolation of contemporary English fiction from the main developments of the novel elsewhere, and hence its relative stagnation" *(The Contemporary English Novel,* p. 9). These three general surveys were all published in the decade of the 1960s, a fact which may account for the lack of perspective necessary to detect minor alternative trends to the major realistic trend we know now as "Movement" fiction. This lack of historical perspective prevented the critics from duly appreciating the work of such writers as Lawrence Durrell, Malcolm Lowry, Samuel Beckett, and William Golding, who had begun their writing careers before the war but who significantly went on afterwards, developing a sort of fiction which may provisionally be included under the general label of "experimentalism."

In "Beckett, Lowry and the Anti-Novel" (p. 89), Ronald Binns makes the same point, insisting on the fact that "the conventional account of the development of the post-war English novel as a movement from pre-war experimentalism to post-war realism has tended to displace or to overlook a good number of writers of experimental stamp—like William Golding or Lawrence Durrell—

who are recognized in critical discussion to be of importance, but held to lie outside the mainstream."

Now, the state of affairs reflected in the above-quoted texts cannot be accounted for simply by pointing to their early dates of publication and to the American nationality of their authors. The books by Karl, Gindin, and Rabinovitz inevitably reflect the influence of an orchestrated campaign in England designed by the mass media to establish the reputation of one particular line both in poetry and fiction, early labeled as *The Movement,* which had a parallel in the so-called "angry" and "kitchen sink" theater of the fifties.

On 1 October 1954, an anonymous leading article entitled "In the Movement," later known to have been written by the literary editor of *The Spectator,* J. D. Scott, appeared in this London periodical. In Blake Morrison's words *(The Movement: Poetry and Fiction of the Nineteen-Fifties,* p. 1), "The article drew attention to the emergence of a group of writers who, it claimed, represented something new in British literature and society. The 'modern' Britain of the 1950s was, the article argued, 'a changed place.' Now it was becoming clear that the 'literary scene' had also been transformed. Literary taste had begun to move in new directions." The appearance of two poetry anthologies in 1955 and 1956 respectively, *Poets of the 1950s,* edited by D. J. Enright, and *New Lines,* edited by Robert Conquest, enlarged the importance of the new movement, while the B.B.C. Third Programme devoted a space to the reading of Movement poetry, and also found an echo in periodicals like *Encounter, The New Statesman,* and *The Times Literary Supplement.*

As Blake Morrison points out and Piedad Frías has amply demonstrated in her unpublished study *Aproximación al estudio de* Lucky Jim: *la obra en su entorno socio-cultural,* the establishment of such novelists and poets as Kingsley Amis, John Braine, Alan Sillitoe, John Wain, David Storey, Philip Larkin, D. J. Enright, Robert Conquest, John Holloway, Elizabeth Jennings, and Thom Gunn was the result, to a great extent, of a conscious campaign launched by the mass media. This effort by the media was stimulated by the social and political situation in England as created by the post-war depression and the compensating euphoria of the first Labour Party in power and of the Welfare State.

If Karl, Gindin, Rabinovitz, and many other critics of the sixties failed to recognize and duly appreciate the importance of a powerful experimentalist current in English post-war fiction it was no doubt because, for political and social reasons, it seemed appropriate to support and develop the one specific literary line which, by holding a concrete class viewpoint (that of the lower-middle class), could easily be identified with the "coming" class and thus with a spirit of change in post-war English society. This spirit of change in turn reflected certain shifts in power and social structure.

The well-known prejudice of Movement writers against intellectualism, the established culture, and cosmopolitanism in general, which led detractors to accuse them of philistinism and "little Englandism," angered and alarmed the older generation of writers. Critics began to speak of England's abandonment of the European mainstream, characterized by the *nouveau roman* in France.

Two decades have elapsed since the publication of the first comprehensive studies of the contemporary English novel, and the perspective thus gained and the work of writers such as Frank Kermode, Bernard Bergonzi, David Lodge, A. S. Byatt, and Malcolm Bradbury enables us to discern at least two other strands of development (of different scope) at work in the fifties, coexisting with the realistic class-conscious writing of the Movement. There was, firstly, what Bradbury and Palmer have called "revival of the social and liberal novel" (p. 12), which has been described in similar terms by Bergonzi *(The Situation of the Novel,* pp. 35–55), and which includes such novels as Angus Wilson's *Hemlock and After* (1952) and William Cooper's *Scenes of Provincial Life* (1950). Secondly, there was a more powerful trend of writers of "quite a different temper, some of them of very great importance (who) were bringing a much more fabulous and speculative mood into post-war English fiction" (Bradbury et al., ibid., p. 12). Bradbury and Palmer mention here Muriel Spark, William Golding, Iris Murdoch, Doris Lessing, and Anthony Burgess, and they add, "In many cases, their best work was to come after the 1950s, and some of their most experimental writing has been their most recent" (ibid., p. 13).

Bradbury and Palmer do not state the characteristics of the group of writers they say have created a revival of the "social and liberal" novel, though we can easily imagine they refer to the literary trend which originated with F. R. Leavis and spread with the help of *Scrutiny* from Cambridge in the 1940s. To the two writers Bradbury and Palmer propose here, Wilson and Cooper, we could add Margaret Drabble, who, as a good pupil of Professor Leavis, seems to be the most contumacious neo-realist with a liberal bent and social concern in England today.

But this liberal trend stemming from Cambridge and the neo-realist trend originating in Oxford around the Amis-Larkin-Wain troika in the 1940s can be separated only with the greatest of difficulties. Both have common roots in the literary generation of the 1930s that Isherwood described in *Christopher and His Kind.* Caught in between the two World Wars and too young to participate in either of them, these writers of the 1930s produced a series of novels about the worlds of the public school and Oxbridge, such as Max Beerbohm's *Zuleika Dobson,* Evelyn Waugh's *Decline and Fall* and *Brideshead Revisited,* Christopher Isherwood's *Lions and Shadows,* and Martin Green's *Children of the Sun.* In these works, the public school and/or the university were recurrently employed as the symbolic microcosm of a sick society in need of revolutionary change (Spender, *The Thirties and after: Poetry, Politics, People). Lucky Jim,* the first "Campus" novel, is also the last "Varsity" novel, as these novels were called in the thirties before the new American term was coined and imported to England (Shaw, "The Role of the University in Modern English Fiction").

Understandably, due perhaps to an excess of modesty, Bradbury and Palmer "forget" to mention in their classification this important trend in the contemporary English novel, in the materialization of which Bradbury himself has played a pioneering role, from his *Eating People Is Wrong* and *The History Man* to *The Rates of Exchange*. Other well-known Campus novels to be mentioned are Howard Jakobson's *Coming from Behind*, Robertson Davies' *The Rebel Angel*, C. P. Snow's *The Masters*, Alison Lurie's *Love and Friendship* and *The War between the Tates*, Thomas Hinde's *High*, and David Lodge's *Changing Places, The British Museum Is Falling Down*, and *Small World*.

Regarding the other "more fabulous and experimental" trend mentioned by Bradbury and Palmer, we must also make several refinements. First, they classify under one single label what may best be considered as two parallel trends with distinctive traits, though, admittedly, with important connections: the tendency towards the fabulous and the fantastic, and the tendency towards formal experimentation. To trace the origin of these two we must again go back to the thirties and forties: novels such as *War in Heaven* and *The Place of the Lion* by Charles Williams, C. S. Lewis's *Out of the Silent Planet, A Voyage to Venus*, and *That Hideous Strength*, J. R. R. Tolkien's *The Hobbit* and *The Lord of the Rings*, and T. H. White's *The Once and Future King* show the vitality in the literature of the thirties, forties, and fifties of the traditional or "romance" fantasy fiction, continued today in the novels of Richard Adams and John Christopher.

This leaves us with a third "experimental trend" within which easily fit the five writers mentioned by Bradbury and Palmer: Muriel Spark, William Golding, Iris Murdoch, Doris Lessing, and Anthony Burgess, as well as Lawrence Durrell, Malcolm Lowry, and Samuel Beckett, whom Bradbury and Palmer mention as precursors of this tendency. But here again more subtle distinctions may be drawn: Beckett, Lowry, and Golding may be said to form a subgroup of writers with strong traits inherited from Modernism and from existentialism, a philosophy which also suffuses the work of John Fowles and Iris Murdoch. Of the latter we can say that she is the first novelist who has consciously tried to offer a more hopeful alternative to the existential void, while John Fowles's existentialism also tends to be hopeful.

However, despite all these groupings we must guard against being led to believe that the experimental and/or fantastic, and the neo-realistic and social-liberal trends are all simple, univocal developments without important and frequent criss-crossings. Even such clearly "experimental" writers as, say, John Fowles and Anthony Burgess may be found to have interesting connections with the Movement fiction of the 1950s, as can be seen in two of their novels, *The Collector* and *A Clockwork Orange*, published respectively in 1963 and 1962.

The protagonist of *The Collector,* Frederick Clegg, as well as the gang of psychopaths in *A Clockwork Orange,* are drawn on the pattern of the inarticulate and aggressive working-class anti-hero characteristic of the "angry" fiction of the fifties. From the apparently harmless and funny Lucky Jim to the dangerous psychopaths in the novels of Fowles and Burgess there is only a turn of the screw: all of them go back to the prototype James Dean made into a symbol of rebellion for a whole generation of "angry young men."

On the other hand, realism-biased Campus novelists like David Lodge also show in their latest fiction a decided bent towards formal experimentation which links them with the most experimental writers. We may sum up the situation by saying that the contemporary English novel in general has been undergoing a steady evolution from the reaction against experimentalism in the fifties to a new form of experimentation which differs in practice from one writer to another.

No doubt, one further reason why critics in the sixties had difficulty in recognizing the real importance of experimental writing in the fifties and early sixties might have been the fact that these experimental writers did not form a clear-cut, straightforward movement or generation in the sense Movement writers were felt to do, sharing aims, attitudes, and poetic faith, for all their disclaimers. In fact, the writing of each novelist mentioned by Bradbury and Palmer as belonging to the "experimentalist" trend shows utterly subjective, individual, and divergent traits. We only have to compare the work of Muriel Spark to William Golding's, or that of Doris Lessing to Iris Murdoch's, to see that these writers do not share characteristic features applicable to all in the same measure. Furthermore, even the individual careers of several of these writers have sometimes taken unexpected turns, which makes their labeling even more problematic (as happens, for instance, with Doris Lessing from a comparison of her first novels, *The Golden Notebook* and *The Grass Is Singing,* to her later *The Summer before the Dark* and *The Memoirs of a Survivor*). Indeed, if there is one single trait shared by all the experimental English writers of the last twenty-five years, it is a common concern with the "craft of fiction," that is, a preoccupation with the nature of fiction and reality which characteristically takes the form of an exploration of a theory of fiction through the practice of writing fiction.

The nineteenth-century realist novel rested on the assumption that the external world could be described univocally, that the writer could draw a faithful picture of nature which would easily be recognized by everybody else as such. The contention of Modernism in the early twentieth century was that it was impossible to describe an objective world because the observer is conditioned by his senses and always distorts the observed, but, in Heisenberg's words, "one could at least describe, if not a *picture* of nature, then a picture of one's *relation* to nature" (Waugh, *Metafiction: The Theory and Practice of Self-*

Conscious Fiction, p. 3). Contemporary self-reflexive writing goes a step further by stressing the uncertainty even of this process.

Again, as Patricia Waugh explains (ibid., p. 10), we see in retrospect the eighteenth- and nineteenth-century hero trying to integrate in a compact social structure, while we view the early twentieth-century Modernist hero as constantly turning his back on society, and struggling to assert his individuality and objective autonomy, thus casting the first shadows on the solidity and subjective reality of this society. The contemporary hero that emerges in the late fifties and sixties seems to assert in an even more thorough sense that reality and history are provisional, that they are simply a series of alternative constructions as artificial and impermanent as fiction itself.

Critics have coined a variety of terms to describe this new type of self-conscious writing: Raymond Federman's "surfiction" (1975), Ronald Binn's "anti-novel" (1979), Robert Scholes's "fabulation" (1967), and William H. Gass's "metafiction" (1970) are among the most currently used, together with such others as "the introverted novel," "irrealism," and "the self-begetting novel." For all their differences and divergent emphases, all these terms point to the basic concern of the contemporary novel with fictionality itself. Making hers William H. Gass's term, Patricia Waugh defines "metafiction" as "a term given to fictional writing which self-consciously and systematically draws attention to its status as an artifact in order to pose questions about the relationships between fiction and reality." And she adds, "In providing a critique of their own methods of construction, such writings not only examine the fundamental structure of narrative fiction, they also explore the possible fictionality of the world outside the literary fictional text" (ibid., p. 2).

This seems to be the basic quality of the dilemma confronting the contemporary experimental novel, the realization that the world as such cannot be "represented," that

> in literary fiction it is, in fact, possible only to "represent" the *discourses* of that world. Yet, if one attempts to analyse a set of linguistic relationships using those same relationships as the instruments of analysis, language soon becomes a "prisonhouse" from which the possibility of escape is remote. . . . In novelistic practice this results in writing which consistently displays its conventionality, which explicitly and overtly lays bare its condition of artifice, and which thereby explores the problematic relationship between life and fiction. (ibid., pp. 3–4)

William Gass has fittingly synthesized the essence of the dilemma confronting all art: "In every art two contradictory impulses are in a state of Manichean war: the impulse to communicate and so to treat the medium of communication as a means and the impulse to make an artifact out of the materials and so to treat the medium as an end" (Waugh, ibid., p. 15).

As Patricia Waugh aptly remarks, "The expression of this tension is present in much contemporary writing but is the *dominant* function in the texts defined here as metafictional" (p. 15). The desire to communicate and the opposed impulse to make an artifact out of their medium are the two extreme poles between which the metafictional writers move. Thus, metafiction may be understood as a mere label covering a vast rank of fictions, from those which tend to sacrifice intelligibility in favor of artistic form to those whose self-reflexiveness is limited by the desire to communicate an intelligible message. Roughly speaking, American fiction has tended to fit into the first half of the spectrum, British fiction into the second half. Within this second half, John Fowles's novels occupy a central position.

The contradictory impulses described by William Gass as "the necessity to communicate and the desire to make an artifact out of the medium" describe the tension at work in the novels by John Fowles. When asked about his early writing, Fowles said to Mark Amory ("Tales Out of School," p. 34), "I tried to scribble a bit at Oxford, but wasn't serious until 1954," and when he first went to a publisher, Jonathan Cape, with *The Collector* in 1963 and was asked if there were any more manuscripts, Fowles answered that there were "about twelve, but only two or three completed" (Amory, ibid., p. 34). Busily writing drafts and rejecting them himself in the 1950s, then, John Fowles must be seen as originally belonging to and stemming from the same literary ferment that gave way to the revival of realism in post-war English fiction, a fact Fowles himself has further acknowledged by admitting to Lorna Sage ("John Fowles," p. 33) the constant pressure on his writing of what he has called the "crushing sort of [English] realistic tradition." On the other hand, he has described his university training in French literature and his later experience as a teacher, as well as his wide reading of contemporary French criticism, as a source of strain, "an opposed pull [between French and English literary traditions, which can be seen] at work in the tragi-comedy of the class battle in *The Collector*" (Sage, ibid., p. 31).

The aim of the present research may be synthesized as the desire to show the specific way in which John Fowles solves this tension between realism—or the necessity to communicate a coherent message—and experimentalism—or the irresistible impulse to transform the medium into a literary artifact. As I hope to show in the analyses of his novels, John Fowles consistently has recourse to the use of metafictional mechanisms to release this tension, and specifically to one major metafictional device: parody or literary inversion.

Readers of the novels of John Fowles have often stressed his protean quality, his astounding capacity to create different styles according to the different requirements of subject matter in every novel; they have also often pointed out the fertility of his imagination and his rare ability to blend personal experience with fantasy, giving his novels a mythical scope. Indeed, *The Collector, The Magus, The French Lieutenant's Woman, Daniel Martin, Mantissa,* and *A*

Maggot are all, in a sense, very different novels, yet all of them bear the mark of their creator. For all their stylistic differences these novels show striking formal and thematic coincidences, so striking that, rather than different, they appear to be remarkably complementary. The complementarity is similar to that offered by the collection of short stories entitled *The Ebony Tower*. In fact, John Fowles had wanted to call this collection *Variations,* but was prevented from doing so by his publisher, who could not see the point in choosing such an irrelevant title for the series. In an interview broadcast by B.B.C. 2 within *The Book Programme*, Robert Robinson ("Giving the Reader a Choice: A Conversation with John Fowles," p. 584) asked Fowles what the significance of his intended title was. Fowles's answer ran as follows: "I think they were variations on the books I had previously done. I wrote them all in two or three months, and I certainly didn't think, 'I'll do a variation on some past story,' but that is how they came out."

We could enlarge this explanation by saying that the short stories within *The Ebony Tower* series not only work as variations on *The Collector, The Magus,* and *The French Lieutenant's Woman,* they also foreshadow his later novels; suffice it to compare "The Enigma" to *A Maggot.* What is more, both the short stories and the novels may be said to complement each other both thematically and formally, as would the musical variations in a symphony, forming an artistic whole.

No doubt, the publisher's reluctance to accept Fowles's proposed title for the series sprang from overlooking one basic axiom of modern deconstructivism, the realization that, as Saussure showed once and for all, language depends on "difference," since "it consists of a structure of distinctive oppositions which make up its basic economy" (Norris, *Deconstruction: Theory and Practice,* p. 32). Drawing on Saussure and Derrida, we can see today the literary text as a linguistic artifact, a polymorphous entity capable of endlessly yielding alternative interpretations and also endlessly subject to alternative rewriting. This is the message John Fowles wanted us to grasp by calling his series *Variations;* that is, alternative writings of one unique, polymorphous text, covering the range of his personal and literary experience. This is precisely the subject matter of his fifth novel, *Mantissa,* and it is in this sense that his six novels—and the short stories—may be said to complement and reflect each other.

As I show in my analysis of the novels, John Fowles's six full-length novels must be viewed as complementary texts offering alternative readings of the same basic ideas. All of them reflect and discuss Fowles's major concern, human freedom, both in relation to the self and to society. The relation of the individual with society is recurrently expressed in terms of a power-bondage relationship, while the question of human freedom in relation to the self is often presented as a hero's quest for maturity, seen from a particularly optimistic existentialist perspective. From the point of view of formal experimentation, each novel consciously assumes and parodies one—or more—particular novel-writing convention, but as we move from *The Collector* to *A Maggot* we also move from a fiction that is predominantly realistic to a much more experimental and specifically metafictional kind of fiction. This may be one reason why, after the success of *The French Lieutenant's Woman,* John Fowles has failed to receive much enthusiastic praise from professional realism-biased critics in England.

Although Fowles pointed out in a recent interview that he "wouldn't say now that I am any longer an existentialist in the social sense, the cultural sense" (Onega, "Fowles on Fowles," p. 64), he admitted at the same time that "when I was younger, when I was well below half of my present age, we all were (existentialists) in England at that time . . . we were on our knees before Camus and Sartre and French existentialism. . . . I quite like the philosophy (existentialism) as a structure in a novel and in a sense I use it."

As is well known, Fowles wrote the first drafts of *The Magus* in the early 1950s, before the publication of *The Collector*. Although it was his first full-scale manuscript, he continued almost obsessively to rewrite it for more than two decades, discarding draft after draft. He finally published a first version in 1964 and a wholly revised one in 1977. Fowles's obsessive rewriting of *The Magus* may be accounted for by its enormous range and scope, for in it Fowles was unconsciously trying to synthesize his whole vision of the world. Indeed, it is no exaggeration to say that he has spent the rest of his literary career trying to rewrite *The Magus,* for, with its neat threefold structure of the (existentialist) hero's quest for maturity, *The Magus* may be said to constitute the nucleus of the writer's thought around which the other novels grow.

Talking about the way in which his novels originate, Fowles has often explained that they usually come out of a single image, "something like a cinema 'still,' capable of evoking the whole film even though there is only one frame, one picture" (Onega, p. 61). Fowles's explanation may help us to accept by analogy the apparently paradoxical fact that his novels may be extraordinarily varied and heterogeneous in content, style, range, and scope and simultaneously homogeneous and simple in their basic meaning and in the principles governing their form.

My contention is that an analysis of the form and meaning of each novel will reveal the tentative way in which Fowles has once and again searched for a definitive answer to two basic questions: What is the meaning and purpose of human life? and, What is the status of reality? Struggling between his existentialist beliefs and his socialist convictions, Fowles hesitates when it comes to deciding whether man is radically free to choose, even death, or damnation, or whether he is socially and biologically determined and conditioned to restrict his freedom in the name of a sense of social responsibility.

Being an agnostic, Fowles tends to express his unique hero's quest for maturity in psychological terms, as a process of individuation. Being a post-Modernist novelist, painfully aware of the fact that his work comes at the end of a very long tradition of writing, he conceives of this quest as taking place within the unreal boundaries of a wholly literary world, which he presents as forming part of reality, for, while his socialist bias inclines him to create an art capable of telling "the real" (*Daniel Martin*, p. 454), his existentialist, more shamanistic and visionary sensibility unconsciously leads him to stress the validity of the unreal. Thus, his novels simultaneously appear as realistic and fantastic, as traditional and experimental, as accurately set in historical time and as epically timeless; while his heroes and heroines are both realistically drawn individuals and archetypal, representative figures.

Explaining how he felt when he wrote a novel, Fowles said in the A.E.D.E.A.N. interview (ibid., p. 65), "You soon learn when you write novels that you are in a prison. I do not deny for a moment that I am in a prison when I am writing a book, but it is really like being in a prison that is perhaps six by four and you think, 'How could I make it a little bit larger?' perhaps seven by five. In other words, you try to create a little bit of freedom, as a prisoner might do in prison circumstances."

Fowles's yearning for absolute creative liberty reflects, in mirror image, his fictional hero's struggle for freedom and echoes the fear of determinism felt by the existentialist. Thus, in a nutshell, Fowles metaphorically synthesizes the thematic core of his obsessive rewriting. By writing symphonic variations of the only conceivable situation—a fictional hero's quest for maturity and freedom—Fowles is telling us that even if liberty proves to be unattainable, it is at least possible to create the illusion of this freedom. But we should not forget that, as we learn from the reading of his novels, for Fowles reality and unreality, the ontological and the fictional, enjoy the same status.

In *The Victorian Multiplot Novel: Studies in Dialogical Form*, Peter K. Garret explains the structure of *Middlemarch* as alternately progressing in time and expanding in space, as the novel's scope alternately narrows in order to concentrate on one of the diverse plots, or widens in order to allow ground for the others that take place at the same time. Using a terminology borrowed from Dr. Lydgate, George Eliot described the dialogical tension created by this alternation as a "systole-diastole" movement. The systole-diastole, shrinking-expanding movements that characterize the multiplot novel may figuratively express the way in which Fowles's novels stand in relation to each other. Like the diverse plots that make up *Middlemarch*, every new novel written by John Fowles recasts ideas already present in *The Magus*, but does so in its own particular way, putting the emphasis on different aspects, thus expanding and altering the original notion and so distinctively adding to the total picture.

Even the curious phonetic similarity existing between "magus" (pronounced [mægas] by Fowles) and "maggot" points to the circularity of Fowles's writing, to the fact that *A Maggot* is indeed another variation on *The Magus,* still another version of the hero's quest. However, the slight phonetic difference between the titles of Fowles's first and last novels also contains a world of difference, the huge stretch that goes from his hesitant and unsatisfying first attempt to express his vision of the world, to the last, masterfully neat and accomplished expression of it. Midway between both, and in dialogical relation to them, stand the other four.

1

The Collector

Critics concerned with establishing the major antecedents to the novel usually single out as such the "confession" and the "picaresque." In their simplest form, these proto-novelistic narrative genres may be said to share two traits in common. One is a first person narrator-character who reports the events of his or her past life in retrospect; the other is an episodic, linear structure following the forward movement of the protagonist, who goes from one adventure to another without ever again having to face the people or the consequences of the situations left behind.

John Fowles's first published novel, *The Collector* (1963), apparently follows the pattern of the "confession." A very simple story, with no subplots to divert our attention, *The Collector* seems at first sight a linear story told from the point of view of one narrator-character (Frederick Clegg), only interrupted by the reading of Miranda's diary.

Clegg's narration can be described as a narrative with internal focalization where the narrator and the focalizer are the same: Clegg speaks in the first person and restricts his observations to his own perception of events, to his own "point of view." Inserted in this first narrative, Miranda's diary functions as an enormous anachrony, within the primary discourse. After the first chapter, Clegg hands over the narration to the only other actor in the story, Miranda, the victim, who gives her own version of her drama.[1]

The function of Miranda's diary, as a recall, is to modify the meaning of the first narrative by offering a divergent interpretation of the story: the handing over of the narrative from Clegg to Miranda thus implies a change of narrative level. Miranda, who was an actor in the first narrative, turns into the narrator in the second version. In this sense, Miranda's diary functions as a metadiscourse,[2] in Gérard Genette's terminology *(Figures III),* which structurally works as a *mise en abyme;* that is, as a mirror-text[3] of Clegg's narrative.

The beginning of the whole story can be traced back to some time during Miranda's last year at school (p. 1), its ending to approximately three weeks after Miranda's death, which takes place sometime after the 7th of December of her second year at the School of Art (p. 282). Chronologically, then, the events that constitute the story take place in the course of three incomplete academic years.

Being both the narrator and the focalizer, Frederick Clegg will tell his tale retrospectively, recording a series of events he lived in the past and which he will try to sum up for us, following a rough linear order, though often digressing to add details about his own background. Thus, he will begin by evoking the first times he watched Miranda during her vacation from boarding school and will go on to tell us about the winning of the pools, the buying of the house, the adaptation of the cellar, the kidnapping, his relation with Miranda, her illness and death. Basically, Clegg will alternate summary with reported dialogue. He will often resort to summary iteratively; that is, instead of telling us about the way he patiently spied on Miranda every day, for instance, he will choose one particular day at random, implying its representative character by locutions denoting habitual actions:

> When she was home from her boarding school I *used to* see her *almost every day sometimes*. (p. 1, my italics)

> I *used to* go and sit in her room and work out what she could do to escape. (p. 25, my italics)

This technique, which is a traditional one in realistic fiction, is also the least mimetic. "Summary" as opposed to "scene" is Plato's recommended narrative style: indirect speech in which the narrator boldly assumes his role of reporting the events in his own words. The effect of such iterative summaries is to quicken the pace of the narrative, while with "scene" story time and narrative time tend to proceed *pari passu*.

Sometimes, Clegg abandons this narrative technique to report a dialogue. In general the dialogues he reports are singulative, that is, they produce once events which only happened once; this is specially the case with particularly significant conversations with Miranda.

By alternating iterative summaries with singulative reported dialogues, Clegg's narrative acquires a peculiar rhythm of its own with alternate quickening and slowing down of the tempo. It was the Russian formalist Boris Eikhembaum[4] who first coined the expression "unity of tension" to differentiate a short story from a novel. Drawing on evidence from the short stories by Edgar A. Poe, Eikhembaum stated that the structure of a short story is similar to that of a lyric poem in that it has a "unity of tension" throughout; the novel, on the other hand, has an epic structure, that is, a structure where tension cannot remain unchanged but must perforce concentrate around certain notable pinnacles. One factor contributing to the slackening or heightening of tension is the pace of the narrative, which can be altered through the alternation of narrative technique.

The Collector, like all novels, is an anisochronous narration in which its peculiar rhythm, in this case in Clegg's narrative, is obtained by the alternation of iterative summaries and singulative reported speeches.

Clegg's reported speeches are heavily marked by declarative phrases and verbs. The narrator often tends to synthesize a remark uttered by himself and even by Miranda in his own words; and he often adds to the report his own reflections and comments on what he or she said:

> "If you let me go, I should want to see you, because you interest me very much."
> Like you go to the zoo? *I asked.*
> "To try and understand you."
> You'll never do that *(I may as well admit I liked the mystery man side of our talk. I felt it showed her she didn't know everything.)*
> "I don't think I ever should."
> Then suddenly she was kneeling in front of me, with her hands up high, touching the top of her head, being all oriental. She did it three times.
> "Will the mysterious great master accept apologies of very humble slave?"
> I'll think about it, *I said.*
> "Humble slave very solly for unkind letter?"
> *I had to laugh; she could act anything.*
> She stayed there kneeling with her hands on the floor beside her, more serious, giving me the look.
> "Will you send the letter, then?"
> *I made her ask again, but then I gave in. It was nearly the big mistake of my life.* (p. 71, my italics)

In a dialogue like this, chosen at random, Miranda's uttered words are isolated from the rest by the use of quotation marks. These indicate the change of level implicit in the narrator's handing over of the narrative to a character, also marked by the use of declarative verbs: *I asked; I said.*

Alternating with Miranda's direct speech we have in this dialogue, firstly, the narrator's own remarks, either between parentheses or in reported speech ("I may well admit"; "She could act anything"; "It was nearly the big mistake of my life"); secondly, the narrator's report of their actions ("Then suddenly she was kneeling"; "I had to laugh"; "She stayed kneeling"); and thirdly, the narrator's indirect report of his own speech ("I made her ask again, but then gave in").

One remark of Clegg's in this dialogue shows that the narrator addresses himself to the reader: "It was nearly the big mistake of my life." This remark functions as an anachrony directed into the future. It is a device the narrator uses to catch our attention, to excite our curiosity by alluding to some hidden fact the narrator already knows and, thus, promises to tell. The paragraph following the one quoted above includes a similar prolepsis:

> The next day I drove up to London. I told her I was going there, like a fool, and she gave me
> a list of things to buy. There was a lot. *(I knew later to keep me busy.)* (p. 71, my italics)

These prolepses are not soliloquizing comments or reflections, but are explicitly
addressed to the reader:

> I used to have daydreams about her . . . nothing nasty, that was never *until what I'll explain
> later.* (p. 10)

> The days spent together . . . *(after the ones I'm going to say about)* are definitely the best I
> have ever had. (p. 11, my italics)

In these two examples, the reader is clearly addressed. Often, the prolepses
also have a specific effect: they heighten the tension by hinting at an imminent
threat or horror:

> She was so changed (that) I managed to forget *what I had to do later.* (p. 81)

> I could have done anything. I could have killed her. *All I did later* was because of that night.
> (p. 102, my italics)

When Clegg tells us that Miranda's beauty allowed him "to forget what I
had to do later" the reader cannot know that he is referring to his decision to
break his promise to release her after a month. Neither can the reader know that
"all I did later" was, simply, to let her die without any medical aid. The reader
doesn't know all these things to which the narrator alludes, and it is precisely
this lack of concretion that makes these prolepses horrifyingly threatening,
while at the same time they increase our desire to know the rest.

So far, we have considered Miranda's diary as a metadiscourse within the
first narrative. As regards its effect on narrative order, the diary acts as an
enormous retrospective anachrony, for in it a different narrator will tell the
same story again. Miranda's narration, like Clegg's, is told retrospectively: she
starts writing on the seventh night of her confinement, a night she tentatively
dates as the 14th of October. Except when she digresses into her own past before
the kidnapping, the gap between story and narrative time is very short, for she
theoretically records in her diary every night the events of the previous day.
This gap is further shortened as the diary reaches its last entry dated "December." At a certain point Miranda lapses from the preterite into the present tense:

> (Evening). He brought a thermometer. It *was* 100 and *now it's* 101. I feel terrible.
> *I've been* in bed all day.
> He's not human.
> Oh God *I'm* so lonely so utterly alone.
> *I can't* write. (p. 256)

The change from the past to the present, like the ending of the chapter with a broken sentence Miranda feels too weak to end, indicates the overlapping of narrative and story time: the end of the story Miranda narrates coincides with the end of her life. Still, as the last but one entry of her diary is dated "7th of December" and the last one simply as "December," we can say that the diary runs from the 14th of October to a day or perhaps a few days after the 7th of December of Miranda's second year at the School of Art, while Clegg's narration continues for several more days—three more weeks, to be precise, as we shall later learn—so that both the beginning and the end of Miranda's narration, and so her present, are included within the past of Clegg's narration. That is to say, Miranda's present is still past with respect to Clegg's present.

In Clegg's first narrative, as has already been seen, narrator and focalizer coincide: the person who "tells" and the person who "sees" are one and the same. The handing over of the narrative to Miranda in the second chapter has interesting implications: Miranda becomes the narrator of her diary, a diary she has hidden under the mattress of her bed in the prison-cellar where it is likely to remain for ages after her death, unless Clegg himself finds it, as, we later learn, he does. This means that if we, as readers, have had access to it at all, it is through Clegg's own reading of it, that is, through his "eyes" and mind. Only by accepting that we have access to the diary through Clegg's own reading can we understand why Clegg's first narrative interrupts itself midway: for Clegg's "confession," his brooding over the incidents of the kidnapping and murder of Miranda, is interrupted when he finds the diary and begins to read it.

After Miranda's diary, Clegg takes up the narration exactly at the point where he had interrupted it. So far, throughout the first and the third chapters, Clegg has insistently reported his tale in the preterite, either by using iterative habitual past or singulative simple past tenses. Reading his report, one has the feeling that the whole drama took place a long time (or, at least, some time) ago. There is nothing in the first three chapters to lead us to relate the death of Miranda in December to our own present. In the fourth chapter, however, and quite unexpectedly, Clegg says, "The days passed, it is now three weeks since all that" (p. 282).

Just as the final remarks of Miranda's diary coincide with her present, so the distance between narrative time and story time shortens first to three weeks, and immediately afterwards they are made to overlap: "I only *put* the stove down there *today* because the room *needs* drying out anyway" (p. 283, my italics). In this complex sentence, the main verb is in the preterite and that of the subordinate clause in the present, as in the preceding quotation, but here the time gap totally disappears with the adverb "today."

Being a metadiscourse within the main one, Miranda's present is included within Clegg's story time, so that the time of her narration and the time of her story coincide in her present though, with reference to Clegg's narration, they have taken place in the past: when Clegg's diegesis and narration overlap in the present, however, his present can only be measured with reference to our own present. Thus, the psychological effect of this degree zero of writing reached at the end of the novel is important: we realize with a pang that Miranda's awful experience and her torturing death took place just three weeks ago: we are not dealing, then, with the confession of a remote crime, but with the account of some horribly near experience, so near indeed that it threatens to stretch into the future: "I have not made up my mind about Marian (another M! I heard the supervisor call her name), this time it *won't be* love, *it would just be* for the interest of the thing and to compare them and also the other thing, which as I say, I *would like to go into* in more detail and I *could teach* her how" (p. 283, my italics). The novel ends with the threat of new kidnappings of young girls like Miranda, but kidnappings that might take place, not only in the story's future, or in Clegg's future, but in our own future: as the gap between narrative time and story time narrows, the threat hanging over Marian's head also threatens the reader: the collector is alive, he is one of us, and is perhaps watching us.

Through this peculiar handling of time, this progressive compression of the distance between story time and narrative time, this funnel technique, John Fowles manages to produce a specific narrative rhythm best described as a progressive heightening of tension which will blow up like a bomb at the very end of the novel, when past and present merge into the future. With delicate symmetry, Miranda's metadiscourse echoes and reflects the timing of the major narration by reproducing its structure.

Technically speaking, Clegg's "confession" takes the form of soliloquy. Soliloquy, as defined by Robert Humphrey *(Stream-of-Consciousness in the Modern Novel,* p. 36), is a narrative technique characterized by two major features: the narrator speaks in the first person with clear syntactic and logic coherence, and he addresses himself to an audience. Syntactic coherence, careful ordering of the sentence through the conventional use of punctuation, and a perfect, logical development of the train of thought are all traits that characterize Clegg's narrative. In fact, Clegg's monologue is painfully clear, structured, systematic: no flow of free association is ever allowed to express itself unchecked, without prompt explanation. We have already seen how the prolepses are openly directed to an implied reader and how they hint, carefully enclosed by brackets or commas, at some information the narrator refuses to give us in full at the moment the association occurs to him, preferring to delay an account of it in the interest of preserving his linear story. Even when Clegg allows an association of ideas to develop, he tries to hide the link between the two elements of the association. Thus, for instance, describing a sadistic dream he has had, in which Miranda cried and knelt for mercy, he says: "Once I let myself dream I hit her across the face as I saw it done by a chap in a telly play. Perhaps that was when it all started" (p. 11). The account of the dream ends here. There comes then a space on the page separating it from the following account, which turns out to be a memory of his family: "My father was killed driving. I was two. That was in 1937. He was drunk, but Aunt Annie always said it was my mother that drove him to drink" (p. 11). Both accounts are apparently highly disparate—the second one appears to inaugurate a digression with no thematic relation to the account of Clegg's dreams of Miranda. There is, however, a strong psychological connection between, on the one hand, Clegg's sadistic fantasies with the woman for whose love he cares, and, on the other, the frustrated love he feels for his mother, who abandoned him to the care of Aunt Annie after the death of his father. As a reading of the novel amply demonstrates, Clegg's unavowed Oedipus complex, fostered by the vicious atmosphere of Aunt Annie's nonconformist household, and the feeling that he is unloved and unwanted, are at the bottom of Clegg's passion for Miranda, a substitute mother who, like his own, simultaneously arouses in Clegg hatred and love, as expressed in his "good" and "bad" dreams. The thematic jump, then, from the day Clegg hit Miranda across the face in a dream, to the account of his father's accident, for which his mother is blamed, is psychologically consistent, and the very fact of wanting to separate them by the device of leaving a space on the page points to Clegg's refusal to admit this subconscious connection. As the chapter progresses, however, and Clegg goes on from the account of his father's death and his mother's neglect to the account of his life with Aunt Annie, Uncle Dick, and Mabel, the subconscious identification of Miranda with his mother recurs once and again. Before her, the only person who had shown any affection for Clegg had been his Uncle Dick: it is therefore significant that the first thing he tells us about him is that he died when Clegg was fifteen. The parallelism with the account of his parental deprivation is striking: "My father was killed driving. I was two. That was in 1937 . . . "; "Uncle Dick died when I was fifteen. That was 1950" (p. 11).

Thus, in a seemingly objective and detached way, Clegg briefly tells us the bleak story of successive deprivations in his childhood. First his father and mother and then Uncle Dick, the only person who cared for his butterflies and who had made him happy by taking him for trips: "Those days (after the ones I'm going to say about) are definitely the best I have ever had" (p. 11).

Here Uncle Dick, Clegg's first substitute parent, is associated with Miranda through the remark in parentheses. Soon afterwards the association is made explicit: "Well, I won't go on, *he was as good as a father to me.* When I held that cheque in my hands, he was the person, *besides Miranda, of course,* I thought of. I would have given him the best rods and tackle and anything he wanted. But it was not to be" (p. 12, my italics). Miranda herself knows that this is Clegg's ultimate reason for kidnapping her, even if he cannot admit it: "You want to lean on me. I feel it. I expect it's your mother. You're looking for your mother" (p. 59).

Clegg's successive deprivations, his unsatisfied yearning for love, have progressively blunted his capacity for affection. To express his love for Uncle Dick, Clegg tells us, he would have *bought* him anything he wanted, now that he was rich, and this is precisely the means Clegg will try to employ to make Miranda fall in love with him: money and objects is all Clegg can give, for he understands love merely as possession: "What she never understood was that with me it was having. Having her was enough. Nothing needed doing. I just wanted to have her, and safe at last" (p. 95). The deprived child must rely on possession: possessing butterflies, possessing money, possessing Miranda, they are all forms of exerting power, a power traditionally denied his social class:

> At the hotel . . . of course they were respectful on the surface, but that was all, they really despised us for having all that money and not knowing what to do with it. They still treated me behind the scenes for what I was—a clerk. It was no good throwing money around. As soon as we spoke or did something we gave the game away. (p. 14)

In Frederick Clegg, then, two major sources of mental derangement merge: his dearth of love and his painful class consciousness. The well-behaved child ("I was never punished at school," p. 13) really hides an enormous desire to prove that he deserves to be loved and cared for, and that he is socially acceptable. It is through Aunt Annie's life-denying nonconformist teaching that Clegg has come to identify love and respectability: he must be well behaved to obtain his aunt's approval. That is, his feeling of social inferiority is so inextricably bound up with his feeling of emotional deprivation, that, in order to be loved, he must first learn the behavior of the class above his own. Typically, the first thing he will do, after "falling in love" with Miranda, will be to behave as he thinks educated people do, going "to the National Gallery and the Tate Gallery" and reading "the classy newspapers . . . so I wouldn't seem ignorant" (p. 19).

The formal way Clegg dresses, his ineffective efforts at educating himself, his profitless readings, his attentive listening to Miranda's lectures on art, are all symptoms that denote his obsession with social respectability—of course, his approach to art and culture with this end in mind effectively prevents him from profitng from the experience:

> "Do you know anything about art?" she asked.
> Nothing you'd call knowledge.
> "I know you didn't. You wouldn't imprison an innocent person if you did."
> I don't see the connection, I said. (p. 43)

In John Fowles's allegory, Miranda's art stands for real life; Clegg's collecting and photographing, for death:

"All photos (are dead). When you draw something it lives and when you photograph it it dies."
It is like a record, I said
"Yes. All dry and dead." (p. 55)

Miranda's implied censure touches the core of Clegg's deficiency as a human being. Behind Clegg's madness lies an incapacity to feel, and to live: Clegg's life is an imitation of life, a life of appearances made up of moral and linguistic clichés. Clegg's use of language thoroughly reflects this stereotyped, lifeless, and deadening quality of his. The very fact that, as a narrator, he chooses to express himself in the traditional convention of the "confession" points to his incapacity to create. It is significant, then, that whatever knowledge he has he has picked up from the pictures or from the media, or has simply heard:

Once I let myself dream I hit her across the face as *I saw it done once by a chap in a telly play.* (p. 11)

I always understood *(from something I heard in the army)* that a gentleman always controls himself to the right moment. (p. 98)

I know you're meant to wash dead bodies, but I didn't like it, it didn't seem right, so I laid her on her bed, and combed her hair and cut a lock. I tried to arrange her face so it had a smile but I couldn't. . . . Then I knelt and said a prayer . . . not that I believe in religion, *but it seemed right.* (p. 274, my italics)

The grim compendium of stereotyped rites he performs with Miranda's body clearly expresses Clegg's obsession with appearances, with "what is right" from a social point of view, not from the point of view of his inner conviction. Significantly, he utters a prayer, after confessing himself an unbeliever, because he senses it to be "right." Significantly too, he cuts a lock of Miranda's hair and tries to make her smile (after her awful death!) to accommodate her death to the stale, stereotyped, romantic ending of a cheap novelette:

It was then I got the idea. . . . All I had to do was kill myself. . . . Post a letter first to the police. So they would find us down there together. Together in the Great Beyond. We would be buried together. Like Romeo and Juliet.
It would be real tragedy. Not sordid. (p. 276)

Clegg's behavior, his ideas about "right" and "wrong," his general knowledge of life, are simply the product of his observation of manners and the media, not the result of his personal convictions and reflections. "Right" and "wrong" simply mean "what most people do," "what everybody believes."

Clegg's language is as dead and stale as his ideas: a neat, well-punctuated language, full of clichés and stereotyped locutions he has picked up. It is a language that exasperates Miranda:

> She wanted a cup of tea. . . . When it was made, I said shall I be mother?
> "That's a *horrid* expression."
> What's wrong with it?
> . . . "It's suburban, it's stale, it's dead, it's . . . Oh!, everything square that ever was. You
> know."
> I think you'd better be mother, I said. (p. 56, emphasis in the original)

Clegg's incapacity to see the point in Miranda's criticism of his expression shows the unbridgeable gap between them both. Her angry reaction to this stale phrase significantly takes the form of swearing—she insults him to shake him into life, but the effort is doomed to failure because Clegg is simply shocked by it. Clegg's dislike of swearing, his idea of propriety, is closely related to his confusion between good and beautiful, ugly and bad. Through George Paston Miranda has learned to separate the two: beautiful or ugly is all-important, good or bad irrelevant:

> At your age one is bursting with ideals. you think that because I can sometimes see what's
> trivial and what's important in art I ought to be more virtuous. But I don't want to be virtuous.
> My charms (if there is any) for you is simply frankness. And experience. Not goodness. I'm
> not a good man. Perhaps morally I'm younger even than you are. Can you understand that?
> He (G. P.) was only saying what I felt. (p. 179)

Frankness, experience, knowing what really matters is what distinguishes G. P. from Frederick Clegg, a man without personal convictions, who accommodates his notions of right and wrong to the narrow popular morality of his social class. Miranda finally understands the quality of Clegg's personality through his stale and stereotyped use of language; a language Peter Conradi (*John Fowles,* p. 36) has characterized as being full of euphemisms:

> The rhetorical figure that characterizes Clegg's language is euphemism, that decorous impreci-
> sion which reveals a world in concealing it. He refers to Miranda not as his prisoner but as his
> guest. Death is "The Great Beyond," and to murder is "to put out." A bikini is a "Wotchermer-
> callit" (when Miranda specifies it, he says "I can't allow talk like that"). "Nice" is a genteelism
> for non-sexual, "garment" for clothes; sex is "the obvious" or "the other thing," naked is
> "stark," and "artistic" often means pornographic. His language is impoverished, and sex
> produces the most hectic ellipses and periphrases.

We might apply to Clegg's use of euphemism the expression "linguistic sensitivity" coined by Ian Watt *(The Rise of the Novel: Studies in Defoe, Richardson and Fielding),* to describe Richardson's prose in *Pamela.* Clegg has a linguistic sensitivity very much like that of Richardson's heroine, who "on hearing her master offer her her dead mistress's clothes is acutely embarrassed and reports in a letter to her parents that when Mr. B. said 'Don't blush Pamela, dost think I don't know pretty maids should wear shoes and stockings,' she 'was so confounded at these words, you might have beat me down with a feather'" (ibid., p. 162). Pamela's "linguistic sensitivity" seems to be a new phenomenon in the eighteenth century, when Mandeville noted that "among well-bred people it is counted highly criminal to mention before company anything in plain words that is relating to this Mystery of Succession" (ibid., p. 163). As Ian Watt points out, this new phenomenon reaches its climax at the end of the eighteenth century when "even *The Tatler* and *The Spectator* were found unsuited to women readers: Coleridge, at least, thought that they contained words 'which might, in our day, offend the delicacy of female ears and shock feminine susceptibility'" (ibid., p. 163).

In Richardson, and in the eighteenth century generally, this linguistic sensitivity is restricted to women, who are increasingly seen as guardians of family morality: the linguistic distinction is based on a biological discrimination, the conviction that only men are subject to sexual passion, that women are immune to it. As Ian Watt amply demonstrates, the double standard of morality applied to man and woman in the eighteenth century, of which this linguistic sensitivity is only a symptom, is a phenomenon closely linked to the development of the middle class.[5] By attaching this linguistic sensitivity to Clegg, then, John Fowles is not only pointing at his incapacity to live, but is also evoking the narrow-mindedness of nonconformism, a Puritanical attitude to life closely connected with the development of the lower-middle class, called by Miranda "the horrid timid copycatting genteel inbetween class" (p. 161).

Clegg's painful attempts at "correction," then, are based on a desire to go up in the social scale. He will consistently try-to employ formal and often old-fashioned terms, such as "the deceased" referring to Miranda's body; or, as Peter Conradi pointed out, "Wotchermercallit" for bikini; or pseudo-learned expressions, such as, "As per usual." Ironically enough, though, his low-class origin often shows in his use of incorrect expressions, such as "like I said" (p. 181); or the typical substitution of adjectives instead of the correspondent adverbs: "she says the young ones don't clean *proper* nowadays" (p. 186); "I did it *scientific*" (p. 282).

Another significant feature of Clegg's use of language is his lack of imagination, his inability to go beyond the literal meaning of words. When Miranda is dying, she keeps calling G. P. Typically, Clegg misunderstands her and thinks she is calling a general practitioner (p. 263). Or again, when Miranda refers to the children of the third world for whom she used to collect money: "'We collected money for them last term, they eat earth.' . . . 'We're all such pigs, we deserve to die,' *so I reckon they pinched the money they should have given in*" (p. 265, my italics).

Clegg's tendency to interpret everything he hears or learns in economic terms further reveals him as an unimaginative square, illiterate, and selfish being, one Miranda describes as the modern equivalent of the eighteenth-century "economic man" (p. 212). Thus, Frederick Clegg, or rather Miranda's Caliban, becomes the representative of a whole social class: the working class G. P. so utterly despised, the class come to maturity under the Labour Party and the Welfare State: "The New People, the new-class people with their cars and their money and their tellies and their stupid vulgarities and their stupid crawling imitation of the bourgeoisie" (p. 207). By identifying Clegg with the New People John Fowles touches the central theme of his allegory: Clegg's kidnapping of Miranda is not simply (as Fowles himself angrily protests in *The Aristos*) the thrilling account of how a petty-minded bank clerk becomes rich with the pools and exerts power over a young and promising art student; it is much more than that, it is a modern allegory of the rape of art by vulgarity and meanness, expressed through the assault of the jealous and ignorant masses—the Many— on the intelligent, the imaginative and the creative Few:

> I see what he (G. P.) feels, I mean I feel it myself more and more, this awful deadweight of the fat little New People on everything. Corrupting everything. Vulgarizing everything. Raping the countryside, as D. says in his squire moods. Everything mass-produced. Mass everything . . . This is what I feel these days. That I belong to a sort of band of people who have to stand against all the rest. I don't know who they are— . . . they're not even good people. They have weak moments. Sex moments and drink moments. Coward and money moments. They have holidays in the Ivory Tower. But a part of them is one with the band. The Few. (p. 208)

The victim of nonconformism, the repressed and love-starved representative of the Many, Frederick Clegg has revealed himself in John Fowles's allegory through his specific use of language. In accordance with the picaresque tradition established by *Lazarillo,* Clegg, like Moll Flanders or Roxana, speaks in the first person, addresses his public and confesses his crime in a neat, intelligible and emotionless way: the characteristics of his prose we have already analyzed—his alternation of summary and reported dialogue; his use of prolepses; his tendency to resort to formal and slightly old-fashioned idiom; his frequent vulgarisms; and, above all, his recurrent euphemisms: they sum up his mental and human deficiencies. Opposed to him, Miranda will try to give us her own version of the tragedy through a different medium: the diary.

By choosing to express Miranda's point of view through the diary, John Fowles is consciously asking us to accept a different set of assumptions. In the first place, the diary is never addressed to an implied reader. But, on the contrary, its message is directed to the writer himself. It is thus a convention traditionally used by heroes in isolation: Robinson Crusoe is the prototypical example.

Although Miranda expects nobody else to read her diary, she feels a strong necessity to communicate with the outside world, and so will try to break her isolation psychologically, by choosing to address some of her entries in the diary to her sister Minny, as if she were writing a letter:

> I can't write in a vacuum like this. To no one. When I draw I always think of someone like G. P. at my shoulder. All parents should be like ours, then sisters really become sisters. They *have* to be to each other what Minny and I are.
> Dear Minny.
> I have been here over a week now, and I miss you very much, and I miss the fresh air and the fresh faces of all those people I so hated on the Tube and the fresh things that happen every hour of every day if only I could have seen—their freshness, I mean. (p. 124, emphasis in the original)

With contrived simplicity John Fowles fuses here two different techniques: the diary and the letter blend into a single form: a diary in which Miranda feigns to write a letter to her sister Minny for the sake of psychological communication. So far, Miranda's consciousness of reality and unreality is intact, she still knows her letter is just make-believe: "Minny, I'm not writing to you, I'm talking to myself" (p. 127).

In *Pamela, or Virtue Rewarded,* Richardson's heroine offers us her version of her attempted seduction by Mr. B. by means of letters: after every encounter with Mr. B., she sits down to inform her parents of the day's incidents by writing a letter to them. As the novel progresses, however, the letter convention breaks down, Pamela's letters unexpectedly turn into her diary. The shift from the letter convention to that of the diary points to Richardson's growing need to devote more and more time to the expression of the workings of Pamela's mind; the answers to the letters become less and less important, as Pamela's writing turns into a kind of cross-examination of her feelings, desires, and intuitions, in a word, as she feels a stronger need for introspection.

From the very beginning of the second chapter of *The Collector,* John Fowles draws upon both conventions. Miranda's primary reason for writing her diary is a need to act: writing is simply a way of making life in the cellar more tolerable: "I can't sleep. I must do something. I'm going to write about the first time I met G. P." (p. 151). Miranda's first attempts at writing are not very successful. We sense the conscious effort she is making when we read the broken bits of thought her stream-of-consciousness is able to build after seven days of confinement. The first entry in the diary simply records the flow of her thoughts as they are forming in her mind:

> It's the seventh night.
> I keep on thinking the same thing. If only they knew. If only *they* knew.
> Share the outrage.
> So now I'm trying to tell it to this pad he bought me this morning.

His kindness.
Calmly.
Deep down I get more and more frightened. (p. 117, emphasis in the original)

Like Clegg's confession, Miranda's first and second entries in her diary are soliloquies. But whereas Clegg's is a conventional account, following a careful logical and grammatical pattern, Miranda's soliloquy, ironically addressed to the "pad" of writing paper Clegg has brought her, is basically a "stream-of-consciousness" device.[6] As such, the ideas she writes down on this paper are simply connected through free associations. While Clegg's aim is primarily to report the events to an audience, assumed to be listening, Miranda's trick of addressing the pad is simply meant to aid her to come to terms with her new situation and to break out of her isolation psychologically.

In the third entry, dated October 16th, Miranda has already passed her first traumatic phase: she is calmer now, she realizes that, whatever Clegg's intentions are, he does not want to assault her sexually, or kill her. As she realizes for the first time that Clegg's intention is simply to "keep" her, she starts feeling the anguish of prolonged isolation: it is now that she tries to break out of her confinement by directing her writings to Minny.

After failing to convince Clegg to allow her to write a letter to her parents, this hope of contacting the outside world finally evaporates; consequently Miranda devises alternative methods to break out of her prison. On the one hand, she tries to escape by diverse means; on the other, she tries to turn reality into fantasy and the unreal into the real. This she accomplishes by experimenting with different literary techniques.

On October 18th, Miranda reproduces in her diary a dialogue supposedly held that morning between Clegg and herself: she does so in direct speech as in a play, using stage directions in italics between parentheses and calling Frederick Clegg "Caliban." This dialogue (pp. 132–33) represents a step in the direction of unreality. At a certain point, Miranda even acknowledges that she is altering the actual dialogue she is reporting: "M. *(I'm cheating, I didn't say all these things—but I'm going to write what I want to say as well as what I did)*" (p. 133, emphasis in the original). That is, Miranda's report is consciously literary: she is creating a fiction out of reality in which both Clegg and herself are the actors, and where the dialogue can be altered and bettered. As soon as she does so she realizes that writing is an art very different from painting: the fact that to write you have to use language for purposes other than communication strikes Miranda as a new revelation: "Words are so crude, so terribly primitive compared to drawing, painting, sculpture" (p. 150).

Miranda's major struggle in the cellar, then, is not a fight for survival in the literal sense. For all its crudity, writing has a healing effect for Miranda she cannot find in painting: she can evoke her past through writing, bring back memories of happy moments at home with Minny, and above all, with G. P. By writing about the external world Miranda hopes to exorcise from her mind the horrible feeling that the other people seem to have lost reality: "The only real person in my world is Caliban" (p. 140); thus, "My emotions are all topsy-turvy, like frightened monkeys in a cage. I felt I was going mad last night, so *I wrote and wrote myself into the other world.* To escape in spirit, if not in fact. To prove it still exists" (p. 157, my italics).

By calling Clegg "Caliban" and reporting their conversation as a stage dialogue and by devoting more and more pages of her diary to an evocation of her past, Miranda tries to evade her real situation, turning it into fiction: after the letters to Minny and the dramatized dialogues, Miranda resorts to other literary devices. One day, after having offended Clegg with a curt remark, she tries to win him back by telling him a fairy tale. It is the tale of "an ugly monster who captured a princess and put her in a dungeon" (p. 187). The tale ends with the ugly monster learning to be good and turning out to be an enchanted prince who eventually married the princess. Miranda's tale functions in the novel as a wish-fulfillment dream: it is a parable to convince Clegg emotionally of his capacity for regeneration. All it does, however, is to confirm Clegg in his love for her and, thus, to strengthen his desire to keep her.

From this day on, Miranda will envisage her confinement as something increasingly unreal, or rather, she will try by every means at her disposal to use literature as a barrier between herself and her bleak reality: her next device was to make a "strip cartoon of him. The Awful Tale of a Harmless Boy. Absurd. But I have to keep the reality at bay" (p. 203). And, in the entry of December 5th, which she addresses to G. P., she refers to her situation as "The Rape of Intelligence. By the moneyed masses, the New People" (p. 251). It is a mocking remark with a heavy load of literary allusion to *The Rape of the Lock,* and in its subtitle to the typical Victorian tracts made out of lurid passion and murder which constitute a vast subgenre of nineteenth-century fiction and which were so appealing to underlings and maids. The fact that Miranda can objectivize her situation to the point of being so ironic about it points to the soundness of her mind, and also to her purpose: we feel the same when she refers to Clegg as "Prince Charming" (p. 236) or as "The Old Man of the Sea" (p. 206). Often, too, Miranda likes to think of herself as "Emma and arrange a marriage for him, and with happier results. Some little Harriet Smith, with whom he could be mousy and sane and happy" (p. 213). She takes the parallelism with *Emma* and her own situation to the point of assigning the characters to her various acquaintances: "Caliban is Mr. Elton. Piers is Frank Churchill. But is G. P. Mr. Knightly?" (p. 218).

The references to Jane Austen, and especially to *Emma,* apart from being a very disingenuous comment by Fowles on the mutual dependence of certain works of art, evoke Jane Austen's major concern in all her novels with the opposition: reality versus appearances. In all of them, the heroine must learn to tell, through trial and error, the fundamental difference between reality and appearances. Reality, for Jane Austen, primarily means a self-knowledge gained through the fruition of virtue. Being real means being true to life; it means the rejection of the apparent, the changing, the fashionable, the fleeting and ephemeral. Learning to be real means learning to see the human value beneath the "pride and prejudice" imposed by social rules. It is, therefore, extraordinarily fitting that, of all English novelists, Miranda should choose Jane Austen as a mirror for herself. Like Emma, Miranda has intrinsic values she has not been able to develop yet: the kidnapping, the confinement, and her relation with Clegg will teach her the lesson, they will alter her vision of reality, her haughty and priggish assumptions, and will lead her to a deep understanding, a grasp of the ultimate reality of life: "It is like the day you realize dolls are dolls. I pick up my old self and I see it's silly. A toy I've played with too often. It's a little sad, like an old golliwog at the bottom of a cupboard. Innocent and used-up and proud and silly" (p. 247).

The maturing of Miranda, the consciousness of her futility, her eventual understanding of life, her losing of innocence, in a word, her anagnorisis, is both welcome and painful, for it brings about the consciousness of human potentialities, but also of human isolation:

> If there is a God he's a great loathsome spider in the darkness.
> *He cannot be good.* This pain, this terrible seeing-through that is in me now. It wasn't necessary. It is all pain, and it buys nothing. Gives birth to nothing. (p. 255, emphasis in the original)

At this stage, Miranda's isolation has deepened; it is not only an isolation from the external world, it is the metaphysical isolation of the existentialist, the vision of the *néant*, of the purposeless and useless void. Miranda's final words before she dies, recorded in the last entry in her diary, sum up her two major concerns throughout her confinement: the question of reality/unreality (or truth/falsehood) and the beastliness of her useless suffering:

> Nothing about last night, him or me.
> *Did it happen?*
> Fever. I get delirious.
> *If only I knew what I have done.*
> *Useless useless.*
> I won't die I won't die.
>
> Dear dear G. P., this (p. 259, my italics)

Her words are echoed by Nicholas Urfe, at the end of *The Magus*, at his point of fulcrum, his moment of anagnorisis: *"Thou shalt not inflict unnecessary pain"* (p. 641, emphasis in the original).

But, of course, Miranda's most sustained literary allusion is in calling Clegg "Caliban." It was Clegg himself who suggested this nickname to Miranda when he said the "F" in his wallet stood for "Ferdinand." In the entry for December 1st, Miranda tells us that she has been "reading *The Tempest* again all the afternoon" (p. 245). Of the whole play the thing that strikes her most is Prospero's contempt for Caliban, "his knowing that being kind is useless" (p. 245). Prospero, like G. P., feels a strong contempt for the half-creatures, or as G. P. would call them, the masses, the Many. Both G. P. and Prospero think that the Many, Heraclitus's *hoi polloi*,[7] should never be allowed to thrive; they ought to be kept in their place and taught hard: they are those "whom stripes may move, not kindness" (p. 245). Miranda knows the radical truth of both Prospero's and G. P.'s positions, but nevertheless she cannot wholly agree to this, for "I feel (beneath the hate and disgust) for my Caliban" (p. 245).

In an interview published by *Counterpoint* (Newquist, "John Fowles," pp. 218–25), John Fowles explained how he started to think about the plot of *The Collector,* after going one night to the opera to see Béla Bartók's *Bluebeard's Castle,* and how a year later he read in the newspapers the case of a girl who had been kidnapped by a boy and kept in an air-raid shelter at the end of the kidnapper's garden for several days in London. These two avowed sources of *The Collector* were literally interpreted by the first reviewers of the novel, who praised it for its thrilling story, and for the clever organization of suspense. Behind the thrill and the horror of the actual kidnapping, however, John Fowles was insistently pointing at something, for him, much more important, and far less obvious, something for which *The Tempest* is the only source. Miranda, with fine sensibility, stresses it in the first entry of her diary: "Power. It's become so *real.* I know the H-bomb is wrong. But being so weak seems wrong now too" (p. 117, emphasis in the original). These words sum up the quality of Miranda's test: the dilemma she has to solve has to do with the right human beings have to exert power over other human beings and with whether the victim of oppression has a right to shake off the yoke by the use of force. Although Miranda knows she is better than Clegg as a human being, she must submit to him, because he controls her physically:

> He is absolutely inferior to me in all ways. His one superiority is an ability to keep me here. That's the only power he has. He can't behave or think or speak or do anything else better than I can—nearly as well as I can—so he is going to be the Old Man of the Sea until I shake him off somehow. It will have to be by force. (p. 222)

At this stage Miranda is considering a course of action which goes against her avowed pacifism and coincides with the position of Prospero and of G. P.: the shaking off of the yoke of tyranny by violence; a tyranny which is the result of Clegg's unexpected winning of the pools: "Stephano and Trinculo are the football pools. Their wine, the money he won" (p. 245). But, as we know, for all her rationalizing the need to use force, when the moment comes to put her logical conclusions into practice striking a final blow at Clegg's head with the axe, she will hesitate and will suddenly stop fighting (p. 92), thus missing her only opportunity to escape. Rather than a simple failure of nerve, though, Miranda's instinctive reaction has to be interpreted, like Conchis's refusal to kill the guerilla men in order to save his life, as her ultimate affirmation of freedom, an existentialist freedom to choose passivity and death, rather than violence and survival: "It's no use. I'm not a hater by nature. It's as if somewhere in me a certain amount of good-will and kindness is manufactured every day; and it must come out. If I bottle it up, then it bursts out" (p. 224).

If there is a basic difference between G. P. and Miranda, between the mature "aristos" and the young "aristos-to-be," it is this. Miranda still keeps intact her idealism, her love of humanity, while G. P. is more concerned with having control of power, even if only as a means of survival in a world dominated by the masses. Miranda dies because she refuses to give up her belief. Fowles will develop this theme at greater length in *The Magus*.

In the preface to *The Aristos*, Fowles explains Heraclitus's theory of the Many *(hoi polloi)* and the Few *(hoi aristoi),* and goes on to explain his real intention in *The Collector:*

> My purpose in *The Collector* was to attempt to analyse, through a parable, some of the results of this confrontation (between the Many and the Few). Clegg, the kidnapper, committed the evil; but I tried to show that his evil was largely, perhaps wholly, the result of a bad education, a mean environment, being orphaned: all factors over which he had no control. In short, I tried to establish the virtual *innocence* of the Many. Miranda, the girl he imprisoned, had very little more control than Clegg over what she was: she had well-to-do parents, good educational opportunities, inherited aptitude and intelligence. That does not mean that she was perfect. Far from it—she was arrogant in her ideas, a prig, a liberal-humanist snob, like so many university students. Yet if she had not died she might have become something better, the kind of being humanity so desperately needs. (p. 10, emphasis in the original)

The solution Fowles proposes to this confrontation between the Many and the Few implies the recognition by the Few that theirs is a privileged status they have got through mere good luck, luck in the family into which they are born and luck in the combination of genes which has given them a superior intelligence. For Fowles, then, being an "aristos" means realizing that you are in a "state of responsibility" (ibid., p. 10) with respect to the masses: it is the task of the Few to educate the Many. Prospero tried to teach Caliban to speak and think, and he succeeded to a certain extent because he was stronger. But all Miranda's efforts at teaching Clegg failed: Miranda tried consistently to teach her Caliban to speak properly; to think seriously and deeply about important matters; to accept sexuality; to understand human friendship; to use his money positively. All her efforts came to nothing because Clegg controlled her physically. Either Clegg was an irredeemable case and Miranda too young a teacher, or we must agree that the tragic outcome of Miranda's benevolent-humanist ideas put into practice expresses Fowles's conviction that Prospero and G. P. were right, that there is no separating the teaching from the punishing. There seems to be confirmation of this suggestion in the *Counterpoint* interview (ibid., pp. 218–19) where Fowles says:

> [In *The Collector*] I also wanted to attack . . . the contemporary idea that there is something noble about the inarticulate hero. About James Dean and all his literary children and grandchildren, like Salinger's Holden Caufield, and Sillitoe's Arthur Seaton (in *Saturday Night and Sunday Morning*). I don't admire beats, bums, punkies, psychopaths, and inarticulates. I feel sorry for them. I think "adjusted" adolescents are better and more significant than "maladjusted" ones. I'm against the glamorization of the Many.

After reading *Saturday Night and Sunday Morning* Miranda herself remarks, "The most disgusting thing of all is that Alan Sillitoe doesn't show that he's disgusted by his young man. I think they think young men like that are really rather fine" (p. 230). By these direct allusions to such anti-heroes as Sillitoe's Arthur Seaton or Salinger's Holden Caufield, Fowles consciously tries to situate his novel within the realistic tradition of English literature of the 1950s inaugurated by Kinsley Amis's *Lucky Jim* and John Wain's *Hurry on Down*. Like James Dixon and his epigone, Clegg is the prototypical lower-class hero jealously conscious of his deficiencies, who tries to thrive in a world that refuses to admit him. Dixon's criticism of established art, his insensibility towards foreign and classical music, or literature, his outspoken defense of the petty, the mediocre, the trivial, and the vulgar are all features inherited by Clegg, but where Dixon's rejection of established values is rebelliously conscious, Clegg's inadequacies are inherent. In both cases, their behavior is a symptom of social maladjustment: both the New People, in *The Collector*, and James Dixon, in *Lucky Jim*, are the result of the politics of the first Labour Government, the product of the Welfare State. Hence, G. P.'s reticences with regard to socialism (p. 207).

In *Lucky Jim*, Dixon is able to climb from his own social position into the upper class with the help of a woman: Christine's love enables Dixon to become Amis's version of the *aristos*. Her uncle Gore Urquhart will give him a better job in London (as opposed to the provinces), and will introduce him to a restricted circle of the elite. Frederick Clegg, like Dixon, wants to better his social position by means of a woman: Miranda symbolizes for him all the remote and alluring appeal of a superior way of life. For Clegg, however, going upwards doesn't mean conforming to the criteria of the upper classes, as is the case with Dixon. It simply means possessing, exerting power, and finally destroying the thing he cherishes, as he has to kill the butterflies to own them.

The Collector was first published in 1963, a decade after the publication of *Lucky Jim,* which may help explain the difference in the handling of the subject. As Robert Huffaker *(John Fowles,* p. 75) has justly remarked, we must not forget that *The Collector* and *A Clockwork Orange* were published only with a difference of months: both novels present the lower-class inarticulate psychopath as the ultimate stage in the thematic line going back to *Hurry on Down, Look Back in Anger,* and *Lucky Jim.* At this stage hypergamy is not enough to assure the adjustment of the maladjusted representative of the Many; neither is there now compassion or sympathy for his misbehavior. In John Fowles's existentialist world, where hazard and the lucky combination of the genes will decide the difference in intelligence, beauty, and wealth among individuals, the control of power by the better-gifted becomes a question of life and death, not of comedy: what Clegg destroyed, and what might have survived with Miranda, is a superior form of living, a "real life" in Jane Austen's terms, a meaningful and ripe life made up of essences, which Clegg at best would only have been able to imitate. In Fowles's allegory, art stands for this superior form of being, collecting for staleness and death:

> I know what I am to him. A butterfly he has always wanted to catch. I remember (the very first time I met him) G. P. saying that collectors were the worst animals of all. He meant art collectors, of course. I didn't really understand, I thought he was just trying to shock Caroline—and me. But of course, he is right. They are anti-life, anti-art, anti-everything. (p. 123)

Although brought up in the French tradition of fiction and an avowed admirer of the *nouveau roman,* John Fowles has admitted to Lorna Sage ("John Fowles," p. 33) the constant pressure on his writing of what he has called the "crushing sort of (English) realistic tradition": "You can see this opposite pull (of French and English literary traditions) at work in the tragi-comedy of the class battle in *The Collector*" (ibid., p. 31).

With these words Fowles places himself in the situation David Lodge has so eloquently described for the modern writer in *The Novelist at the Crossroads.* As I hope to have shown in my analysis of the novel, *The Collector* exemplifies both the French (or innovating) and the English (or traditional) influences simultaneously at work at every level, linguistic, structural, and thematic: the deft handling of the confession, the diary and the letter conventions; the pastiche-like quality of the cliché-ridden language of Clegg, together with constant references to literature as well as the insertion of the tale of the Ugly Monster and the story captions, all point to the conscious effort of the author to fictionalize his narrative, to write a novel which is first of all, and avowedly, a fiction. At the structural level, the startling use of time and space, the *mise en abyme* Miranda's metadiscourse represents, and the funnel technique he uses to compress the distance between narrative and story time to reach a zero degree of writing at the very end of the novel, show Fowles's ability to reach beyond the boundaries of the Western tradition of fiction into experimentalism. Behind the paraphernalia of literary allusion and Victorian pastiche, behind the apparently trivial situation and the realistic depiction of character, we already sense the disingenuous grin of the man who, a few years later, will write the opening of the famous chapter 13 of *The French Lieutenant's Woman:*

> I do not know. The story I am telling is all imagination. These characters I have created never existed outside my own mind. If I have pretended until now to know my characters' minds and innermost thoughts, it is because I am writing in (just as I have assumed some of the vocabulary and "voice" of) a convention universally accepted at the time of my story: that the novelist stands next to God. He may not know all, yet he tries to pretend he does. But I live in the age of Alan Robbe-Grillet and Roland Barthes; if this is a novel, it cannot be a novel in the modern sense of the word. (p. 85)

2

The Magus

The most straightforward reading of *The Magus*[1] offers a modern version of the myth of the hero's quest for maturity. Structurally, the novel unfolds like a triptych: it is divided into three sections. The first one, from chapters 1 to 9, shows the hero still in his homeland, at the crucial moment in his evolution from adolescence into manhood when he has finished his university training at Oxford and is trying to orient his life. This part ends with his decision to abandon England in search of a job in a remote island in the Aegean, that is to say, with the hero's "call to adventure" and the "crossing of the first threshold" (Campbell, *The Hero with a Thousand Faces*).

The second, and by far the largest, section of the book goes from chapters 10 to chapter 67, and in it the hero undergoes the different phases of trial and testing that constitute his ritual initiation into knowledge. The third section, covering chapters 68 to 77, may be read as the hero's return, his maturity achieved.[2]

From the very beginning, then, Fowles consciously organizes his tale along traditional lines, but uses the convention—as he has done with the diary and epistolary traditions in *The Collector*—for his own particular ends: *The Magus*, while sharing the traditional quest structure, diverges from it in the characteristics of the hero and of his quest. First of all, as we will see, Nicholas's journey, like the journeys of Daniel Martin and of Mr. Bartholomew, has a baffling double status, as it takes place simultaneously in a physical and in a mental domain. As happens in *Daniel Martin* and in *A Maggot*, the physical journey moves forward and echoes the traditional mythological hero's quest, whereas the mental journey follows its own psychological logic and is best described as a fictionalization of the process of individuation of the self, in Jungian terms.

The double nature of the journey is reflected at the narrative level. The main story is narrated retrospectively in the first person by an adult narrator-character, thus adding to the circularity: by allowing Nicholas Urfe to report the tale of his own life in retrospect we are assured from the start that he did return safely from his adventure. At the same time the fact that the narrator is the mature hero speaking about himself when he was still untaught and purblind produces a constant irony similar to that created in *Great Expectations,* where Pip the adult narrator must report the adventures, fears, and feelings of Pip the child, from the latter's perspective and without anticipating later events. The resulting effects of this narrative structure will be further explored in *Daniel Martin.*

Below this narrative level, a metadiscourse containing the story of Conchis's life is narrated by Conchis in the first person, who thus exchanges his role of narrator with Nicholas. At a higher level, however, a third extra-heterodiegetic narrator, identifiable with the author, gnomically comments in two metalepses at the end of the novel on the moral of the whole course of events.

From a thematic point of view, the situation Urfe has experienced with Alison in England, the situation he is experiencing with Lily at Bourani, and the situation Conchis describes when he narrates his life bear clear-cut analogies, so much so that both the metadiscourse and the metatheater may be considered as inverted *mises en abyme* of the primary discourse.

In *Le récit spéculaire,* Lucien Dällenbach defines the *mise en abyme*[3] as a structural reality whose essential property is its capacity to reflect the whole discourse in mirror image, and thus to uncover its formal structure and to enhance the intelligibility of the literary work. The simplest kind of *mise en abyme* is represented by "le blason dans le blason" (ibid., p. 38), a shield that contains within itself the design of a shield. This is the type of reflection we find in *The Murder of Gonzago,* where Claudius sees enacted the murderous act he himself committed with King Hamlet. A more complex kind of reflection is "la réflexion à l'infini," symbolized by the box of Quaker oats, which shows a box of Quaker oats, which . . . *ad infinitum;* while the third type, or "réflexion paradoxale," is a sort of reflection where the fragment is supposed to include the work of which it is a part.

Now, if we take the main story (Alison and Nick) to represent the material; and the masque (Lily and Nick) to represent the psychological aspects of reality; and we add to them Conchis's story (Lily and Conchis) as an inverted mirror image of the first, we may understand *The Magus* as one tale containing three variations of the same story, told from complementary perspectives which, when mixed in the all-enveloping literary text, offer a polymorphous unique whole.

The fact that it is so difficult to separate these three theoretically different "variations" points to one important structural characteristic of the novel, namely that the *mises en abyme* it contains are not "concentrating," but, on the contrary, are *mises en abyme éclatées.* According to Mieke Bal *(Narratologie,* p. 106), the *mise en abyme concentrante* is a story within the story, a resumé of the principal story which is contained within the principal one; the *mise en abyme éclatée,* on the other hand, functions inversely, by scattering rather than concentrating its elements within the main story, that is, by dispersing the elements of the story-resumé throughout the principal story.[4]

With these definitions in mind we may say that both the masque and the metadiscourse function in *The Magus* as *mises en abyme éclatées,* that is, as *mises en abyme* whose elements are not linearly developed, but rather appear scattered and intertwined with the elements of the main story and with the elements of each other, forming an inextricable unity.

As we know, the masque develops at Bourani only over weekends and stops during weekdays when Nicholas has to work as a teacher at the Byron school; so it follows a discontinuous temporal course, further altered whenever Conchis takes on the role of narrator to tell his life. In general, two devices are used within the masque: portrait-like staging of iconic scenes by secondary actors, such as the double hunting of the satyr, the apparition of Robert Faulkes, or of the jackal-headed Anubis, or the enactment of the persecution of the Greek guerilla men by the German troops. The way in which these iconic scenes function in the masque is similar to the way in which the literary icons function in the metadiscourse; that is, by symbolically encapsulating one particular point later to be expanded and explained either in the masque or in Conchis's narration.

The other device in the masque is the performance of the *Three Hearts* story by Nicholas himself and the twins. Properly speaking, only this part of the masque may be said to constitute a *mise en abyme* of the primary story, while the iconic scenes, by interrupting its development, and intertwining with it, with the metadiscourse and even with the main story, scatter their punctual meaning in all directions. Sometimes these iconic scenes function as vivid analeptic materializations of something Nicholas has just read or heard at Bourani, as is the case with the apparition of Robert Faulkes; but the iconic scenes also often precede the account, standing as mute proleptic icons, whose meaning will only be gathered much later. This is what happens, for instance, when Nicholas is assaulted and made prisoner by the German troops and is accused by one of the guerilla men of being *prodotis,* a "traitor" (p. 379). Later on Nicholas will hear the story of the three guerillas from Conchis's lips and will learn that the person who was considered a traitor was Conchis himself, but we must not forget that Nicholas has behaved treacherously with Alison and with women in general, so that the meaning of the iconic scene expands itself in all directions, offering a wealth of possible interpretations.

The way in which these iconic scenes function, as well as the function of the iconic tales Conchis tells, is very similar to the way in which images may be used impressionistically. By the impressionistic use of images Robert Humphrey *(Stream-of-Consciousness,* p. 77) understands "the description of an immediate perception in figurative terms which expands to express an emotional

attitude toward a more complex thing." Like the images used impressionistically, the meaning of the narrative and theatrical icons "figuratively expand to
express an emotional attitude towards a more complex thing," which is exactly
what happens when Nicholas hears the word *prodotis*.

The combination of the formal alternations of elements from the masque
with elements of the discourse and the metadiscourse, plus the polymorphous
metaphorical expansions of meanings effected by the iconic tales and scenes,
endlessly pointing to various, more complex levels of reading, is what has
sometimes produced a baffling effect on the readers of *The Magus*. These
readers feel, as it were, lost in a centerless maze which leads them nowhere.
The effect may be frustrating, but we must not forget that, from a structural
point of view, the *mise en abyme éclatée* neatly echoes the thematic message
of the novel.

It is within this centerless maze that Nicholas Urfe has to progress. In the
mythological version of the hero's quest, the hero is generally endowed with
several outstanding features, by which he can be easily recognized and which
will ensure his survival through the dangerous journey. Often the mythological
hero is a god's son, or has been miraculously begotten or saved, or is related
in some way to a certain divinity. Often, too, the hero's name points to his
divine or supernatural condition.

In *The Magus* the hero's name—Nicholas Urfe—has no supernatural connotations but, although it has been related by Fowles ("Foreword," p. 9) to
"earth," primarily evokes the world of literature: "The wishful tradition is that
our family came over from France after the Revocation of the Edict of Nantes—
noble Huguenots remotely allied to Honoré d'Urfé, author of the seventeenth-
century best-seller *L'Astrée*" (p. 15). The hero's ancestry, wishfully connected
with a well-known and reputed writer and with a tradition of dissent, has later
developed into the prototypical representative of the English upper-middle-class
to which Miranda also belongs. Nicholas Urfe's ancestry, then, is established
in mock-heroic terms as a combination of real and not-so-real wishful *data*.

The only son of middle-class parents with precise ideas about "Discipline,
Tradition and Responsibility" (p. 15), but also the true born inheritor of a French
and literary tradition, fostered by the postwar atmosphere at high school and
Oxford, and the reading of a novelist such as D. H. Lawrence, Urfe soon finds
himself living two different and opposed lives: "I went on leading a double life
in the Army, queasily playing at being Brigadier 'Blazer' Urfe's son in public
and nervously reading *Penguin New Writing* poetry pamphlets in private"
(p. 16).

The parallelism between Urfe's position and that of Miranda Grey at this
stage is striking: both are the children of middle-class parents with means; both
have had the best possible educational opportunities; both feel ashamed of their
parents for different reasons (Urfe of his father; Miranda of her mother and

aunt); and both have artistic talent. In the preface to *The Aristos* (p. 10), Fowles speaks disparagingly of Miranda, calling her a "prig," a beautiful and intelligent young woman, proud of her natural gifts, who still lacks the necessary insight. Urfe is also one of these snobbish university students. "Prig" is the word that comes to mind when we hear of Nicholas's membership of the Oxford club "Les Hommes Revoltés: A club whose members devoted themselves to drink, very dry sherry, and (as a protest against those shabby duffel-coated last years of the 'forties')," to wear "dark-grey suits and black ties for our meetings" (p. 17).

The desire to create a fashionable club of this sort with its pompous French name and the effort to mark off their members from the common run of mortals by the adoption of "expensive habits and affected manners" (p. 17), reveal Urfe as the prototype of the upper-middle-class with a sensitivity toward tradition and "class" that he so thoroughly despised in his parents, while his disgust and contempt for "those shabby duffel-coated last years of the 'forties'" (p. 17) links him with G. P. in the latter's rejection of the "New People," the duffel-coat, the corduroy jacket with leather-patched elbows and the bicycle instead of a car being the symptomatic symbols that characterized the "angry generation" of the late forties and fifties.

The association of the "angry young men" with a wider class struggle was, according to Blake Morrison *(The Movement,* p. 58), "one reason why the group established itself so quickly in the years 1953–1955," but also the reason why the literary generation of the 1930s reacted so aggressively to the emergence of the Movement. "Philistinism," "little Englandism," "provincialism," and "social concern" were labels liberally bestowed upon the Movement writers by their analyzers and detractors. They all point to the Movement's rejection of the Modernist ideas of art and culture, that is of elitism, cosmopolitanism, and technical experimentation.

Nicholas Urfe's nervous reading of the *Penguin New Writing* series is in sharp contrast to James Dixon's boredom with the Welches' "arty get-togethers" and his anger with a reading of Anouilh, compare Amis's remark on "filthy Mozart," while Urfe's admiration for Greek culture is directly opposed to Philip Larkin's "A Greek statue kicked in the privates" (ibid., p. 59).

Before taking the decision to leave England, Urfe has tried a first job as a teacher in a "minor public school in East Anglia" (p. 18); he boastfully tells us that he got the job because the only two other applicants were "redbrick." However, the drab, monotonous, and unheroic life he leads at the school proves too hard a trial for the young man of aspirations:

> The mass-produced middle-class boys I had to teach were bad enough; the claustrophobic little town was a nightmare; but the really intolerable thing was the common-room. Boredom, the numbing annual predictability of life, hung over the staff like a cloud. And it was real

boredom, not modish *ennui*. . . . I could not spend my life crossing such a Sahara; and the more I felt it the more I felt also that the smug, petrified school was a toy model for the entire country and that to quit the one and not the other would be ridiculous. There was also a girl I was tired of. (p. 18)

Like so many Modernist and post-Modernist writers, Nicholas Urfe feels the necessity of breaking out of the narrow boundaries of his barren homeland in search of transcendence. Here, in mythological terms, is the origin of his "call to adventure." But Urfe's protest that it was "real boredom, not modish *ennui*" is heavily qualified by his last, reluctant statement that "there was also a girl I was tired of." At this stage, again and again, Urfe presents himself as an intelligent but spoiled young man who wants to lead a full, creative life, but for the wrong reasons and primarily for the sake of impressing others.

In "Collectors and Creators: The Novels of John Fowles," John Mellors says "The rules of the game are flexible, but it almost always involves a conflict between collector and creator, the two classes into which Fowles divides mankind" (p. 65). Although essentially true, the statement needs qualification. If Frederick Clegg is a particularly awesome exponent of the human tendency to "collect" and Miranda of the potentialities of a "creator-to-be," Nicholas Urfe may be said to bring together in his own person these two tendencies: thematically, *The Magus* can be viewed as the inversion of *The Collector*. Using the Dickensian technique of focalizing the same themes from different points of view in subsequent novels, Fowles undertakes to analyze in *The Collector* and *The Magus* the clash between the lower- and upper-middle classes from two complementary perspectives. In *The Collector,* as we have seen, Fowles studies the negative effects of a nonconformist, mediocre, lower-middle-class upbringing on a shy, orphaned and unintelligent youth, and how the unexpected winning of the pools threatens to dislocate the balance of power between the "many" and the "few." In this novel, the sympathy is wholly on Miranda's side, the beautiful and clever art student who represents the highest potentialities of the human being. In *The Magus,* on the other hand, Fowles makes the vulgar, mediocre but appealing Alison (representative of the man in the street) the innocent victim, and Nicholas, the upper-middle-class snob with a polished upbringing and a superior intelligence, the aggressor.

One outstanding feature of Frederick Clegg is his incapacity to have a normal sexual relation with Miranda or with any other woman: he kidnaps Miranda because he is madly in love with her—throughout the novel he protests that his is a pure, uncontaminated love, devoid of sinful fleshly cupidity. Nicholas Urfe, on the other hand, is a Don Juan type, a Lovelace obsessed with taking to bed as many girls as possible and boastful of his incapacity for "love." For all his protests, Urfe is primarily presented as a "collector": "I didn't collect conquests, but by the time I left Oxford I was a dozen girls away from virginity.

I found sexual success and the apparently ephemeral nature of love equally pleasing" (p. 21). Both Clegg and Urfe suffer from a basic deficiency. Clegg's portentous capacity to love a single woman eternally is transmuted into Urfe's reckless changing of sexual partners. "Learning" for Clegg involves learning how to go beyond his monomaniacal fixation on Miranda and develop sexually, and this he does in an awful and ironic way: he develops sadistic and voyeuristic attitudes and, when Miranda dies, is able to focus his "interest" on another girl without falling in love with her ("this time it won't be love" [p. 283]). Urfe's reaching of maturity, on the other hand, must involve a recognition of Alison's worth, the rejection of sex as an end in itself, and his acknowledgment of love.

Nicholas Urfe, then, synthesizes in himself some of the outstanding "creative" characteristics of Miranda: the artistic bent, the love of transcendence, the superior intelligence and breeding; but also has the basic "collecting" quality of Frederick Clegg. He is, in a word, the "aristos-to-be" blinded by pride and folly. John Mellors's statement then, that the "collector and (the) creator (are) the two classes into which Fowles divided mankind" (ibid., p. 65) might be qualified by saying that, in the case of Urfe rather than classes of people, the "collector" and the "creator" represent deep human traits to be encountered simultaneously in the same person. This point is crucial, for it explains why Miranda is unable to teach Clegg while Conchis succeeds in his teaching of Urfe:

"Are you elect?"
"Elect?"
"Do you feel chosen by anything?"
"Chosen?"
"John Leverrier felt chosen by God."
"I don't believe in God. And I certainly don't feel chosen."
"I think you may be."
I smiled obviously. "Thank you."
"It is not a compliment. Hazard makes you elect. You cannot elect yourself." (p. 87)

In John Fowles's modern version of the mythical quest, then, the hero bears the marks of the superior being even though he still doesn't know it himself; like the mythological hero, his character is marred by a blemish: his inconsiderate and rakish sexual feats and his incapacity to love. This he will learn through the ordeals of the quest.

The first stage of the mythological journey, the "call to adventure," says Joseph Campbell *(The Hero,* p. 58), "signifies that destiny has summoned the hero and transferred his spiritual center of gravity from within the pale of his society to a zone unknown. This fateful region of both treasures and danger, may be variously presented: as a distant land, a forest, a kingdom underground, beneath the waves, or above the sky, a secret island, lofty mountain-top, or profound dream state; but it is always a place of strange fluid and polymorphous beings, unimaginable torments, superhuman deeds, and impossible delight."

In the novel, the distant land of torments and delight is Greece; to it Urfe is driven by an irresistible impulse and when he finally lands on it he finds that his expectations are surpassed by reality. Urfe's first contact with Greece is described in wholly metaphorical terms, which underline its mythical quality:

> It was like a journey into space. I was standing on Mars, knee-deep in thyme, under a sky that seemed never to have known dust or cloud. I looked down at my pale London hands. Even they seemed changed, nauseatingly alien, things I should long ago have disowned. (p. 49)

This world of superhuman purity which "seemed never to have known dust or cloud" is also a world of potentially simultaneous good and evil:

> When that ultimate Mediterranean light fell on the world around me I could see it was supremely beautiful; but when it touched me, I felt it was hostile. It seemed to corrode, not cleanse. . . . It was partly the terror, the stripping-to-essentials, of love; because I fell totally and for ever in love with the Greek landscape from the moment I arrived. But with the love came a contradictory, almost irritating feeling of impotence and inferiority, as if Greece were a woman so sensually provocative that I must fall physically and desperately in love with her, and at the same time so calmly aristocratic that I should never be able to approach her. (p. 49)

So, from the start, Urfe senses this "Circe-like" quality of Greece, its potential benignity and its potential aggressiveness, which is the essential quality of the "unknown" in mythical terms. To express his ambivalent love-hatred for Greece, Urfe uses a simile which is extraordinarily apt, for it anticipates in a verbal icon the kind of trial the hero will undergo. The comparison of Greece to an ever-enticing, every-denying woman also works towards our identification of the changeable Lily/Julie/Vanessa figure with Greece. Urfe stresses this identification by using a technique of personification elsewhere: "What Alison was not to know—since I hardly realized it myself—was that I had been deceiving her with another woman during the latter part of September. The woman was Greece" (p. 39). And again: "To get through the anxious wait for the secondary stage not to develop, *I began quietly to rape the island*" (p. 63, my italics).

From his arrival in Greece on October 2nd to "a Sunday late in May," Urfe lives on Phraxos a sterile life of loneliness and depression. His relation with Alison is more and more feeble: he only thinks of her at "moments of sexual frustration, not regretted love (p. 54). By December he is determined to "cut (Alison and London) away from (his) life" (p. 54). Simultaneously he deepens his relationship with Demetriades, a somewhat caricatured modern equivalent of the mythological defenders of the boundary, who will help him in his reckless pursuit of amoral sexual gratification. Demetriades takes him to a brothel in

Athens to which Urfe would later return by himself, and at Christmas the hero even indulges in some "Gide-like moments" (p. 57). At the same time, Urfe dreams of becoming a world-famous poet: "But then, one bleak March Sunday, the scales dropped from my eyes . . . the truth rushed down on me like a burning avalanche. I was not a poet" (pp. 57–58).

The burning of his poems and the diagnosis of syphilis are the tangible outcomes of his two self-destructive primordial occupations during the winter. Still, Urfe is too blind to see his failures from the right perspective: he indulges in self-pity *("Je suis maudit,"* p. 59), and decides that his life is too sterile to be worth living any more. The reasons for his suicide are wholly romantic and aesthetic, a way of "creating" something at last: "It was a Mercutio death I was looking for, not a real one. A death to be remembered, not the real death of a true suicide, the death obliterate" (p. 62). The comments are those of the mature narrator in retrospect. At that stage Nicholas was unable to see the "intensely false—in existentialist terms, inauthentic" (p. 62) quality of his suicide, and thus the contrast in which it stands with regard to Alison's real and authentic desire to die:

> I don't want to live any more. I spend most of my life not wanting to live . . . I'm only happy when I forget to exist. When just my eyes or my ears or my skin exist. I can't remember having been happy for two or three years. Since the abortion. (p. 42)

From a mythical point of view, Urfe's "inauthentic" death symbolizes the descent into the "belly of the whale" which, according to Campbell *(The Hero,* p. 90) symbolizes "the idea that the passage of the magical threshold is a transit into a sphere of rebirth." In the novel, Urfe's token suicide and the burning of his poems as well as the feeling that the only way on is "down, down and down" (p. 63) stresses the idea that "the passage of the threshold is a form of self-annihilation" *(The Hero,* p. 91) previous to his entry into the sacred place where he will undergo an important metamorphosis before he is reborn.

In medieval iconography the gargoyles at the entrances of the cathedrals are symbols of the guardians of the threshold: they stand in resentful animosity against those who dare cross the boundary without the appropriate mood, but will not touch the initiate, as the whale will safely vomit the hero it has swallowed.

When Urfe approaches Bourani for the first time he finds on the beach a pair of footfins, a towel, and a paperback anthology of English poetry. Some lines from "Little Gidding," from poems by Auden and by Ezra Pound have been underlined: these lines are all gargoyle-like warnings for the hero, summing up in a verbal icon the essence and quality of what is to come. In them the aim and form of the hero's trials are synthesized. They all stress the danger and exhaustion of the journey to hell prior to the acquisition of knowledge of self which culminates the journey. At the same time, the fact that the warnings take the form of poems also points to the basic quality of the realm the hero is entering: the polysemic world of literature. The incongruous notice Nicholas soon after finds with the words *Salle d'attente* "in the sort of position one sees *Trespassers will be prosecuted* notices in England" (p. 71) bears a similar double warning. The notice also confirms the hero in his intuition that he has finally come to the "realm," as it explains Mitford's warning, "Beware of the waiting-room" (p. 45).

When Nicholas jumps over the broken barbed-wire fence that offers a token protection to Bourani, he enters a mysterious realm where he is to be confronted by a series of ordeals intended in principle to test and adjust his notion of reality. During his first visit to the villa, Conchis explains the meaning of the word "Bourani":

> "Two hundred years ago it was their [the Albanian pirates'] slang word for gourd. Also for skull." He moved away. "Death and water." (p. 83)

In Conchis's interpretation, the skull stands for death, the gourd for water. Thus, Bourani may be said to contain the two opposed principles of life and death, but this is not the meaning with which the word "skull" is used elsewhere in the novel. It is often used to suggest, rather, the inner, mental or psychological potentialities of man. Thus, after the incident in the Earth, when Nicholas is left locked up for half an hour, he finds after his release two "clues" hanging from a tree: a doll in rags and a human skull. Nicholas interprets the doll quite easily: "The doll was Julie, and said that she was evil, she was black, under the white innocence she wore" (p. 459), but is undecided about the interpretation of the skull: "Alas, poor Yorick. Disembowelled corpses? Or Frazer . . . *The Golden Bough?*" (p. 460).

With these possible interpretations in mind, Nicholas walks away. As he does so, the adult narrator comments: "The skull and his wife swayed in a rift of breeze. Leaving them there, in their mysterious communion, I walked fast away" (p. 460). This comment on the "mysterious communion" of "the skull and his wife" shows that the mature Urfe has solved his doubts in the direction of the third possibility. Julie is neither a symbol of death nor of sadistic slaughter, but belongs, like Frazer's "dolls in sacred woods" (p. 460), to the realm of myth and fantasy: that is, to the realm of the psychological.

The psychological nature of Bourani is further enhanced by the poem Urfe writes during his first weekend stay at the villa:

> From this skull-rock strange golden roots throw
> Ikons and incidents; the man in the mask

Manipulates. I am the fool that falls
And never learns to wait and watch,
Icarus eternally damned, the dupe of time . . .
(p. 95)

The skull-rock from which "golden roots throw ikons and incidents" may literally refer to the *head*land on which the villa is set, but its "golden roots" suggest golden hair, and it is from them that "ikons," that is, symbols, and incidents spring.

Over and over again, the psychological entity of Bourani is stressed. So, for instance, when Urfe first knocks at the door of the villa, he has "a *déjà vu* feeling of having stood in the same place, before that particular proportion of the arches, that particular contrast of shade and burning landscape outside" (p. 78), which contrasts with his strong awareness of coming backward to reality after leaving the "domain": "Yet I enjoyed the walk back to school. . . . In a sense I re-entered reality as I walked" (p. 157).

Similarly, John Fowles has explained the etymology of "Conchis" saying that by it he meant to suggest "echo-catching, sea-murmuring" qualities, but, as Barry N. Olshen points out *(John Fowles,* p. 41), it also "carries an obvious pun on conscious(ness)." It is, therefore, easy to agree with this critic when he says that

> the symbolic names, in combination with the geographical metaphors . . . , already provide more than sufficient indication that the journey from London to Phraxos and back to London is a journey of self-discovery, to be interpreted as both external and internal reality. It is at once a physical reality, that is, an actual journey over space and time, and a metaphorical account of a nonphysical, experimental reality, that other kind of trip over the inner landscape of the mind. (ibid., p. 41)

After the discovery of the objects on the sand, and following the quotation of the line from "Little Gidding," "We shall not cease from exploration" (p. 69), Urfe immediately starts gathering information about Bourani and its mysterious owner, Maurice Conchis. From the start, the difficulty of establishing a one-sided, univocal truth about him becomes apparent. Conchis is alternately described as a German collaborationist, a patriotic major, a retired musician, a cynical man and an atheist and, simply, as a man who cherishes his privacy. Neither can Urfe himself describe his looks: he feels incapable of guessing his age and alternately thinks he might be "slightly mad, no doubt harmlessly so" (p. 79). But "then he changed . . . he wasn't mad after all" (p. 30). Perhaps he was "simply an old queer" (p. 85), or "a transvestite" (p. 90): Conchis was "somehow not contemporary . . . , his whole appearance was foreign. He had a bizarre family resemblance to Picasso; saurian as well as simian . . . the quintessential Mediterranean man" (p. 81), and later Urfe will describe him as "Picasso imitating Ghandy imitating a buccaneer" (p. 139). Nevertheless, his manners suggest "the quick aplomb of a conjurer" (p. 80).

All these and other efforts Urfe makes at describing the ever-changing nature of Conchis and his doubts about his sexual tendencies point to the two basic qualities of the "magus": his protean nature, on the one hand, that is, an inherent capacity for transformation to match the polymorphous quality of reality and, on the other, his bisexual condition, which points to his godlike nature and also perhaps to his double role of both wiseman and trickster. Fowles himself has explained in the foreword to the revised edition (p. 10) the intended meaning of these two basic qualities of Conchis: "I did intend Conchis to exhibit a series of masks representing human notions of God, from the supernatural to the jargon-ridden scientific; that is, a series of human illusions about something that does not exist in fact, absolute knowledge and absolute power." Conchis's masks express, then, the novel's basic message that absolute knowledge is unattainable, that reality, and our notions of God, are constructs made up of human illusions.

Having recognized the simultaneously physical and psychological nature of the hero's quest we might analyze the form it actually takes. Throughout the second section of the novel Nicholas Urfe will wildly try to find his Ariadne's thread in the maze set out for him by the Magus: he will insist in separating illusion from reality, lies from truth, the apparent from the actual. He will write letters, will study archives, will ask questions, will compare reports and will write down names, dates, and places, refusing, in a word, to admit the polymorphous nature of reality, which is precisely what Maurice Conchis wants him to learn. From the start, Conchis insists that what is going on at Bourani must be taken as a mere entertainment, belonging to the realm of the unreal. This is why he gives Nicholas a book entitled *Le masque français du dixhuitième siècle* with a passage marked out for reading. After having done so, Nicholas comments:

> All that happened at Bourani was in the nature of a private masque; and no doubt the passage was a hint to me that I should, both out of politeness and for my own pleasure, not poke my nose behind the scenes. I felt ashamed of the questions I had asked at Agia Varvara. (p. 165)

At its surface level, the passage works as a reality-enhancing mechanism: by openly acknowledging the fictive quality of Conchis's experiments, the passage gives Nicholas a pleasurable feeling of knowing where he stands. When Nicholas tells Conchis that he has already read the passage, the latter says: "It is only a metaphor, but it may help" (p. 166). Nicholas takes this remark literally and is further reassured. But, of course, *Le masque français* is a metaphor of the masque organized by Conchis in the same way Conchis's masque is a metaphor of the real world. This blurring of the boundaries between fiction and reality becomes clearer if compared to Conchis's explanation of his reason for burning all the novels within his reach:

> "Why should I struggle through hundreds of pages of fabrication to reach half a dozen of very little truths?"
> "For fun?"
> "Fun!" he pounced on the words. "Words are for truth. For facts. Not fiction."
> "I see." (p. 96)

Nicholas says "I see," but, of course, he does not, at this stage, understand the real meaning of Conchis's words, his warning that Nicholas's own "struggle through several hundreds of pages" in the godgame will not be a question of amusement, but something serious and truth revealing.

Conchis's remark, then, again emphasizes the blurring of boundaries between literature and nonliterature, literature symbolizing the mythical, archetypal, and psychological side of man. To mature, Nicholas must be able to understand the essentially polymorphous nature of truth and the futility of drawing boundaries between literature and nonliterature, that is, between the real and the unreal, the ontological and the psychological. Metaphorically, then, we can say that Nicholas will mature the day he is able to interpret his life creatively, not literally, as he has been doing so far. Before coming to Bourani, Nicholas thought he knew very well what sort of man he was and what he wanted to be in life; he also had set ideas about his parents, about English society in general, and about Alison in particular. The function of the masque will be to shatter Nicholas's absolute convictions by showing him the complexity of truth and by testing his capacity to accept both reality and fantasy.

By burning all the novels within his reach and by dedicating the rest of his life to "truth" and "reality," not fiction, Conchis is performing an act similar to that carried out by the friends of Don Quixote with his books of chivalry: old fiction is burned only to allow Don Quixote himself to live a real life which, after all, is only a further fiction. Like Mr. B. in *A Maggot*, Conchis burns his books in order to be able to create a "real fiction," a masque which will permit Urfe to mature as a man. But, of course, not only the masque at Bourani is a fiction: the outer world, Athens, and England are also fictional places described in a novel entitled *The Magus*. Nicholas Urfe himself is just a fictional character like Don Quixote and the span of his life is included within *The Magus* in the same way as Don Quixote's "real" adventures, as opposed to the fictional adventures of his books of chivalry, are included in *El Quijote*.

Bearing Dällenbach's definition of the *mise en abyme* in mind, it is easy to see the events organized by Conchis at Bourani as primarily a reenactment of the relation between Alison and Nicholas, in which Julie plays the role of Alison but where the premises are inverted: Nicholas fails to understand the real value of Alison beneath her commonness, he doesn't value the love she offers him and refuses to admit that he loves her in his turn. Consequently, Julie will perform throughout the masque the role of a delicate, innocent, rare, and intelligent young woman, little versed in sexual matters, who seems to be offering him the opportunity to share a unique romantic experience. From the start, Julie and Alison come to represent in Nicholas's mind two quite disparate personalities: "I sat on the bunk again. (Alison) pulled off her jumper and shook her hair free. I invoked the image of Julie, but somehow it was a situation that Julie could never have got into" (p. 262).

Alison and Nicholas had become sex partners from the very first day they met, their love, whether avowed or not, developing later. In the masque the reverse situation is enacted: Julie will captivate Nicholas first, delaying the fulfillment of his sexual aspirations till the very end of their relation. At the same time, the successive metamorphoses of Lily into Julie and finally into Dr. Vanessa Maxwell will be accompanied by shocking revelations about her sexual capacity, which will progressively corrode Nicholas's earlier notions about her virginal innocence and purity, ending up in climactic lovemaking the night before the trial. The inversion is, then, very neat: thematically, the Julie-Nicholas relationship acts as the symmetrical mirror image of the Alison-Nicholas relationship: while the latter exists in the realm of physical reality and takes place within what Olshen *(John Fowles, p. 41)* described as the "actual journey over space and time," the former exists in the psychological realm and belongs to "that other kind of trip over the inner landscape of the mind" (ibid., p. 41).

Thematically and structurally, then, the masque may be seen as a *mise en abyme* of the main story in *The Magus.* But what is its real aim? Robert Huffaker *(John Fowles,* p. 58), among others, has analyzed the close connection between Jung's theories of the archetypes and the development of the godgame:

> The godgame is initiation ritual, dramatized fiction, and several other things; but in *reality,* the metatheatre is an elaborate psychodramatic application of Jung's psychology to Nick's individual case. Jungian analysis aims to bring about a consciousness of one's mental processes and to rescue modern man from his own facelessness—a rescue which Nick needs badly. (emphasis in the original)

From Huffaker's point of view, the aim of the masque is to help Nicholas control his own behavior, "by helping him to understand his unconscious feelings and drives, but also to appreciate their suggestions of truth, their universal beauty, and their function in motivating him to happiness, kindness, and creativity, as well as to sorrow, cruelty and destructiveness" (ibid., p. 58). Conchis's task, then, is to help Nicholas become aware of the fact that the unknowable, the mysterious, "does exist within the human mind." Huffaker concludes:

By allowing the individual person to retain his faith in the beauty and efficacy of his own irrational nature, Jung's method would bring the neurotic to harmony and creativity by reinforcing his individuality. The theory is designed to help man become his own magus—to exult in his own unconscious drives and to use them for his own happiness and creativity—and for the happiness of his fellow-man. (ibid., pp. 58–59)

The highlighting of the literary and psychological quality of the world in which Nicholas Urfe is made to move should enable us to understand the peculiar characteristics of the ordeals the hero will have to endure at Bourani. First of all, Nicholas is attracted to Bourani in much the same way that fairy-tale children are attracted to the witch's chocolate house: a book of English poetry; a towel with the musky scent of sandalwood; the enigmatic *salle d'attente* notice; the rumors about Conchis, are all sure enough lures for the excitement-starved Urfe. In the villa the role of the gems/gold/chocolate/candy of the fairy tales is now played by a series of "authentic" works of art: the "authentic" Modigliani and Bonnards, a maquette by Rodin, a Pleyel harpsichord, and even the fifteenth-century Venetian window which, Urfe realizes with a pang, is the very same window Fra Angelico painted in *The Annunciation,* besides a series of authentic-looking ancient Greek vases and Edwardian "curiosa," including a picture of Conchis's long-deceased fiancée. Conchis gives Urfe all kind of details about the form in which he came to own these works of art, implying by the way that he possessed many others, and Nicholas believes him. So, from the start, the villa is presented as a sort of tabernacle of the fine arts and Conchis as an artist himself, a wonderful musician who further captivates him with his music.

Art would have been enough to allure Urfe, but to art Conchis adds another vital source of attraction: mystery, the expectation of the strange and unknown:

He was standing in the doorway, giving me his intense look. He seemed to gather strength; to decide that the mystery must be cleared up; then spoke.
"I am psychic."
The house seemed full of silence; and suddenly everything that had happened led to this. (p. 100)

What puzzles Urfe most is Conchis's ability to baffle him, to disprove his conclusions and expectations. The result of this endless bafflement, of this never knowing what Conchis is really at, produces in Nicholas a mixed feeling of attraction and fear:

I was increasingly baffled by Conchis. At times he was so dogmatic that I wanted to laugh, to behave in the traditional xenophobic, continental-despising way of my race; at times, rather against my will, he impressed me—not only as a rich man with some enviable works of art in his house. And now he frightened me. It was the kind of illogical fear of the supernatural that in others made me sneer; but all along I felt that I was invited not out of hospitality, but for some other reason. He wanted to use me in some way. (p. 102)

Attraction and fear, the two basic feelings aroused by any fairy tale or gothic story,[5] are already felt by Urfe during his first visit to Bourani. The combination of these two will constitute Conchis's only weapon to ensure the return of Urfe to the villa weekend after weekend. But, having once aroused his interest, Conchis has to provide new means of maintaining it. In keeping with the literary quality of their world, Conchis will entertain Urfe by telling him stories, thus entering the field of yet another literary genre, the didactic master-pupil colloquy. Nicholas is aware of this didactic purpose of his host, and he expresses it with the image of the Victorian picture:

> In some way we (Julie and Nicholas) were both cast now as his students, his disciples. I remembered that favourite Victorian picture of the bearded Elizabethan seaman pointing to sea and telling a story to two goggle-eyed little boys. (p. 311)

Like the sages and the prince in *The Seven Sages,* Conchis teaches Nicholas by telling him stories with a clear-cut moral. Thus, in essence, the training of Urfe at Bourani may be said to consist of two major exercises: telling of stories and participation in the masque.

The overall structure of *The Magus* can easily be seen as linear by virtue of the discourse narrated by Nicholas Urfe. Within this linear development, the central episodes corresponding to his visits to Bourani disrupt the linear development by the introduction of a second narrator: at Bourani Nicholas sometimes hands over the narrative role to Maurice Conchis, who in his turn narrates his own life story to Nicholas and also tells him tales. Thus, the roles of narrator and listener are reversed: Nicholas listens and Conchis narrates. From a structural point of view, these alternations imply a change of narrative level similar to the one we found in *The Collector.* When Nicholas hands over the narrative role to Conchis the linearity of the primary discourse is arrested and the narrative time altered. The stories Conchis narrates either refer to episodes of his own life or are tales, and so must be viewed as heterodiegetic digressions, digressive anachronies, unrelated in principle to the diegesis. If there is a relation between them and the story of Urfe's life, it is simply analogical.

In *Narratologie* (pp. 107–9), Mieke Bal describes the function of the diagrammatical icon as identical to the function of the *mise en abyme,* with one difference: while the *mise en abyme* analogically reflects the whole discourse, the icon only reflects part of it.[6] With this definition in mind we may say that the stories and the tales Conchis tells function as diagrammatical icons of concrete points Conchis wants Nicholas to understand. Thus, the first time Nicholas refuses to tell him anything about Alison, Conchis unexpectedly tells him the tale of the Swiss and the goats. With the image of the beautiful Bonnard picture still in mind, Urfe has mentally rejected Alison as a desirable reality, in favor of the ideal woman painted by Bonnard: "I thought of the Bonnard; that was reality; such moments; not what one could tell" (p. 99). Although Nicholas does not utter this thought, Conchis seems to know what he is thinking, for he then says:

> "Greece is like a mirror. It makes you suffer. Then you learn."
> 'To live alone?"
> "To live with what you are." (p. 99)

And then Conchis starts telling Urfe how he once knew a Swiss who had come to end his days at Phraxos. He was a man who "had spent his life assembling watches and reading about Greece" (p. 99). He had one hidden passion, goats, and one day he decided that to be a shepherd on a remote island in Greece was all he wanted in life: "He was alone. No one ever wrote to him. Visited him. Totally alone. And I believe the happiest man I have ever met" (p. 99).

The tale of the Swiss-turned-shepherd is the literary materialization of the sentence "to live with what you are," which analogically reflects precisely what Urfe, who misunderstands the correct use of art, has failed to do with Alison. Alison has always fallen short of his expectations because Nicholas expects her to embody his own idea of woman, and cannot take her for what she really is. By telling him the tale of the Swiss at this precise moment, Conchis is rejecting his point of view, but is also giving us a clue for the interpretation of the following move in the masque: no sooner has Urfe mentally compared Alison to the Bonnard girl than Conchis leads him to the table where stands a large picture of Lily in her Edwardian dress. Conchis tells him that she died a long time ago, and that she was his fiancée. A little later, downstairs, Conchis shows him a glass cabinet which contains various antique objects with only one thing in common, their obscenity, and among them, another picture of the Edwardian girl. The display of obscene "curiosa" makes Urfe wonder about the perverted sense of humor or the simple bad taste of their owner. Neither the reader nor Nicholas is able at this stage to gather the connection between these obscene objects and the ethereal, virginal-looking Edwardian girl, nor between this girl and the naked girl in the Bonnard picture. However, Conchis has carefully drawn the analogies: if Lily is to come to life at all (as she later will) she must do so by stepping out of the picture, for she is Urfe's ideal woman come real, and the fact that she is surrounded by obscene objects is a warning that we should not trust her virginal appearance. Thus the display of the "curiosa" and the pictures of the Edwardian girl already forerun the essential meaning of the metatheater.

If Urfe wants to enjoy the unique experience of seeing the ideal woman become flesh, he must allow the blurring of boundaries between the real and the unreal; the logical and the psychological. Conchis is very clear on this point from the beginning, when he reprimands Nicholas for behaving like a porcupine, which prefers to starve to death rather than lay back its protective spines. To the incredulous Urfe's question, "You . . . travel to other worlds? . . . In the flesh?" (p. 106), Conchis's answer is unequivocal: "If you can tell me where the flesh ends and the mind begins, I will answer that" (p. 106).

Toward the end of the second section, after having passed through the nightmare of the trial, Nicholas Urfe returns to Bourani, and to "The Earth," the atomic refuge used by the actors as a hiding and resting place. There he finds several costumes used for the masque and also Conchis's directions taken in part from *The Tempest* and *Othello* and also from the Marquis de Sade. With them there is a story entitled "The Prince and the Magician" which Nicholas takes to be "a fairy story on them" (p. 550). The tale of "The Prince and the Magician" sums up the essence of Conchis's teaching as regards the reality-unreality question, and thus synthesizes at the end of the second section the quality of the transformation undergone by the hero.

A young prince, the story runs, is told by his father that princesses, islands, and God, do not exist. But then he meets a man with his coatsleeves rolled back who convinces him that his father lied. The stranger presents himself as God. When the prince goes back to the palace and explains the incident, the king tells him that, in reality, the stranger is only a magician, and that all kings and gods are merely magicians. On hearing that, the prince is distressed:

> "I must know the real truth, the truth beyond magic."
> "There is no truth beyond magic," said the king.
> The prince was full of sadness.
> He said, "I will kill myself." (p. 552)

But when he saw the awful face of death and remembered "the beautiful but unreal islands and the unreal but beautiful princesses" (p. 552), he decided he could bear the burden of uncertainty. As soon as the prince accepts as the only truth the fact that there is no absolute truth, he starts turning into a magician himself. Peter Wolfe *(John Fowles, Magus and Moralist,* p. 119) fittingly sums up the moral of the tale: "No reality underlies appearance; the phenomena is all. Truth and reality do not exist objectively but inhere, instead, in the perceiver."

The story of "The Swiss and the Goats" and the tale of "The Prince and the Magician," respectively opening and closing the second section of the novel, encapsulate within themselves the two major ideas Conchis wants to impress on Nicholas's consciousness: that to be happy, man must know himself and live with what he is; and that there is no reality outside the boundaries of the perceiver or, to put it in Fowles's own words (foreword to the *The Magus,* p. 10), that "absolute knowledge and absolute power [do] not exist in fact." These two theoretical principles give rise in practice to two major questions: the first, the nature of the individual's relationship to other human beings and to himself; the second, the nature of freedom. In order to show Urfe the importance of these two questions, Conchis will again resort to the telling of a story, in this case the story of his own childhood, youth, and manhood, which he will combine with the metatheater.

Conchis tells Urfe the story of his own life as a real story, insisting that it did really take place, admitting at the same time that the masque is only an entertainment, a fictional make-believe whose only *raison d'être* is the performance itself. In practice, however, it is absolutely impossible to separate the story from the masque, as in both of them Lily and Conchis play major parts, so that, again, "real" story and "fictional" metatheater function as inseparable aspects of a polymorphous reality. Furthermore, as both the story and the masque develop, we see how the story of Conchis's life becomes more and more fictional, and the masque more and more disquietingly real. Thus, after the revolting account of the battle of Neuve Chapelle, Urfe has a strange feeling of listening to a fictional rather than a real report of the war:

> The horrors of Neuve Chapelle had been convincing enough as he described them, yet they turned artificial with this knowledge of repetition. Their living reality became a matter of technique, of realism gained through rehearsal. It was like being earnestly persuaded an object was new by a seller who simultaneously and deliberately revealed it must be second-hand: an affront to all probability. (p. 127)

Julie described the masque as "in one way . . . a sort of fantastic extension of the Stanislavski method. Improvising realities more real than reality" (p. 338).

One of the reasons why the story of Conchis's youth sounds inauthentic is the abundance of analogies with Nicholas's life: Conchis, like him, had an artistic bent; he gave piano concerts at the age of nine and had hoped to become a first-rate harpsichordist, as Nicholas had hoped to become a poet. But, then, at the age of fifteen he had had a nervous breakdown and when he was twenty he had decided, as Nicholas had just done, that he was "not going to fulfill (his) early promise" (p. 113). Where Urfe had become a member of Les Hommes Revoltés, a futile romantic endeavor, Conchis had founded the Society of Reason and contributed greatly to the writing of its Manifesto, which stressed the possibility of human progress only through the cultivation of reason. Just after his nervous breakdown, when he was fifteen, Conchis met Lily, one year his junior, and a pure, platonic love developed between them, helped by their mutual fascination for music. Conchis describes Lily as "a Botticelli beauty. Long hair, grey-violet eyes . . . A sweetness without sentimentality, a limpidity without naivety. She was easy to hurt, to tease. And when she teased, it was like a caress . . . Lily was a very pretty girl. But it was her soul that was *sans pareil"* (p. 115).

Now, it is easy to see how the relationship between Conchis and Lily reflects, in mirror image, that between Nicholas and Alison. As they grow together, Conchis begins to love Lily physically too. But she goes on treating him "as a brother" (p. 116) and in the same way the frustration Nicholas feels with Alison leads him to indulge in fanciful dreams about a virginal ideal woman, Conchis starts having erotic dreams: "She became in my mind at night the abandoned young prostitute. I thought I was very abnormal to have created this second Lily from the real one" (p. 116).

At the end of their relationship, when Conchis returns from the war, a deserter but a free man, Lily is unable to understand his motives. Her exemplary death from the typhoid fever she had caught at the hospital where she worked as a war-nurse synthesizes her unflinching devotion to duty: her soul *sans pareil* only amounted to this. This episode of Conchis's life, then, reflects, in an inverted form, the affair between Alison and Nicholas, and also synthetically anticipates the relation to come between Lily and Nicholas, anticipating its bathetic *denouément*. Again, Nicholas is aware of the didactic purpose in the story: "It was finally much more like a biography than the autobiography it purported to be; patently more concealed lesson than true confession" (p. 133). The parallelism is carried further by another aspect of Conchis's activities: his interest in birds, which analogically reflects Urfe's rakish interest in "collecting" girls. Conchis "came to birds through sound" (p. 113), and in due time turned into an expert ornithologist and an avid collector of bird sounds:

> As soon as I had ornithologically exhausted the tundra of the extreme north I crossed the Varangerfjord and went to the little town of Kirkenes. From there, armed with my letter of introduction, I set out for Seidevarre. (p. 297)

At this stage, then, Conchis has reached the phase of "collector" which, we are led to suppose, is attained when man relies for his knowledge of reality only on his senses. Thus, Conchis's statement that he "came to birds through sound" is not unimportant. The temptation to collect bird sounds is basically of the same sort as that of Frederick Clegg to collect butterflies, or that of Charles Smithson to collect ammonites, or that of Daniel Martin and his friend Anthony to collect orchids. Or again, of the same sort as Nicholas's temptation to collect girls. Collecting for Fowles is essentially evil for it exhausts itself in the passion to collect, but also, because it is a passion only fed through the senses. The story of Alphonse De Deukans, which Conchis inserts within the story of his life, presents the picture of the arch-collector, the man who "has devoted all his life to his collecting of collections," someone who "collected in order to collect" (p. 117).

An immensely rich aristocrat with a fantastic château in eastern France, De Deukans symbolizes one of the alternatives open to man: to close himself up in the "Ebony Tower" and consume himself in the relish of possession. Among the millions of beautiful objects De Deukans had in Givray-le-Duc was Mirabelle, *la Maîtresse-Machine,* a mechanical puppet devised for the Sultan of Turkey as a substitute for a real sex partner:

> De Deukans cherished her most because she had a device that made it unlikely that she should ever cuckold her owner. Unless one moved a small lever at the back of her head, at a certain pressure her arms would clasp with vice-like strength. And then a stiletto on a strong spring struck upwards through the adulterer's groin. (pp. 177–78)

Mirabelle stands as the symbol of the hideous egoism of all collectors, but also points directly to the life-killing effects of Urfe's attitude to women in general and to Alison in particular.

When Conchis went to Givray-le-Duc for the first time, he was "shocked, as a would-be socialist. And ravished, as an *homme sensuel"* (p. 177). In this brief comment Conchis synthesizes the essence of the "collector": he is *l' homme moyen sensuel,* the intrinsic materialist, a man who only lives to satisfy his sensual desires, in this case, his hunger for beauty, which he must feed through his senses, watching, touching, possessing, not through his imagination. So the collector is the least imaginative of men, for in order to exist he must tangibly possess the objects that obsess him. This is exactly what Clegg meant when he said that "having her was enough" (p. 95), and this is why, when Givray-le-Duc is destroyed by the fire, De Deukans commits suicide.

The refusal to remain simply a collector, a passive consumer of fictions, is what makes Conchis burn all his novels: he must destroy them in order to be free to create his own fictions. And we must not forget that Nicholas only realizes the real value of Alison when he gives up hope of ever touching or seeing her again.

The day Givray-le-Duc is burned to ashes and De Deukans kills himself, Conchis tells us he was "in fact in the remote north of Norway, in pursuit of birds—or to be more exact, bird-sounds" (p. 296). With this simple remark Conchis makes two stories within the story of his life coincide chronologically, which will turn out to be basic for the teaching of Urfe: the story of De Deukans, and the story of Henrick Nygaard, the Norwegian ship's engineer gone mad who lived retired in Seidevarre. Henrick Nygaard was a Jansenist and so believed in divine cruelty—he had the conviction that God had elected him to be punished and tormented and so lived like an anchorite in a log cabin in the wood. When Conchis offers him his medical aid, Nygaard tries to kill him with an axe:

> It seemed incredible to me that a man should reject medicine, reason, science so violently. But I felt that this man would have rejected everything else about me as well if he had known it—the pursuit of pleasure, of music, of reason, of medicine. That axe would have driven right through the skull of all our pleasure-oriented civilization. Our science, our psychoanalysis. To him all that was not the great meeting was what the Buddhists call *lilas*—the futile pursuit of triviality. (p. 306)

After the episode of the axe, Conchis is able to spy Henrick Nygaard one night, calling on God, knee-deep in a stream:

> Something was very close to him, as visible to him as Gustav's dark head, the trees, the moonlight on the leaves around us, was to me. I would have given ten years of my life to have been able to look out there to the north, from inside his mind. I did not know what he was seeing, but I knew it was something of such power, such mystery, that it explained all. And of course Henrick's secret dawned on me . . . He was not waiting to meet God. He was meeting God, and had been meeting him probably for many years. He was not waiting for some certainty. He lived in it. (p. 308)

After this extraordinary experience, Conchis abandons all interest in collecting bird sounds. The sight of Henrick Nygaard in the water, contemplating God in his mind's eye, convinces him of a radical truth, the complexity of reality: "that great passive monster, reality, was no longer dead, easy to handle. It was full of a mysterious vigour, new forms, new possibilities" (p. 309).

Henrick Nygaard rejecting "what the Buddhists call *lilas*" (one cannot help noticing the heavy pun on "Lily") in favor of the essential, and then creating it in his own mind, stands at the opposite pole to De Deukans. The visionary aesthete confronts the sensual materialist. At the same time, by rejecting any kind of established convention—comfort, a family, society, medicine, etc.— and choosing illness and poverty and suffering as a way of life, Henrick Nygaard teaches Conchis another fundamental truth: that man is free. This is the last lesson Conchis has reserved for Urfe, and to illustrate it he will select the main strand from the story of his life.

During Urfe's first weekend at Bourani, Conchis tells him how he enlisted during the First World War, although he hated the very idea of it. That is, he chose a course of action strictly in opposition to his convictions and desires, influenced by the pressure of society and of Lily. Near the end of the second section of the novel, after Nicholas has undergone the climactic session of the trial, he goes to the delegation of the British Council in Athens and agrees to go to dinner with various people he finds annoying and boring. No sooner has he taken this decision than a line of the report read at the trial comes to his mind:

"He seeks situations in which he knows he will be forced to rebel" (p. 555, emphasis in the original). This association of ideas stresses the analogy between the young Conchis and Nicholas. Conchis's first step towards maturity takes place when, after having survived the horrors of the battle of Neuve Chapelle, he is able to articulate his unconscious resistance to the war by deserting, thus acknowledging his real self. The fact that he is reported as officially dead consequently symbolizes his ritual death and rebirth to a new, more mature life. The clearer result of his experience of the war is a radical conviction in the value of human life:

> I was without shame. I even hoped the Germans would overrun our positions and so allow me to give myself up as a prisoner.
> "Fever. But what I thought was fever was the fire of existence, the passion to exist. I know it now. A *delirium vivens*." (p. 129)

"The passion to exist" is the first axiom Nicholas, who has just committed his token suicide, must learn to appreciate. And this is precisely what he does when, after the trial, he is left with a loaded gun at Monemvasia: "Standing on the old bastion, I fired the remaining five bullets out to sea. I aimed at nothing. It was a *feu de joie,* a refusal to die" (p. 534).

Clearly, an understanding of "what you are" produces a *delirium vivens,* the passion to exist, the refusal to die. By rejecting the social standards that justify the war, Conchis has proved that man is free to choose his own way; he has rejected convention and social dictatorship and has affirmed the right of the individual. But still he has behaved according to the biological law that teaches man to preserve his life. This is why Conchis later has difficulties in understanding Nygaard's resolution to reject comfort, security, art, and anything that in principle makes man's life happy. However, Nygaard was only exchanging physical comfort for psychological bliss. But to cherish liberty as the only real good of man is a lesson Conchis will only learn much later, during the Second World War, in an episode of his life he fittingly entitled *ELEUTHERIA.*

During the German invasion of Greece in 1941, a troop of Austrians commanded by a German lieutenant called Anton Kubler took charge of Phraxos. Kubler was sensitive to art and a tolerant man. Life in Phraxos developed in a quasi-normal way until the S. S. Colonel Dietrich Wimmel came with his *Raben* to stiffen the morale of the Austrian soldiers. When four soldiers were shot by the guerillas, Colonel Wimmel ordered eighty villagers to be picked at random and shot in revenge. They would only be spared if the guerillas were found out; somebody betrayed them and the three guerillas were horribly tortured in the presence of Conchis, then the Major of Phraxos. When the guerilla leader was captured, he cried *eleutheria,* and went on repeating this word until his tongue was burned out.

Conchis who, as we know, was a deserter and a pacifist, could not understand the guerilla leader, just as he had been unable to understand Henrick
Nygaard years before. But when Colonel Wimmel asked Conchis to club the
guerillas to death and so spare his own life and those of the remaining seventy-
nine hostages, light dawned on him:

> In (my world) life had no price. It was so valuable that it was literally priceless. In his, only
> one thing had that quality of pricelessness. It was *eleutheria:* freedom. He was the immalle-
> able, the essence, the beyond history. He was not God, because there is no God we can know.
> But he was a proof that there is a God that we can never know. He was the final right to deny.
> To be free to choose . . . He was every freedom, from the very worst to the very best . . . The
> freedom to disembowel peasant girls and castrate with wire-cutters. He was something that
> passed beyond morality, but sprang out of the very essence of things—that comprehend all,
> the freedom to do all, and stood against only one thing—the prohibition not to do all. (p. 434)

Conchis understands this basic truth and refuses to kill the men; in consequence
he and the seventy-nine hostages are shot, but, miraculously, Conchis survives:
he is given up for dead, then rescued and healed. This second death and resur-
rection can be symbolically interpreted as the descent into hell which finds its
parallel in Urfe's subterranean trial. There Nicholas is confronted with the same
dilemma: to take revenge on Lily by flogging her, or to use his liberty by
refusing to undertake any action. Conchis's and later Urfe's understanding of
the—existentialist—freedom of man is what turns them into "elect."

In all, the stories Conchis narrates convey three major lessons: know thy-
self, as the Swiss shepherd did; don't limit yourself to just one side of reality,
as both De Deukans and Nygaard did, but, on the contrary, learn (like the
prince-turned-magician) to appreciate its polymorphous nature; and use freedom
discriminatingly. The three lessons are interrelated, as they sum up complementary aspects of man's one great need: to understand his position in the world.
And this is what Urfe finally does:

> All my life I had turned life into fiction, to hold reality at bay; always I had acted as if a third
> person was watching and listening and giving me marks for good and bad behaviour—A god
> like a novelist, to whom I turned like a character with the power to please, the sensitivity to
> feel slighted, the ability to adapt himself to whatever he believed the novelist-god wanted.
> This leechlike variation of the super-ego I had created myself, fostered myself, and because
> of it I had always been incapable of acting freely. It was not my defence; but my despot. And
> now I saw it, I saw it a death too late. (p. 539)

This understanding, brought about by the belief that Alison has killed herself,
amounts to a point of fulcrum. Using the metaphor of the character performing
for an omniscient author, Urfe ironically tries to express his feeling of "being
watched," "an experience," says Barry N. Olshen (ibid., p. 38), "that reverber-
ates throughout the novel." For this critic

it suggests his continual need to perform for others and to be evaluated by others, It points, in the Sartrean terms of his own account, to his "bad faith," that is, to his incapacity to accept responsibility for the deeds he freely performs. *The Magus* is designed to indicate that the revulsion Nicholas feels at his "nothingness," his feeling of divorce between himself and the world, results from a misguided attitude and not from a fact of nature, not from the human condition. It is in this respect that *The Magus* parts so radically from the French existentialist novels to provide a more optimistic approach to daily life.

Urfe's incapacity to accept responsibility for his free acts, his tendency to turn life into fiction, rejecting the real in favor of the unreal—as the octopus did—is Urfe's major sin, generated by his shortsighted interpretation of reality. If Nicholas is to be healed he must learn to distrust his senses and to foster his imagination. This part of his training will be achieved through his involvement in the masque.

Side by side with the telling of tales and of episodes of Conchis's life, the display of the masque at Bourani enacts materially the morals encapsulated in the iconic stories, in order to provide a concrete realization of the theoretical lessons imparted by them. Thus, after Conchis has spoken of his long-deceased fiancée, Lily fleetingly appears at the villa: her scent, first, then her glove, then herself; and after listening to the report of the Battle of Neuve Chapelle, Nicholas has the experience of hearing the *"finest drone of men"* creeping down from the hillside and then realizing with a shock that what they were singing was "Tipperary." After the ear, the reliability of the sense of smell is also tested: *"an atrocious stench that infested the windless air, a nauseating compound of decomposing flesh and excrement"* (p. 134), and, the following day, the sense of sight when, after having read the seventeenth-century story of Robert Foulkes, rapist and murderer, Foulkes appears before Nicholas, dressed in black with a white-faced little girl:

> As I listened to him [Conchis], I thought. The incidents seemed designed to deceive all the senses. Last night's had covered smell and hearing; this afternoon's, and that glimpsed figure of yesterday [Lily], sight. Taste seemed irrelevant—but touch . . . how on earth could he expect that what I might touch was "psychic"? (pp. 143–44)

Quite accurately, Nicholas himself interprets the incidents as devices "designed to deceive all the senses." And, as he intuitively guesses, touch is the most important sense and the most difficult to deceive in a man who has circumscribed his relation with women to a mere sexual contact: Lily's role in the masque will be, then, to convince Nicholas of the fact that it is possible to touch a woman who only exists in his imagination.

Analyzing "The Ebony Tower," Robert Huffaker (ibid., p. 117) stresses the analogy between the plot of the novella and the situation described in the epigram to it, which is taken from the eighth-century romance by Chrétien des Troyes, *Yvain*. "The epigram," Huffaker says,

> describes the archetypal quest to the knight who, often leaving a lover behind, reaches some mysterious master's castle and gains entry against dubious odds . . . Once inside the castle, the knight usually becomes somehow involved with at least one nubile damsel—more often *two*—rarely more. Of the customary two, one is distant and desirable, the other accessible and less attractive—occasionally not pretty at all, but haggish instead. Sometimes the hag is transformed; *sometimes the two maids prove to be one;* but the hero usually discovers to his eventual surprise that the master is not as mysterious, nor the princess as distant, as he had supposed. Almost inevitably, she at last becomes available whether he decides to keep her or not. (my italics)

Huffaker's analysis explains the mysterious triangle formed by the old painter and the two young women at Coëtminais. Henry Breasley, the seventy-seven-year-old expatriate British painter and Diana (the Mouse) and Anne (the Freak) are, in Huffaker's words, "contemporary versions of the medieval castle's two damsels. The Mouse, a talented art student, is initially distant and mysteriously attractive; the Freak, a skinny refugee from the drug scene, is the "absurd sex-doll" with an air of easy availability. One is ideal, the other reality" (ibid. p. 119).

Now, the parallelism between Huffaker's description of the situation in "The Ebony Tower" and that in *The Magus* is striking: Nicholas, like David Williams, has had access to the "domain" of an old and mysterious man and there he is confronted by two girls. Lily, like the Mouse, is mysteriously attractive and distant; Rose, like the Freak, is felt to be much more easily available, as her use of a bikini and her lying in the sun without its upper part suggests: "Once more I was shocked: this was not just the latest clothes fashion, but behaviour years ahead of its time" (p. 349).

In "The Ebony Tower" the Mouse, Huffaker says, stands for "the ideal," the Freak, for "reality." We may agree that Lily stands for the ideal in *The Magus*, but what exactly is the role of Rose in the plot? Isn't the role of reality played by Alison? In the medieval romance, Huffaker says, "sometimes the two maids prove to be one," and we could add, because they are symbolic figures representing two opposed principles of woman in the abstract: the virginal white lily and the red rose of passion of the Victorians are, like the medieval damsels of the romance, two complementary *twin* aspects of the *anima* which, as Jung has explained, is the female archetype within the male psyche. If we accept this interpretation of Lily and Rose we may understand why they are identical twins, only distinguishable through the scar Lily has on her wrist, and also why she insists that she has no sisters: "I have no sister" (p. 205), "I was an only child" (p. 208).

Lily and Rose exist within the unreal boundaries of Bourani as the embodiments of two complementary aspects of woman whose reality is only archetypal and psychological. This fact explains why Urfe is alternately attracted by both of them, for while his conscious drives him to choose Lily, who stands for the virginal aspect of woman, his unconscious is simultaneously attracted by Rose, who stands for the whore. Fowles will further use this basic, archetypal symbolism of the twins in the novels to come. In *Daniel Martin* he will toy with the idea, multiplying the couples of women: besides the "Heavenly Twins" Nell and Jane, the reader will encounter the "Fairy Sisters" Marjory and Miriam, and also Nancy Reed's twin sisters, Mary and Louise. In *Mantissa* we will find a Muse who has the power to split into a white Dr. Delfie and a black Nurse Cory, who are physically identical, except for the color of their skins, while in *A Maggot,* Fowles will expand the symbolism of the "twins" to cover the archetypal triangle formed by Mr. B., Rebecca, and Dick.

At the end of the novel, Mrs. de Seitas emphasizes the wholly psychological nature of her daughters: "My daughters were nothing but a personification of your own selfishness" (p. 610). In contrast to them, Alison, like Sarah in *The French Lieutenant's Woman,* or like Jane in *Daniel Martin,* or like Rebecca in *A Maggot,* or like any Fowlensian "real" woman, simultaneously possesses in herself the potentialities of the lily and the rose, of the virgin and the whore, expressed in her baffling double nature:

> She had two voices; one almost Australian, one almost English. . . . (p. 23)

> She was bizarre, a kind of human oxymoron. (p. 24)

> . . . innocent-corrupt, coarse-fine, an expert-novice. (p. 28)

The triangle formed by the ("real") Muse, and her mental projections, (the white) Dr. Delfie and (the black) Nurse Cory in *Mantissa* is of the same kind as the triangle formed by (the real) Alison and her anima potentialities, (the white) Lily and (the red) Rose (of passion), as the green pot of flowers Nicholas finds on the tombstone of Maurice Conchis, at St. George's, indubitably indicates: "in which sat, rising from a cushion of inconspicuous white flowers, a white arum lily and a red rose" (p. 559). The "inconspicuous white flowers" are, of course, *Alysson maritime . . . parfum de miel . . .* from the Greek *a* (without) *lyssa* (madness) . . . in English: *Sweet Alison* (p. 566, emphasis in the original). As the flower pot suggests, one lily and one rose make the Alison, the real (without madness) woman.

During the climactic trip to Mount Parnassus Nicholas has had the opportunity to realize the apparently paradoxical "oxymoronic" double nature of Alison, but he has been incapable of interpreting it. First, during the night in the wooden hut, while Alison tempts him into sex with her, Nicholas thinks, as she caresses him, "It's like being with a prostitute, hands as adept as a prostitute's" (p. 263). But the following morning, during the descent, as they stop by a pool in a clearing of the wood, when Alison runs naked through the long grass to take a bath in the ice-cold water, and then sits on the grass with a garland of wild flowers around her head, like "a Queen of May," Nicholas suddenly feels her Eve-like innocence: "She was sitting up, turned to me, propped on one arm. She had woven a rough crown out of the oxeyes and wild pinks that grew in the grass around us. It sat lopsidedly on her uncombed hair; and she wore a smile of touching innocence" (p. 268).

This archetypal scene, which foreruns a similar one in *A Maggot,* expresses Alison's archetypal anima potentialities, also expressed by Lily's progressive transformations, and by the fact that both Lily and Alison are in turn alluded to as Astarte, "mother of mystery" (p. 205), and Ashtaroth "the Unseen" (p. 566), two names for the goddess Isis, symbol of the changing moon and so symbol of woman. Urfe only understands this after the session of "disintoxication":

> The metamorphoses of Lily ran wildly through my brain, like maenads, hunting some blind-ness, some demon in me down. I suddenly knew her real name, behind the masks. Why they had chosen the Othello situation. Why Iago. Plunging through that. I knew her real name. I did not forgive, if anything I felt more rage.
> But I knew her real name. (pp. 530–31)

Lily's real name is, of course, "Alison," as Nicholas himself intuited long before: "I did love her (Alison), I wanted to keep her *and* I wanted to keep—or to find—Julie. It wasn't that I wanted one more than the other, I wanted both. I had to have both" (p. 269).

While the godgame starts at the level of the conscious with the blurring at Nicholas's senses of smell, hearing, and sight, each "turn of the screw" implies a progressive delving into the hero's unconscious, ending up in the phantasma-goric subterranean trial in which the actors, who are elaborately masked, are made to represent particular symbolic and mythical figures. The disguises the characters have at the trial offer the critic a wealth of alternative readings: Rosicrucianism, the Cabbala, the Tarot, Waite's Hermetic Order of the Golden Dawn, Masonic ritual, the Greek Eleusian Mysteries, ancient Egyptian mythol-ogy, and Christianity, among others. But any research in this direction would only satisfy the source-seeker. The wealth and variety of mythological, reli-gious, and symbolic allusion interspersed in the godgame is best analyzed as simply a rich metaphor for Jung's theory that archetypes in the collective uncon-scious are timeless and universal. "By presenting Nick with aesthetic, mythic, and historical images from the human consciousness," says Huffaker (ibid., p. 60), "the godgame applies Jung's 'individuation' process." He adds:

Jungian individuation aims to give a person awareness and courage to behave as an individual rather than as the kind of imitator Nick has become. Jung calls such self-deluding poses as Nick's literary persona, collective behaviour which only appears individual. The Latin *persona* was originally an actor's mask; unmasking so often, the godgame players encourage Nick to do the same. Individuation also seeks to replace unconscious behaviour with conscious action.

To replace unconscious behavior with conscious action is exactly what Nicholas has to learn if he wants to free himself from the necessity of having "a god like a novelist . . . watching and listening and giving (him) marks for good and bad behaviour" (p. 539), that is to say, if he wants to outgrow his incapacity to accept responsibility for his free acts.

After the trial, Nicholas is curtly dismissed by Conchis and told that the experiment is over. In Athens first, then in Rome, Subiaco, and later in England, Nicholas tries to undo the labyrinth in order to maintain a link with Conchis and to recover Alison. After the sterile meeting with Leverrier, Nicholas becomes aware for the first time of his—existential—loneliness:

> I looked around, to try to find somewhere I might hypothetically want to know better, become friendly with; and there was no one. It was an unneeded confirmation of my loss of Englishness; and it occurred to me that I must be feeling as Alison had so often felt: a mixture, before the English, of irritation and bafflement, of having the same language, same past, so many things, and yet not belonging to them any more. Being worse than rootless . . . speciesless. (p. 574)

His earlier blinding assumptions of reality having been shattered, Nicholas stands alone, experiencing the same feeling of rootlessness, and specieslessness, felt by Charles Smithson at the end of *The French Lieutenant's Woman*. What he feels amounts to a bout of that nauseating angst felt by the existentialist confronted by a vision of his own futility and of the meaninglessness and purposelessness of life. When Nicholas finally traces Mrs. de Seitas, and so the thread back to Alison, she comforts him and mothers him in a sense, but refuses to tell him where Alison is. Instead, she presents him with a beautiful old Chinese plate she had bought with Alison. The plate's design is a "Chinaman and his wife, their two children between them" (p. 624). Mrs. de Seitas's comment when she hands him the plate points to the fact that Nicholas is not yet prepared to meet Alison. She says, "I think you should get used to handling fragile objects. And ones much more valuable than that" (p. 624).

The Chinese plate with the happy family functions as the iconic image of what may give meaning to Nicholas's existence: it offers him an unheroic, quotidian life, far removed from his literary speculations, but which, when accepted in all its implications as the Swiss shepherd had done, may turn into a source of happiness. However, instead of following the advice the Chinese plate mutely offers, Nicholas involves himself in a pathetic relationship with a young

Scottish art student, an untidy, mongrel-like, love-starved seventeen-year-old girl whose company Urfe tries to buy:

> I'm offering you a job. There are agencies in London that do this sort of thing. Provide escorts and partners . . . You're temporarily drifting. So am I. So let's drift together. (p. 635)

Nicholas offers Jojo what he believes to be a "clean" relationship: no sex, just friendship and mutual company. As a matter of fact, however, Nicholas behaves with her as egotistically as he had always behaved with women: he uses Jojo to lick his wounds, to help him out of his dreadful loneliness without realizing that she too has feelings, desires, and sorrows as any human being does. When, to his distress, Jojo tells him that she is desperately in love with him, Nicholas understands for the first time the real meaning of Mrs. de Seitas's words about the "only sin," the only crime man can commit: *Thou shalt not inflict unnecessary pain* (p. 641, emphasis in the original).

After Jojo slips out of his life, Nicholas considers again life without Alison: an empty cereal packet, with a picture of "a nauseatingly happy 'average' family" (p. 643), again offers him in a silent icon the plastic image of the way in which he can give his life meaning. Nearby, the Bow plate mutely offers him the same solution: "The family again; order and involvement. Imprisonment" (p. 643). The sight of the plate and of the cereal packet seem to help Nicholas make up his mind to go away from London and from his past, to start a new life in the country. As he is packing, Nicholas lifts the Bow plate carelessly off its nail, and it slips and breaks in two across the middle:

> I knelt. I was so near tears that I had to bite my lips savagely hard. I knelt there holding the two pieces . . . I raised the two pieces a little to show her (Kempt) what had happened. My life, my past, my future. (p. 645)

Nicholas with the broken pieces of his past, present, and future in his hands constitutes John Fowles's living icon of the existentialist. The whole novel seems to have been moving in the direction of this picture. After it the narrative freezes. Breaking the rules of narrative decorum, an extra-heterodiegetic narrator identifiable with the author opens the chapter immediately following this episode with a metalepsis, that is to say, with a break of narration, to comment in a carefully apersonal, and thus gnomic, aside, on the situation of the hero. The authorical digression is an open reflection on the image of the kneeling Nicholas:

> The smallest hope, a bare continuum to exist is enough for the anti-hero's future; leave him, says our age, leave him where mankind is in its history, at a crossroads, in a dilemma, with all to lose and only more of the same to win; let him survive, but give him no direction, no reward; because we are waiting, in our solitary rooms where the telephone never rings, waiting

for this girl, this truth, this crystal of humanity, this reality lost through imagination, to return; and to say she returns is a lie.

But the maze has no centre. An ending is no more than a point of fulcrum in sequence, a snip of the cutting shears. Benedick kissed Beatrice at last; but ten years later? And Elsinore, that following spring?

So ten more days. But what happened in the following years shall be silence, another mystery. (p. 645)

This metalepsis foreruns bolder intrusions of the author in the novels to come. Structurally, it serves to confirm our impression that the boundaries between fiction and reality are wholly artificial for, as Genette (*Narrative Discourse. An Essay in Method,* p. 245),[7] quoting Borges, explains: "The most troubling thing about metalepsis indeed lies in this unacceptable and insistent hypothesis, that the extradiegetic is perhaps always diegetic, and that the narrator and his narratees—you and I—perhaps belong to some narrative."

Thematically, it sums up the author's conviction that, for the contemporary hero, the end of the quest is the quest itself, and the aim of life, the bare act of living. For him future, past, and present merge in an eternal "waiting" as the involuted structure of the metatheater tried to show. This is the deeper meaning of the mysterious notice board at Bourani, and of Mitford's cryptic warning, "Beware of the waiting-room," a meaning Urfe intuited in the poem he wrote during his first weekend at Bourani: "I am the fool that falls/And never learns to wait and watch . . ." (p. 95).

"Waiting, always waiting" (p. 643) is what Urfe has to learn to do all through the weary summer and autumn before he is allowed to meet Alison once more on All Hallows Eve. And when he is dismissed from Bourani, he is given a rush basket with food for two and a note with just one word: *Perimeni,* "she waits" (p. 449).

When, finally, Nicholas is allowed to meet Alison again at Cumberland Terrace, he has the feeling that the row of statues of classical gods are watching him from their pedestals, very much in the same way he had always felt watched either by Conchis and his theatrical jury or by that "god like a novelist" he had always sensed behind him "watching and listening and giving him marks for good and bad behaviour" (p. 539). But, then, suddenly,

The final truth came to me. . . . There were no watching eyes. The windows were all as blank as they looked. The theatre was empty. It was not a theatre. They had perhaps told her (Alison) it was a theatre, and she had believed them. Perhaps it had all been to bring me my last lesson and final ordeal. . . . The task, as in *L'Astrée,* of turning lions and unicorns and magi and other mythical monsters into stone statues . . . It was logical, the perfect climax of the godgame. They had absconded, we were alone. (pp. 654–55)

As Nicholas intuits, the "absconding" of the gods is the perfect climax of the godgame, for it brings about Nicholas's realization that, in Fowles's own words (foreword, p. 10), Conchis's masks "representing human notions of God (are only) a series of human illusions about something that does not exist in fact." Nicholas's acceptance of the fact that the classical gods of Cumberland Terrace are only stone-gods is the final proof that the hero has been healed, that he can now see reality as it is, for learning, like the hero in *L'Astrée*, to turn "lions and unicorns and magi and other mythical monsters into stone statues" (p. 655) is, as Huffaker points out (ibid., p. 59), learning to interpret symbols hermeneutically instead of literally, that is, as actual symbols, and thus, learning to separate life from fiction, failure to do which has been Urfe's overriding sin; but it also means learning to accept his existential loneliness, and the major truth that there is no applause by a watching god, no final reward, beyond the passion to exist.

In *"The French Lieutenant's Woman's* Man: Novelist John Fowles" (p. 60), Richard B. Stolley relates the following anecdote:

> In response to a gentle letter from a New York lawyer, dying of cancer in a hospital, who said he very much wanted the couple to be reunited, Fowles wrote back, "Yes, they were." On the same day he got a "horrid" letter from an American woman who angrily demanded, "Why can't you say what you mean, and for God's sake, what happened in the end?" Fowles replied curtly: "They never saw each other again."

This anecdote sums up the controversy aroused by the "real" meaning of the final meeting of Alison and Nicholas at Cumberland Terrace. Most critics have interpreted the ambiguous ending positively, basing their opinion on the quotation from the *Pervilium Veneris* that closes the novel, which, translated, means, "Tomorrow he who has never loved will love, and he who has loved, tomorrow will love." In fact, however, the ending, as the anecdote suggests, is absolutely open, as open as the ending of *The French Lieutenant's Woman*. There is no reasonable way of knowing whether Nicholas and Alison will be able to build up a renewed happy relationship (even if we admit that they met again) or not. The intruding author already warned us in the metalepsis that "a bare continuum to exist is enough for the anti-hero's future," and this is what John Fowles does with his hero, consciously leaves him "at the crossroads" in the eternal dilemma of endlessly having to decide how to use his liberty in the next act.

From the structural point of view, the openness of the ending is enhanced by a further metalepsis, accompanied by a distortion of the time-scheme. As he had already done in *The Collector*, Fowles suddenly removes the gap between narrative and story time: the last paragraph is written in the present tense, and reported in a neutral, impersonal way by the author in person, who intrudes again to give his final, metaleptic, atemporal and thus, gnomic, comment: "She is silent, she will never speak, never forgive, never reach a hand, never leave this frozen present time. All waits, suspended" (p. 656).

As the shift from the preterite to the present and future tenses suggests, past, present, and future merge in the authorial comment to provide a formal linguistic equivalent of the thematic axiom synthesized in the words "all waits, suspended."

Alison frozen in an eternal present is John Fowles's verbal icon for the final truth he has tried to develop through the whole novel, namely, that the aim of the quest is the quest itself. To imagine happy or sad endings beyond this moment would be to enlarge *The Magus* by adding to it a further fiction.

The French Lieutenant's Woman

When *The French Lieutenant's Woman* first appeared in 1969, the critics immediately welcomed it as an extraordinary example of the revival of the historical novel in England, while at the same time lamenting John Fowles's inexplicable indulgence in what seemed an uncunning and haphazard sort of literary experimentation. Thus Walter Allen, while admitting that *The French Lieutenant's Woman* was "a most interesting novel [and] a genuine achievement," held the view that "it is, first and foremost an historical novel of an old-fashioned form" ("The Achievement of John Fowles," p. 66).

Allen denies Fowles any "innovatory inventiveness" stressing the fact that the use of a twentieth-century narrator to focus a nineteenth-century story is a well-worn literary device: "In fact, Fowles here is merely taking advantage of hindsight in his interpretation of character and scene as historical novelists have always done, as Scott, for example, does in *Rob Roy* and George Eliot in *Adam Bede*" (ibid., p. 66).

Walter Allen reserves a final rebuff for those critics—mainly American—who have applauded the appearance of *The French Lieutenant's Woman* as a breakthrough in narrative technique: "One can only assume that an acquaintance with classic English fiction is no longer a pre-requisite for reviewing novels" (ibid., p. 66). Allen's impatient remark is absolutely to the point: it is true that when John Fowles makes his twentieth-century narrator omnisciently comment on his nineteenth-century protagonists he is drawing on a convention as old as the novel itself. Indeed, the point of interest is not the newness of the devices used, but the particular aim that lies behind Fowles's use of them in this concrete novel, something Walter Allen fails to realize: "The significance of *The French Lieutenant's Woman* doesn't lie in its 'experimental' features. These are much more apparent than real and, in my view, are a big boring herring" (ibid., p. 67).

Similarly, Prescott Evarts, Jr. ("Fowles' *The French Lieutenant's Woman* as Tragedy," p. 57) fails to see any consistent or intelligible purpose in Fowles's experimentalist flights, beyond a mere mannerism:

> *The French Lieutenant's Woman* is a mannerist tragedy set in Victorian times. It is fraught
> with the distortions and lack of symmetry that are associated with Mannerism, as it revolted
> against Renaissance form. Fowles has followed many of the Victorian conventions while at
> the same time making them obscure, troubled and illogical.

And he concludes,

> A retrospective authenticity is achieved in spite of and in conflict with the self-conscious
> modernism of the narrator. One is tempted to admire the historicity at the expense of the total
> experience. (ibid., p. 58)

If Evarts contents himself with admiring "the historicity at the expense of the
total experience," stricter Victorian specialists are much more reluctant to accept
the intrinsic value of even this aspect of the novel. Thus, Patrick Brantlinger
("The French Lieutenant's Woman: A Discussion," p. 347) castigates Fowles
for confusing Victorian duty with sexuality, charging him with the sin of
anachronic distortion—"the notion that sexuality is the 'primum mobile' of
history is a peculiarly modern, post-Freudian, and apparently popular form of
lopsidedness," while Ian Adam in his section of the same article *("The French
Lieutenant's Woman:* A Discussion," p. 344), accuses the author of "irksome
pedantry" and expresses his surprise that although "as an experimental novel
The French Lieutenant's Woman is disarmingly old-fashioned," he finds that
John Fowles doesn't seem to feel "any evident worry about imitative form."
No more than Cervantes imitating the books of chivalry, one might add.

The implicit accusation that John Fowles openly and shamelessly imitates
old conventions, trying to cheat us into accepting them as new, springs from
one common misunderstanding: the insistence on viewing *The French Lieutenant's Woman* primarily as a historical novel on which futile and illogical attempts at experimentation have been made at random. Significantly, Evarts
realizes that "Fowles is ironic about everything," but he dismisses the insight
by adding that "the narrator renders the whole experience ironic, making the
Victorians seem overclever and pedantic, being aggressive and assertive for no
clear reason at all" (ibid., p. 58).

As Robert Burden ("The Novel Interrogates Itself: Parody and Self-Consciousness in Contemporary English Fiction"), among others, has pointed out,
every work of art must solve in one way or another the tension created by the
opposed pulls of two elements at work in its creation: tradition and innovation;
that is, the pressure on the work of art of the inherited past and the simultaneous
necessity to break new ground. Burden quotes from Claudio Guillén to support
his thesis:

> A cluster of conventions determines the medium of a literary generation—the repertoire of
> possibilities that a writer has in common with his living rivals. Traditions involve the competi-

tion of writers with their ancestors. These collective coordinates do not merely permit or regulate the writing of a work. They enter the reading experience and affect its meaning. The new work is both a deviant from the norm (as crime is based on an attitude toward accepted social custom) and a process of communication referring to that norm. (ibid., p.133)

Burden's contention is that in the case of the contemporary English novel "this tension is often solved through a self-conscious relationship of the new work to past forms" (ibid., p. 133), and indeed, we may say that this is the case of *The French Lieutenant's Woman.*

Instead of trying to judge Fowles's achievement by his ability to create new fictional devices, we should judge his capacity to use the well-known devices inherent in the particular literary tradition he selected for *The French Lieutenant's Woman,* and above all the effects of their use on the novel, for only through them will we be able to grasp the author's real aim.

From the beginning John Fowles places his tale within the tradition of the Victorian novel, choosing for it an omniscient narrator. As the first chapter opens up we are confronted with a narrator who freely addresses himself to the reader, and who carefully situates the action of the novel on "one incisively sharp and blustering morning in the late March of 1867" (p. 1). The morning, we shall soon learn, is that of the 26th. At the same time the narrator locates his action spatially by describing the quay of Lyme Regis, which he further situates on the south coast of England. With a somewhat pedantic but enthusiastic erudition, the narrator digresses then on the beauty of the Cobb, only to stop to address the reader:

I exaggerate? Perhaps, but I can be put to the test, for the Cobb has changed very little since the year of which I write; though the town of Lyme has, and the test is not fair if you look back towards land. (p. 1)

In book 3 of *The Republic* Plato refers to two narrative modes: one in which the poet himself is the speaker and does not attempt to hide his presence; and another in which the speaker tries to efface himself, by assuming the personality of some character. The first type Plato calls "pure narrative," the second "imitation" or *mimesis.* Although Plato clearly held the former to be the only real narrative mode, the twentieth century, influenced by the ideas of Henry James and his epigones, has become increasingly used to regarding the hiding of the narrator as a *sine qua non* for producing an effect of realism.

Henry James's angry question (referring to the Victorian novel), "But what do such large loose baggy monsters with their queer elements of the accidental and the arbitrary, artistically *mean?"* ("Preface to *The Tragic Muse,"* p. 84), sums up the rejection by the new era of Victorian literary craft and also points to their failure to grasp the real aim of the Victorian novel. The Victorians were, above all, realists. If they wrote a novel they had to show in it a perfect replica not only of the actions of men but also of these actions set against their proper social background. And they thought that this task was possible. The technical solution to their endeavor was two-fold: they invented the multiplot, and sublimated the role of the omniscient narrator. The dialogical form of the multiplot (Garret, *The Victorian Multiplot Novel: Studies in Dialogical Form*) allowed the Victorian novelist to create a fictional microcosm in which the actions of the different members of a given community were allowed to develop quasi-simultaneously. The omniscient narrator, with his godlike capacity to alternately adopt the point of view of every one of his characters, ensured an "objective" rendering. For all the complaints of Henry James (and of the Modernists after him), absolute objectivity was the aim the Victorian novelist strove for, with very much the same seriousness of purpose to be found in James's own work. This is the basic concern behind the opening paragraph of chapter 29 in *Middlemarch*, when George Eliot puts an end to her description of the growing differences arising between Dorothea and her husband, which the narrator has so far been describing from the heroine's perspective, in order to allow Casaubon to express his own point of view about the matter:

> One morning, some weeks after her arrival at Locwick, Dorothea—but why always Dorothea? was her point of view the only possible one with regard to this marriage? I protest against all our interest, all our effort at understanding being given to the young skins that look blooming in spite of trouble; for these too will be faded, and will know the older and more eating griefs which we are helping to neglect. In spite of the blinking eyes and white moles objectionable to Celia, and the want of muscular curve which was morally painful to Sir James, Mr. Casaubon had an intense consciousness within him, and was spiritually a-hungered like the rest of us. *(Middlemarch, p. 312)*

If we accept, then, that the primary aim of the Victorian narratorial frame-breaks was to give an impression of realism, we should agree that the breach of narrative level produced by the narrator's rhetorical question in *The French Lieutenant's Woman*, "I exaggerate?," functions in a seemingly Victorian fashion. Indeed, rather than breaking the illusion of realism, the narrator's aside enhances it, producing what Barthes has called an *effet du réel*, as it makes the 1867 fictional Cobb appear historically real, a mere ancestor of the actual Cobb everyone can still see standing in 1967.

Fowles's breach of the narrative frame in this case is aimed at blurring the boundaries between fiction and reality. By making us accept the action of the novel as part of the historical past of Lyme Regis, we as readers implicitly accept the reality of such action, and what is more, the reliability of the narrator, who presents himself to us as an impartial—if somewhat erudite and pedantic—historian.

Many other minor narratorial intrusions in the novel function in the same way, and there is no doubt that it is this kind of frame-break that Walter Allen and the other critics mentioned above had in mind when they said Fowles's experimentation was painfully old-fashioned. Similarly, a great number of footnotes in which the narrator undertakes to explain to the reader some detail of the Victorian world have the same general aim: to suggest the objectivity of the narrator, by stressing the strictly historical quality of his interest in the events. Thus, when after having said that Charles Smithson had returned from his journey abroad "a healthy agnostic," the narrator adds, "though he would not have termed himself so, for the very simple reason that the word was not coined (by Huxley) until 1870, by which time it had become much needed" (p. 18). The effect of this footnote may be two-fold: it may either anger the reader, if he happens to be a Victorian scholar, as an unnecessary and platitudinous comment whose only justification is the narrator's desire to show off; or it may baffle the unknowing reader with the wealth and accuracy of the narrator's historical knowledge. But in any case the digression will work toward the building of the illusion that the narrator is first and foremost a historian who has undertaken to narrate events that really took place in the historical past.

Evidently, minor breaks of the frame like the ones so far discussed do not work to destroy the illusion of reality but paradoxically to reinforce it. In Patricia Waugh's words,

> Although the intrusive commentary of 19th century fiction may at times be metalingual (referring to fictional codes themselves), it functions mainly to aid the readerly concretization of the world of the book by forming a bridge between the historical and the fictional worlds. It suggest that one is merely a continuation of the other, and it is thus not metafictional. *(Metafiction,* p. 32)

Soon, however, the narrator of *The French Lieutenant's Woman* seems to be intent on furthering as far as possible our "willing suspension of disbelief." Thus, when he proleptically comments on the longevity of Ernestina Freeman, a fact her parents were never to know, and says, "Had they but been able to see into the future! For Ernestina was to outlive all her generation. She was born in 1846. And she died on the day that Hitler invaded Poland" (p. 29). Only by an enormous effort of the will can the reader accept the coincidence of dates as historically accurate. In the same way the appearances of Luther, Erasmus of Rotterdam, the Earl of Surrey, and numberless other historical figures in *The Unfortunate Traveller* undermine its realism, the allusion to "the day Hitler invaded Poland" has the faint smack of that devilish irony Prescott Evarts, Jr. found so irritating and gratuitous, and we start to wonder what is Fowles's narrator *really* at. Patricia Waugh may again help us to guess his real purpose:

> One method of showing the function of literary conventions, of revealing their provisional nature, is to show what happens when they malfunction. Parody and inversion are two strategies which operate in this way as frame-breaks. The alternation of frame and frame-break (or

the construction of an illusion through the imperceptibility of the frame) provides the essential deconstructive method of metafiction. (ibid., p. 31)

If we still entertain doubts about whether Patricia Waugh's words apply to *The French Lieutenant's Woman* or not, we only have to wait till we reach the often-quoted first paragraph of chapter 13. The narrator has ended the previous chapter with a rhetorical question in the best Victorian fashion:

Who is Sarah?
Out of what shadows does she come? (p. 84)

His answer in chapter 13 acts as a major frame-break, shattering to its foundations the illusion of realism created so far:

I do not know. The story I am telling is all imagination. These characters I have created never existed outside my own mind. If I have pretended until now to know my characters' minds and innermost thoughts, it is because I am writing (just as I have assumed some of the vocabulary and 'voice' of) a convention universally accepted at the time of my story: that the novelist stands next to God. He may not know all, yet he tries to pretend that he does. But I live in the age of Alain Robbe-Grillet and Roland Barthes; if this is a novel, it cannot be a novel in the modern sense of the word. (p. 85)

After so much care even to assume "some of the vocabulary and 'voice' of" the Victorian period; after the mass of historical detail and reference with which the narrator has tried to bury the fictionality of his created world, this paragraph in chapter 13 destroys the painfully built illusion as a draught of wind would scatter a house of cards. "One method of showing the function of literary conventions, of revealing their provisionality, is to show what happens when they malfunction," Waugh has said, and this is one clear example of the malfunctioning of the convention of the omniscient narrator.

In agreement with post-Modernist metafictional practice, John Fowles has built an illusion only to break it, to show us its provisionality, its intrinsically fictional character. But as he undermines the realist convention, his novel turns into something else: "If this is a novel, it cannot be a novel in the modern sense of the word" (p. 85). For the new something he is creating, the narrator offers us several labels:

So perhaps I am writing a transposed autobiography; perhaps I now live in one of the houses I have brought into the fiction: perhaps Charles is myself disguised. Perhaps it is only a game. Modern women like Sarah exist, and I have never understood them. Or perhaps I am trying to pass off a concealed book of essays on you . . . what you will. (p. 85)

The reader, who has been flung out of the convention as remorselessly as Mrs. Poultney was flung out of Paradise, stares incredulous and hurt at the new possibilities the narrator seems to be offering: all of them hide a new treachery, a further blurring of the boundaries between reality and illusion, but focused from a wholly unexpected angle. First, the narrator tries to make us believe he is John Fowles in person, by saying that "perhaps I now live in one of the houses I have brought into the fiction," something we know to be exact: John Fowles wrote the manuscript of *The French Lieutenant's Woman* in a house in Lyme Regis described in the novel as "The Dairy." But surely John Fowles and the narrator, like Ernestina and Hitler, belong to two different ontological levels, and we know, with the help of Wayne Booth, that we cannot and should not confuse the flesh and blood writer called John Fowles with the implied author in *The French Lieutenant's Woman*. Neither should we confuse the narrative levels to which the narrator and the characters respectively belong, a snare the narrator tries to lure us into when he adds, "Perhaps Charles is myself in disguise."

By trying to blur the boundaries between the narrative levels within which the narrator and the characters respectively move, and between the narrative level and the ontological level of the flesh and blood writer, the narrator is implicitly conferring on author, narrator, and characters the same, fictional status. But, of course, taking *The French Lieutenant's Woman* as simply a transposed autobiography, or identifying John Fowles with the narrator and the narrator with Charles Smithson, is not the only alternative: "Perhaps it is only a game . . . what you will" (p. 85).

By breaking the Victorian frame John Fowles had been building as far as chapter 13, the author is making us reflect on this literary convention as what it simply is: a provisional frame, created by the combined work of the author and "the willing suspension of disbelief" of the reader. By offering us as an alternative the possibility that *The French Lieutenant's Woman* may be the autobiography of a flesh and blood writer called Charles Smithson disguised as John Fowles, the author is pointing to a basic post-Modernist and specifically deconstructivist contention: the advisability of seeing the everyday reality as a construct similar to that of fiction, and as such, similarly "written" and "writable." This is why the narrator shamelessly says that Ernestina died the same day that Hitler invaded Poland, mixing up the historical and the fictional futures. This is why, too, when the narrator describes Mary's beauty, he refers incidentally to "Mary's great-great-grand-daughter, who is twenty-two years old this month I write in, [and who] much resembles her ancestor; and her face is known over the entire world, for she is one of the more celebrated younger English film actresses" (pp. 68–69). Or again, when later on Sarah buys a Toby jug and the narrator says that it is the same one that came to be his own:

> Those two purchases had cost Sarah ninepence in an old china shop: the Toby was cracked, and was to be recracked in the course of time, as I can testify, having bought it myself a year

or two ago for a good deal more than the three pennies Sarah was charged. But unlike her, I fell for the Ralph Leigh part of it. She fell for the smile. (p. 241)

Patricia Waugh has written of this episode:

Sarah and the Toby jug appear to have the same ontological status as the narrator. This brings the reader up against the paradoxical realization that normally we can read novels only because of our suspension of disbelief. Of course, we *know* that what we are reading is not "real," but we suppress the knowledge in order to create our enjoyment. We tend to read fiction as if it were history. By actually appearing to treat fiction as a historical document, Fowles employs the convention against himself. The effect of this, instead of *reinforcing* our sense of a continuous reality, is to split it open, to *expose* the levels of illusion. We are forced to recall that our "real" world can *never* be the "real" world of the novel. So the frame-break, while appearing to bridge the gap between fiction and reality, in fact lays it bare. (ibid., p. 33, emphasis in the original)

The same effect is produced when Fowles makes Sarah live in the house of Dante Gabriel Rossetti and work there as a model and an assistant. But perhaps the most baffling confusion of ontological and narrative levels is obtained when the author appears in person as a character in the novel, a stranger who sits facing Charles in the first-class compartment of his London train and scrutinizes the hero while he is asleep, trying to make up his mind about the appropriate ending of the novel. Like Fowles, the stranger is a bearded fellow in his forties, and has "something rather aggressively secure about him" (p. 346). At the beginning the narrator describes this man from the perspective of Charles, referring to him in the third person, but then, all of a sudden, he surprises the reader by using the first person, and identifying with the stranger:

[The stranger's look] is precisely, it had always seemed to me, the look an omnipotent god—if there were such an absurd thing—should be shown to have. Not at all what we think of as a divine look; but one of distinctly mean and dubious (as the theoreticians of the *nouveau roman* have pointed out) moral quality. I see this with particular clarity on the face, only too familiar to me, of the bearded man who stares at Charles. And I will keep up the pretence no longer.

Now the question I am asking, as I stare at Charles, is not quite the same as the two above. But rather, what the devil am I going to do with you? (p. 348)

By introducing this bearded fellow as the author, only to identify with him later on, the narrator is challenging our assumptions about the convention of omniscient narration, trying to lure us into believing that narrator and author are one and the same. But, as Elizabeth D. Rankin ("Cryptic Coloration in *The French Lieutenant's Woman,*" p. 197) has remarked,

It is a mistake to assume, as Allen does, that behind that *persona* is the naked face of John Fowles. What is actually exposed when the narrator's *persona* is dropped is simply another *persona:* the novelist's. That is, Fowles has created a "novelist" who acts as a "narrator" but from time to time speaks openly as "novelist." An implied author, to use Wayne Booth's term, is discernible in the ironic distance which separate John Fowles from the "novelist."

Rankin is drawing here the same conclusion we intuitively drew when, at the beginning of chapter 13, the narrator says that "perhaps I now live in one of the houses I have brought into the fiction" (p. 85), that is, we may understand that the narrator is simply referring to an "implied author," not to John Fowles himself. But on the second occasion this implied author appears in the novel, when he is made to stand "leaning against the parapet of the embarkment" opposite the residence of Dante Gabriel Rossetti and is adjusting his watch to gain an extra quarter of an hour that may enable him to give us a second version of the ending, the narrator explicitly refuses to identify with him. More than that, he presents the bearded fellow as belonging to the same ontological level as Dante Gabriel Rossetti, who, despite the identity given him in the novel, is primarily a historically real Pre-Raphaelite painter. And, furthermore, the narrator protests that, while he is a man "who refuses to intervene in nature," the author is "the sort of man who cannot bear to be left out of the limelight [and] has got himself in as *he really is*," adding, "I will not labour the implications that he was previously got in as he really wasn't" (p. 394). That is, giving a final turn of the screw, the narrator tries to convince us now that, although he has also got himself under different masks, the bearded fellow is John Fowles in the flesh, who has been able to find his way into the fiction, even though "in spite of appearance, [as] a very minimal figure" (p. 394).[1]

As with Rossetti, Hitler, the architect who owns Millie's cottage, or Mary's film-star great-great-grand-daughter, the author's stepping into the fictional world of *The French Lieutenant's Woman* functions as a major frame-break, underlining Derrida's contention that all is included within the text, that even the author is born with the text and lives as long as the text is being written, a theme Fowles will develop at length in his fifth novel, *Mantissa*.

One way in which John Fowles undermines the convention of the omniscient narrator, then, is confusing ontological and narrative levels, giving the writer, the narrator, and the character the same fictional status. Another, more ironic way of obtaining the same effect is to show the real limitations of his avowedly omniscient narrator, who is likely to remark openly on his inadequacy as such, either by admitting that he doesn't know what happened at a certain moment, or by stressing his lack of skill as a writer. Thus, for instance, when referring to Sam and Mary's intended meeting at Coombe Street, he says: "Whether they met that next morning, in spite of Charles's express prohibition, I do not know" (p. 117). In this example the reader may take the remark as overscrupulousness on the part of the narrator, who would want to make clear his purpose of limiting his report to the objective facts to which he has had access, very much in the same way a Victorian novelist would pretend to open a door and enter a room before allowing himself to describe its contents. But on other occasions the narrator's remarks seem strangely unfit, as when, after quoting from a florid and enthusiastic article published in the *Edinburgh Review* on a Victorian best-seller, *The Lady of La Garaye,* the narrator adds, "Surely as pretty a string of key mid-Victorian adjectives and nouns as one could even hope to light on (and much too good for me to invent, let me add)" (p. 100). Here the parenthetical remark works to convince us of the authenticity of the poem, but only by simultaneously stressing the fictionality of the rest, as it presents the narrator as primarily an "inventor" (i.e., a creator) if of somewhat diminished powers.

Again and again the narrator speaks to affirm the fictionality, instead of the reality, of his created world: "But at last the distinguished soprano from Bristol appeared, together with her accompanist, the even more distinguished Signor Ritornello (or some such name, for if a man was a pianist he must be Italian" (p. 112). The narrator's insecurity about the name of the pianist produces a nagging effect, as it turns what we were willing to believe to be a sort of overscrupulousness into wantonness and irresponsibility not completely devoid of playfulness. A playfulness that comes to the fore when, after cheating us into believing that Charles and Ernestina eventually married, he says, "They begat, what shall it be—let us say seven children" (p. 292).

In these examples the insecurity the narrator shows works to undermine one particular aspect of the Victorian convention of omniscience: according to it, the narrator's role is that of the faithful historian—as he always narrates in the retrospect, the reader may assume that he knows beforehand the course events will take as well as the consequences derived of his characters' actions. By denying the reader this security of knowledge about the past, the narrator is both undermining our confidence in his reliability as a historian and stressing the radically fictional nature of his reported world.

In all these examples, then, as in many others to be found throughout the novel, the narrator turns the Victorian convention of the omniscient godlike narrator upside down, or in more technical terms, he uses the convention parodically. Robert Burden (ibid., p. 135) has defined parody in contrast to pastiche as "a mode of imitation in subversive form," while pastiche is defined as "a nonsubversive form of imitation, one which depends on systems of borrowing: a patchwork of quotations, images, motifs, mannerisms or even whole fictional episodes which may be borrowed, untransformed, from any original in recognition of 'the anxiety of influence.'" The task of parody, therefore, is to assume well-known forms or styles of the past in order to underline their obsolescence and limitation. This is precisely the function of the narrator's asides and footnotes in *The French Lieutenant's Woman* and no other is the intentional confusion of ontological and narrative levels. Only by admitting that *The French*

Lieutenant's Woman is a sustained parody of the Victorian novel can we properly account for the narrator's pedantry and overbearing erudition. Indeed, the narrator's elaborate style, denounced by the early critics as a naïve and immature attempt to imitate the Victorian idiom, appears now as sustained and deliberate pastiche; that is, pastiche used as such to stress, in Robert Burden's words, "the ironic awareness that language, literary form, themes and motifs regularly come to the writer in, so to speak, second-hand form" (p. 135).

> Perhaps you suppose that a novelist has only to pull the right strings and his puppets will behave in a lifelike manner; and produce on request a thorough analysis of their motives and intentions. Certainly I intended at this stage (Chap. Thirteen—unfolding of Sarah's true state of mind) to tell all—or all that matters. But . . . I know in the context of my book's reality that Sarah would never have brushed away her tears and leant down and delivered a chapter of revelation. (p. 85)

Fowles denies here the capability of the author to create his fictional world according to his particular whim: once created, the characters behave according to their own personality: "It is only when our characters and events begin to disobey us that they begin to live" (p. 86).

The Victorians believed that the created world was perfectly ordered; that it was continuously watched over by an all-knowing Providence; that not even a sparrow fell without God's acquiescence and knowledge. The godlike narrator of Victorian fiction was built on similar premises. But for John Fowles "there is only one good definition of God: the freedom that allows other freedoms to exist. And I must conform to that definition" (p. 86). Clearly, then, Fowles is offering us the only possible version of the godlike narrator he can give: one who, like the twentieth-century post-existentialist God, asserts his existence by his nonintervention:

> The novelist is still a God, since he creates. . . . What has changed is that we are no longer the gods of the Victorian image, omniscient and decreeing; but in the new theological image, with freedom our first principle, not authority. (p. 86)

Chapter 13 must be viewed, then, as a sort of enormous reappraisal of our assumptions: a convention has been destroyed only to allow another convention to take its place. Fowles has given us the criteria by which we should judge his ability to conform to the newly chosen frame: instead of a replica of the "real" world we are offered now a wholly fictional world, but we must not forget that for Fowles fiction and reality enjoy the same status:

> Fiction is woven into all. . . . I find this new reality (or unreality) more valid. . . . You do not even think of your own past as quite real; you dress it up, you gild it or blacken it, censor it,

> tinker it . . . fictionalize it, in a word, and put it away on a shelf—your book, your romanced
> autobiography. We are all in flight from the real reality. That is a basic definition of *Homo
> sapiens*. (p. 87)

Having stated the real aim underlying the devious use John Fowles makes of the
Victorian convention of omniscience, we may turn to the question of whether
Fowles's ideas on the nature of reality and God are also reflected at the thematic
level. As John Fowles himself commented to Richard B. Stolley *("The French
Lieutenant's Woman*'s Man: Novelist John Fowles," p. 59), the plot of *The
French Lieutenant's Woman* sprang from "no fixed plan, [I had] only a vague
idea of the way it was going. There was the outcast woman and a respectable
man would fall in love with her. That was the first stage. Then it happened that
the respectable man was engaged to another girl, and all sorts of things came
out of that." The Victorian theme of the seduced and rejected woman, visualized
in the image of a mysterious woman looking out over a rough sea at the end of
the Cobb, seems to be the pivot around which the whole novel developed. This
theme, which goes back to Richardson and the Gothic romance, developing later
into the historical romance, has been pointed out by Ronald Binns ("John
Fowles: Radical Romancer," p. 331) as the novel's major source:

> Fowles's third novel contains all the characteristic properties of the historical romance, includ-
> ing the Persecuted Maiden, the motif of flight, and dramatization of "history—real history, as
> distinguished from legend and myth," backed up by an impressive array of documentation.

As Ian Watt *(The Rise)* has amply demonstrated, the myth of the seduced
and abandoned maiden is closely linked to the rise of the middle class and
reflects the impact of the new mercantile philosophy: woman is regarded as a
property of man, and her virginity is the only means of assuring the legitimacy
of the descent. When Pamela rejects the advances of Mr. B., she assumes a
totally new middle-class behavior, utterly foreign to the rural medium, where
virginity didn't have any particular significance. In *The French Lieutenant's
Woman* the subplot focusing on the engagement of Sam and Mary is partly
meant to highlight this difference in sexual behavior. Referring to Mary's long-
lost virginity, the narrator comments with his accustomed pedantic accuracy:

> The prudish puritanity we lend to the Victorians, and rather lazily apply to all classes of
> Victorian society, is in fact a middle-class view of the middle-class ethos. . . . The hard—I
> would rather call it soft, but no matter—fact of Victorian rural England was that what a simpler
> age called "tasting before you buy" (premarital intercourse, in our current jargon) *was the rule,
> not the exception.* (p. 234, emphasis in the original)

Allied to the middle-class myth of the necessity of virginity were two other closely related notions: the Puritans' literal interpretation of the biblical words, "flesh of one's flesh," which in practice meant that a woman should either marry the man who had taken her maidenhead or no other, even if, as in the case of Tess of the d'Urbervilles, the man was a rake and a rapist. The other notion is what Ian Watt has called the double standard of morality, that is, the belief that there should be different criteria for judging the behavior of man and woman because, while man was by nature subject to physical passion, woman was immune to it. The narrator points to this biological discrimination in the summary of Victorian traits he makes at the beginning of chapter 35: "Where it was universally maintained that women do not have orgasms; and yet every prostitute was taught to simulate them" (p. 232).

In the novel, Ernestina Freeman embodies all the clichés attributed to the Victorian middle-class maiden: she is not only technically a virgin, she regards sex with such disgust that she had developed a mechanism to stop her mind from digressing into anything connected with sex: "I must not" (p. 30). As the narrator remarks:

> It was not only her profound ignorance of the reality of copulation that frightened her; it was the aura of pain and brutality that the act seemed to require, and which seemed to deny all that gentleness of gesture and discreetness of permitted caress that so attracted her in Charles. . . . Ernestina wanted a husband, wanted Charles to be that husband, wanted children; but the payment she vaguely divined she would have to make for them seemed excessive.
>
> She sometimes wondered how God had permitted such a bestial notion of Duty to spoil such an innocent longing. (p. 30)

Ernestina's assumptions neatly sum up the nineteenth-century middle-class attitude to marriage that Ian Watt has described as the combination of "a tremendous fascination for marriage and every detail connected with it for the heroine (and) an equally striking horror of any sexual advance or reference until the conjugal knot is tied" (*The Rise*, p. 155). For Watt this attitude to marriage is typical of Puritanism, and reflects "the assimilation of the values of romantic love to marriage," attributing "supreme spiritual importance to the relation of man and wife" (ibid., p. 155), a relation which thus is surrounded by the halo of idealization conferred to celibacy by Catholicism.

Drawing on the ideas of the double standard of morality and of the biological difference of woman, the fictional heroines stemming from *Pamela* and *Clarissa* develop a new stereotype of the feminine role, which Ian Watt (ibid., p. 161) synthesizes as follows:

> The model heroine must be very young, very inexperienced, and so delicate in physical and mental constitution that she faints at any sexual advance; essentially passive, she is devoid of any feelings towards her admirer until the marriage knot is tied—such is Pamela and such are

most of the heroines of fiction until the end of the Victorian period.

If her nature was not distorted, the passionless Victorian maiden would never give way to the temptation to yield to a socially inappropriate partner: her natural lack of sexual appetite protected her, while man could at best hope to learn to control his impetuous lust with the help of his intelligence and his notion of duty, or, even better, to find a legal outlet for it through marriage. Thus matrimony was inextricably bound up with economic and social status. A woman would only make that payment which seemed so excessive to Ernestina if it ensured a rise in the social scale. For, as Ian Watt remarks (quoting Dr. Johnson's words), it was "regarded as a 'perversion' for a woman to marry beneath her" (ibid., p. 164).

Ernestina Freeman stands in the novel for the Puritan ideal of the middle-class woman, and Sarah Woodruff for its reverse: she is the fallen woman, one who has distorted her nature, allowing passion to obfuscate her reason and her notions of morality and propriety. For such a woman, the only course left was repentance, never redemption. Accepting her lot with incomprehensible alacrity, Roxana says after refusing to marry one of her lovers, "After a man has lain with me as a Mistress, he ought never to lye with me as a wife" (Defoe, *Roxana, or the Unfortunate Mistress,* p. 192). Defoe's novel is a faithful report of the only course open to the scarlet woman: a fallen woman can only be redeemed by marrying the man who has seduced her, but such a man would be a fool to do so. Initially free from the torments of remorse, Roxana takes the only course of action left to a woman in her situation: she progresses in her corruption, making the best economic profit she can out of it.

Roxana's motives were understandable by eighteenth-century standards: greed for money could pervert a woman to the point of making her silence her conscience and feign a passion she could not possibly feel. But no amount of money would satisfy the more sensitive, romantic and pathetic Victorian woman: as in *Tess of the D'Urbervilles,* seduction and abandonment always provide the turning point in the development of tragedy.

At the beginning of *The French Lieutenant's Woman* we find Sarah in the familiar role of the seduced woman, but, as we learn a little later, not only does she not hide her shame, but she seems to take a positive pleasure in being the butt of contempt and rejection. Sarah's behavior is indeed shocking and her motives incomprehensible and obscure.

Just before he gives up further pretense of omniscience, the narrator ends chapter 12 by asking himself, "Who is Sarah? Out of what shadows does she come?" (p. 84). This is the same question Charles will try to answer from the very first moment he sees her facing the wind, enveloped in her dark clothes, "a figure from myth" (p. 9) oddly out of place in the quay of Lyme Regis. Mrs. Talbot, the affectionate lady for whom Sarah used to work as a governess, often sees her in her mind's eye as one of the heroines of the romantic literature of her adolescence and specifically as the protagonist of "an actual illustration from one of Mrs. Sherwood's edifying tales [which] summed up her worst fears. A pursued woman jumped from a cliff. Lightning flashed, revealing the cruel heads of her persecutors above, but worst of all was the shrieking horror of the doomed creature's pallid face and the way her cloak rippled upwards, vast, black, a falling raven's wing of terrible death" (p. 49).

From the start, then, Sarah is presented in wholly literary terms both as "a figure of myth" and as the stereotyped persecuted maiden of Gothic romance. When Charles meets her for the second time, the medium where he finds her is again described in strictly literary terms. The place is that part of the Lyme Regis wood called The Undercliff, and more precisely the eastern part of it known as Ware Commons. Charles has gone to The Undercliff in search of ammonites for, like all John Fowles's immature heroes, he is still a collector; Sarah habitually goes there to enjoy its solitude.

The narrator describes The Undercliff as "an English Garden of Eden" (p. 62) and to express its beauty he uses images borrowed from Renaissance art: "It is the ground that Botticelli's figures walk on, the air that includes Ronsard's songs" (p. 63). However, if from the narrator's and Charles's points of view The Undercliff is a nineteenth-century English version of the Garden of Eden, for the Puritan inhabitants of Lyme Regis and especially for Mrs. Poultney, Ware Commons inevitably evokes Sodom and Gomorrah, not only because it is the "nearest place to Lyme where people could go and not be spied on" (p. 80), but also because "the cart-track to The Dairy and beyond to the wooded common was a *de facto* Lovers' Lane" (pp. 80–81). On top of that, Ware Commons is the place where on "Midsummer's Night young people should go with lanterns, and a fiddler, and a keg or two of cider ... to celebrate the solstice with dancing" (p. 81). Although, in the narrator's words, the Donkey's Green Ball is "no more than an annual jape," in the minds of "the more respectable townsfolk one had only to speak of a boy and a girl as 'one of the Ware Commons kind' to tar them for life. The boy must thenceforth be a satyr; and the girl, a hedge prostitute" (p. 81).

Thus, The Undercliff is both the idyllic *hortus conclusus* of medieval romance, and the heathen wood of the satyr and the nymph; an Arcadia of bucolic chivalry and the meeting place for dyonisiac orgies. It is in this atmospheric place that Charles finds Sarah at the brink of the abyss, but peacefully asleep:

> There was something intensely tender and yet sexual in the way she lay; it awakened a dim echo in Charles of a moment from his time in Paris. Another girl, whose name he could not even remember, perhaps had never known, seen sleeping so, one dawn, in a bedroom over-

looking the Seine. (pp. 64–65)

Charles's contradictory feelings of simultaneous tenderness and sexual attraction fittingly correspond to the double image given of The Undercliff: like the wood, which is Sarah's natural environment, Sarah has in herself the double nature of the pathetic yet provoking persecuted maiden imagined by Mrs. Talbot and, as we are later to learn, consciously assumed by Sarah herself.

The second time Charles meets Sarah in the wood something significant happens: as he approaches her, she slips on the muddy path and falls to her knees, thus giving Charles the opportunity to put into practice his as yet unconscious desire to help her. But as he chivalrously steps forward to raise her from the mud, he contemplates her face and again associates it with the faces of "other foreign women—to be frank (much franker than he would have been to himself) with foreign beds" (p. 105).

So, again Charles's noble and not-so-noble sentiments are simultaneously aroused. From the start, too, Charles senses a sort of ambiguity in Sarah, a feeling that "the girl's silent meekness ran contrary to her nature; that she was therefore playing a part" (p. 92), a realization that, for all her tears and subdued talk, her eyes revealed "an intelligence, an independence of spirit . . . a silent contradiction of any sympathy; a determination to be what she was" (p. 105). Alternately, Charles thinks of Sarah as Emma Bovary (p. 106), as the Virgin Mary (p. 121), as tempting Calypso (p. 125), and as he becomes more interested in her, he becomes uneasily aware of his being "about to engage in the forbidden (and that) she was a woman most patently dangerous" (p. 128).

Charles's first reaction to his bafflement is to try to find a rational explanation. He discusses Sarah with Dr. Grogan, the village physician and, like him, a convinced Darwinian. According to Dr. Grogan, Sarah's behavior can only be explained as madness: she is subject to masochistic fits of "obscure melancholia" (p. 134), that is, as the twentieth-century narrator later explains, "the mental illness we today call hysteria . . . : a neurosis or psychosis almost invariably caused, as we now know, by sexual repression" (pp. 201–2). The rational side of Charles immediately accepts this explanation; and, moreover, he uses it as a pretext to cover his less rational, more instinctual and pleasurable impulses towards Sarah:

> He had been frank enough to admit to himself that it contained, besides the impropriety, an element of pleasure; but now he detected an element of duty. He himself belonged undoubtedly to the fittest; but the *human* fittest had no less certain responsibilities towards the less fit. (p. 144, emphasis in the original)

The eighteenth-century rationalists, and the Victorians after them, viewed man in Platonic terms as the combination of rationality and the passions, where, in Pope's words (*The Poems of Alexander Pope*, III, i, 68–69),

> Passions, like elements, tho' born to fight,
> Yet, mix'd and soften'd, in his work unite:
> These 'tis enough to temper and employ;
> But what composes Man, can Man destroy?
> Suffice that Reason keeps to Nature's road,
> Subject, compound them, follow her and God.

The balanced man was one who managed to control the black horses of passion with the iron fist of rationality directed by Nature and God; hence, allowing reason to yield to the impulses of passion was both unnatural and sinful. The Gothic literature of the eighteenth and nineteenth centuries was primarily a fictionalization of the revolt and rebellion of passion against virtue. It is in this context that we should interpret Charles's foreboding that he is entering forbidden and dangerous territory.

As in the tale of Laurentini in *The Mysteries of Udolpho,* or that of Beatrice in *The Monk,* the temptation Sarah represents for Charles amounts to the release of the hold of rationality on the brutish instinctual passions inherent in the nature of man. That this is so is clear from Charles's reaction after the climactic sexual encounter with Sarah at the Endicott Family Hotel: the consummation brings him not only the satisfaction of sexual desire, but also "a whole ungovernable torrent of things banned, romance, adventure, sin, madness, animality" (p. 304), and this is why, too, when he recovers his senses, he is seized by "an immediate and universal horror" (p. 305).

As the narrator ironically remarks ("precisely ninety seconds had passed since he had left her to look into the bedroom," p. 304), Charles only loses control for ninety seconds, but this minute and a half is enough to change the whole course of his existence. The effects of his act are described by the narrator in apocalyptic terms:

> [It] was like a city struck out of a quiet sky by an atom bomb. All lay razed; all principle, all future, all faith, all honourable intent. Yet he survived, he lay in the sweetest possession of his life, the last man alive infinitely isolated . . . but already the radioactivity of guilt crept through his nerves and veins. (p. 305)

Still, Charles believes that Sarah has only yielded to his impetuous lust, that he is the possessor, and she the victim, for,

> Charles was like many Victorian men. He could not really believe that any woman of refined sensibility could enjoy being a receptacle for masculine lust. He had abused her love for him intolerably. (p. 307)

His real catharsis comes a little later when he realizes that his assumptions about her were illusory, that she was no outcast maiden with a turned ankle and nobody to protect her, but, on the contrary, an unnaturally passionate virgin who had lured him into an irreversible situation for her own private and devilish ends. In short, that he was not the possessor but the possessed: "But for what purpose. Why? Why? Why? Blackmail! To put him totally in her power!" (p. 307).

Charles's first reaction after this realization is wholly Victorian: he sees Sarah as a succuba, a satanic figure, similar to the fiendish heroines of Gothic fiction, bent on his possession and destruction:

> And all those loathsome succubi of the male mind, their fat fears of a great feminine conspiracy to suck the virility from their veins, to prey upon their idealism, melt them into wax and mould them to their evil fancies . . . these, and a singing back to credibility of the hideous evidence adduced in La Roncière appeal, filled Charles's mind with apocalyptic horror. (pp. 307–8)

As in so many plots and subplots of the traditional Gothic novel, Charles sees Sarah's tremendous fascination as that of a demon lover who hides her real nature behind a pathetic and weak appearance in order to draw the hero's sympathy, eventually to put him in her power.

So far Charles has believed in his free will. The realization that Sarah has been playing the role of victim and outcast in order to possess him has the effect of plunging Charles into a fit of deterministic despair. Like Lieutenant Emile de la Roncière, he feels trapped and played with by a dangerous neurotic. Led by the tempting hand of Sarah, Charles has fallen into the hellish realm of passion only to find his naked self surviving in a world deprived of "all principle, all future, all faith, all honourable intent" (p. 305).

But just as the experiences undergone by Miranda and Nicholas in *The Collector* and *The Magus* brought about their existentialist awareness of the nature of the self, so Charles's rejection of the Augustan principle of rationality conveys a similar intuition. For all his feeling that he has been tempted and used for ignoble and selfish reasons, Charles comes to see Sarah as the necessary cross on which man has to be crucified to be truly himself:

> He had thought sometimes of Sarah in a way that might suggest he saw himself crucified on *her;* but such blasphemy, both religious and real, was not in his mind. Rather she seemed there beside him, as it were awaiting the marriage service; yet with another end in view. For a moment, he could not seize it—and then it came. To uncrucify! (p. 315, emphasis in the original)

As was the case with Nicholas Urfe, Charles eventually reaches beyond the feeling of betrayal to the notion of necessary pain as prerequisite to the fruition of human freedom. During his trial, strongly reminiscent of the above-quoted passage, Nicholas underwent a "cure of disintoxication" through which he achieved his emotional separation from Julie/Lily. Without the benefit of anything of the sort, Charles initiates his painful process of individuation of the self, mistaking Sarah for freedom, or rather, believing that he would only be able to achieve his freedom with and through her: "Sarah on his arm in the Uffizi did stand, however banally, for the pure essence of cruel but necessary . . . freedom" (p. 317).

The rest of the novel is a fictionalization of the way in which Charles completes his transformation from the Victorian gentleman into the modern existentialist. Drawing on the ideas of the epoch, the narrator presents his process of maturation wholly in Darwinian terms: the last heir of a long line of landed aristocrats living at the ebb of the industrial revolution, Charles Smithson is presented in the novel as the last exemplar of a species in danger of extinction. If he is to survive he must adapt to the new conditions which seem to be especially appropriate for the proliferation of the middle class. From this point of view, his plans to marry Ernestina Freeman, the wealthy heiress of a self-made middle-class tycoon, appear to be the inevitable liaison of blue blood and money, and especially so after Charles loses hope of inheriting the title and the fortune of his uncle when Sir Robert decides to marry.

Before he knew Sarah, marriage to Ernestina seemed the only possible course of action, although it inevitably entailed his transformation from a gentleman into a businessman, a possibility that threatened to materialize after the interview with Mr. Freeman (who offered Charles a partnership in the family business). Just before he takes the crucial step of visiting Sarah in Exeter, Charles imagines his future with Ernestina: they have a long, quiet, happy life together, they found a large family and he finally becomes a businessman: "His own sons were given no choice; and their sons today still control the great shop and all its ramifications" (p. 292).

It is to this drab foreseen future that Sarah seemed to be offering an alternative. Indeed, as Charles was painfully to learn, Sarah's offer never went beyond the realization that he was free to choose Ernestina, convention, safety, and rationality, or reject them and so choose damnation. Although Charles comes to understand the theoretical principle of necessary freedom during his tormented soliloquy in the church at Exeter after the climactic encounter with Sarah, he will be made to wait, again like Nicholas Urfe, to learn the real implications of this liberty. Deprived of the presence of Sarah, Charles will undergo one after another the ordeals decreed by social convention. He will lose Sam, lose the respect of his equals, and he will have to endure the revenge of Mr. Freeman by signing a document which precludes his every marrying again (and which, most significantly, denies him the right to be called a gentleman). Only after two long years of desperate waiting will Charles be allowed—by a combination of fortune and remorse (Sam sees Sarah and anonymously informs Charles's prosecutor of her whereabouts)—to contact Sarah again.

A lot has been written about the two versions of this last meeting. Once again breaking the illusion of verisimilitude, the narrator openly informs us that he has decided to give us two alternative versions of the novel's ending in order to preserve his objectivity, thus taking to its final consequences his former contention that "I do not fully control these creatures of my mind, any more than you control . . . your children, colleagues, friends, or even yourself" (p. 87).

But, as Christopher Ricks ("The Unignorable Real," p. 24) has pointed out, two alternatives are as restrictive as one, given the infinite possibilities of behavior of the characters, free from the narrator's coercive hand:

> To reduce the infinity to two alternatives is no less manipulatory or coercive—though because of its quasi-abnegation it is far more congenial to modern taste—than was the Victorian novelist's reduction of this infinity to one eventuality.

That is, for all his protests of nonintervention, the narrator can only hope to produce an *illusion* of freedom, above all when, as he ironically concedes, "it is futile to show optimism or pessimism, or anything else about it, because we know what has happened since" (p. 348).

To deprive us of any clue that might help us to guess which of the two is the "real" ending, the narrator tosses a coin, allowing hazard to decide for him the order in which the two versions shall be reported. But, of course, nobody is there to see on which side the coin has fallen.

The version the narrator tells in the first place has been called by the critics the "romantic" or "happy ending." According to it, Charles's intuition that Sarah was not at all mad, that she loved him truly and deserved to be pitied and loved, turns out to be correct. In this light her dragging Charles down into the gutter, making him an outcast as she herself was, is to be interpreted as the necessary bitter pill that would put them both on the same footing, and the two years of painful wait and reliance on hazard to reunite them, as an unshakable faith in the justice and watchful care of a pitiful God:

> "But why? Why? What if I had never . . ."
> Her head sank even lower. He barely caught her answer.
> "It had to be so."
> And he comprehended: it had been in God's hands, in His forgiveness of their sin. (pp. 392–93)

The second version the narrator tells presents what the critics have called the "modern" or "existentialist" ending. In it Sarah remains the satanic figure of Charles's worst fears. Like Frederick Clegg, she is obsessed with possessing, with exerting power over other creatures:

> She could give only to possess; and to possess him—whether because he was what he was, whether because possession was so imperative in her that it had to be constantly renewed, could never be satisfied by one conquest only, whether . . . but he could not, and would never, know—to possess him was not enough. (p. 397)

According to this ending, Sarah is one more version of John Fowles's manipulator, and the novel a "variation" on John Fowles's recurrent theme, as Rosemary M. Laughin ("Faces of Power in the Novels of John Fowles," p. 71) points out:

> In *The Collector*, a man exercises power over a woman in a physical way only. In *The Magus* a man manipulated another man physically and psychologically primarily through women. In *The French Lieutenant's Woman*, it is a woman, Sarah, who captures and controls a man, Charles, psychologically and sexually.

In *The Collector*, as we have seen, the outcome of physical force on Miranda is death, but we must not forget that Miranda dies only after she learns that she is not "a hater by nature" and that she cannot use force against Clegg, thus choosing death to the alternative of violence. In *The Magus* the effect of Conchis's manipulation of Nicholas is to allow him to grow from a collector of women into a mature existentialist hero. In the second ending of *The French Lieutenant's Woman* Sarah's exertion of power on Charles will likewise provide the means for Charles to reach beyond convention to the ultimate truth of the existentialist intuition:

> To realize that life, however advantageously Sarah may in some ways seem to fit the role of Sphinx, is not a symbol, is not one riddle and one failure to guess it, is not to inhabit one face alone or to be given up after one losing throw of the dice; but is to be, however inadequately, emptily, hopelessly into the city's iron heart, endured. (p. 399)

If in the first ending chance is presented in Victorian terms as the means by which a watchful Providence works to punish and reward, in the second ending action becomes a matter of personal choice: the painful revelation of Sarah's egotism works as his "cure of disintoxication": Charles abandons Sarah and chooses unhappiness and freedom.

With these considerations in mind, Robert Burden (ibid., p. 151) has written that "the second of the two endings fulfils the logic of the narrative at a deeper level" and that for this reason this second ending must be viewed as the "real" ending of the novel. Elizabeth D. Rankin (ibid., p. 205) takes a similar line, observing that: "(1) it is the only ending which is not undercut by the novel and (2) it is the logical conclusion toward which the novel has been moving since page one. . . . It is also the ending which the rest of the novel requires, for it completes the evolutionary process Charles has had to go through to become an existentialist."

In "Ambiguously Ever After" (p. 153), David Lodge offers Jonathan Culler's suggestion that every narrative operates according to "a double logic":

> Namely a logic of events, according to which a novel pretends to unfold a sequence of events that have already happened, revealing a chain of cause and effect, and a logic of coherence, according to which the characters and their actions confirm or complete a certain pattern of meaning.

We may adopt Jonathan Culler's useful terminology instead of the tentative expressions of Robert Burden (the logic of the narrative at a deeper level) and Elizabeth D. Rankin (the logical conclusion toward which the novel has been moving, or, the ending the rest of the novel requires), for all of them point to the same thing: the realization that John Fowles's second ending conforms to the logic of coherence instead of conforming, as the traditional realist novel usually does, to the logic of events.

In Fowles's first ending the actions of the characters are presented as the result of a chain of causes and effects: repentance and suffering winning God's pardon, Lalage unites Charles and Sarah. But in the second, existentialist, ending the actions of the characters conform to a different logic: the necessity to trim the characters' actions to the subtle pattern of meaning John Fowles has been weaving from the very first page. The novel proposed the fictionalization of the way in which a Victorian gentleman was able to metamorphose into an existentialist, and this is what we are left with in the second ending: a mature hero, free and with fully developed new qualities which will allow him to survive in the new medium. At the thematic level the logic of coherence displaces the logic of events; at the structural level the narrator's contention that God is revealed in His nonintervention is further reflected in the fact that the last ending is the only "open-ended" one.

Both the "Victorian" ending imagined by Charles during his train trip to Exeter, and the "romantic" ending offered by the narrator, are closed endings projecting themselves into the future, whether this future is plastically realized as a large family and Charles's turning into a businessman, as happens in the first case, or whether it is left to the reader's imagination to draw a picture of the happy future of the triangle formed by Sarah, Charles, and Lalage, as happens in the second case.

In the last ending, past and future merge into the present moment. Charles walks out of the residence of Dante Gabriel Rossetti with no preconceived ideas about his future, knowing that every step he will take from now on will be the result of a personal, though difficult, choice:

> And at the gate, the future made present, (Charles) found he did not know where to go. It was as if he found himself reborn, though with all his adult faculties and memories. But with the baby's helplessness—all to be recommenced, all to be learnt again! (pp. 397–98)

Charles's discovery that life is a succession of nows is one he had already intuited in London, after the frustrating and disgusting episode with the prostitute named Sarah:

> Now he had a far more profound and genuine intuition of the great human illusion about time, which is that its reality is like that of a road—on which one can constantly see where one was and where one probably will be—instead of the truth: that time is a room, a now so close to us that we regularly fail to see it. (p. 278)

By reducing Charles's future to the present moment the second ending presents itself as one containing within itself all those infinite alternatives Christopher Ricks referred to when he accused the narrator of manipulation. In this sense, this ending may be said to function as the abrupt time-breaks at the end of *The Collector* and *The Magus,* opening up for the characters a whole range of alternative possibilities of behavior, thus making true the narrator's desire of nonintervention.

By starting as a Victorian novel and then developing from this into a post-Modernist metafictional parody of Victorian conventions, *The French Lieutenant's Woman* may be said to occupy a somewhat isolated position in the history of English fiction. Echoes of the sentimental novel, of Tennyson, Jane Austen, Dickens, George Eliot, Arnold, John Stuart Mill, and a hundred other nineteenth-century writers and thinkers massively press on the novel with the shameless pleasure of conscious and deliberate pastiche,[2] but only one Victorian novelist is openly acknowledged as a direct, major influence: at a certain moment in the novel, the narrator refers to Thomas Hardy and to the unhappy triangle formed by the writer himself, his cousin Tryphena and his wife Lavinia. As the narrator points out, Hardy had to choose between an obscurely unnatural and socially disadvantageous marriage to his beloved Tryphena or a socially appropriate match with Lavinia Gifford. For reasons not yet fully revealed, Hardy chose the second course of action, only to regret it the rest of his life. As the narrator further observes, the personal drama provided Hardy with one recurrent theme for his novels and, we may add, for his *Wessex Tales.*

As I have shown elsewhere ("Amor y muerte en *The Wessex Tales,* de

Thomas Hardy"), five out of the seven tales in this series are stories of matrimonial unhappiness in which frustration and disharmony are the outcome of a mistake in the choice of partner. Recurrently a hero or a heroine, faced with having to choose between love and social advantage, mistakes social profit for happiness and condemns himself or herself to a sterile and frustrating marriage. On other occasions, when the hero falls in love and decides to attach himself to the beloved one, tragedy often arises due to social and psychological barriers. It seems as if in Hardy, no matter how you choose, human happiness is always threatened by the combined forces of social convention and bad luck.

The French Lieutenant's Woman reproduces, then, a Hardian situation: if Charles chooses Ernestina his felicity will be blighted by the memory of Sarah, as he well understands in his mental reconstruction of this possibility; but choosing Sarah does not necessarily imply choosing happiness, as he is painfully to learn. Charles's inability to foresee how miserable he will be by choosing Sarah is similar to Jude's inability to understand fully the terms of his relationship with Sue Brideshead: Jude and Charles make the same mistake of trying to make the women they love conform to their own idea of them. Charles becomes aware of this fact at the end of the novel, after his solitary journey abroad, when "he became increasingly unsure of the frontier between the real Sarah and the Sarah he had created in so many such dreams" (p. 367).

Charles's words echo Frederick Clegg's "good and bad dreams" of Miranda and point to Sarah's ability to appear both as victim and manipulator, expressing her radical ambiguity, similar to Alison's "oxymoron quality" in *The Magus,* to Jane's "opacity" in *Daniel Martin,* and to Rebecca's condition of both virgin and whore in *A Maggot.* The double nature of John Fowles's heroines, often developed more elaborately in the splitting into twins, expresses the archetype of woman that was synthesized in Swinburne's poem as the virginal white lily and the red rose of passion. This archetype appears recurrently in Victorian fiction and is present throughout in *Jude the Obscure.* As in *The French Lieutenant's Woman,* we may say that the source of strain and unhappiness stems in them from the man's inability to grasp fully the complexity of the woman, and from his insistence that she conform to his own illusory idea of her.

We may carry further the parallels between *Jude the Obscure* and *The French Lieutenant's Woman:* both Sue and Sarah are unusually intelligent, they consider themselves equal to men, care nothing for conventions, and are at a given point identified with the prototype of the New Woman. Both of them provoke tumultuous passions in their respective lovers, but would only yield to them as a means to keeping them in their power: Sue to make Jude forget about Arabella; Sarah to separate Charles from Ernestina. At the end of the novels, both of them abandon their lovers after they have turned the situation upside down, placing their lovers in the position they themselves were in, and most important of all, they are both responsible for their lover's leap into the void, having seen the radical absurdity of life, which causes Jude's lapse into nihilism and suicide and Charles's conversion to existentialism.

The echoes of Hardy in John Fowles's novels are deep and pervasive. Not only, as we have seen, at the thematic level, but also structurally, in the way *The French Lieutenant's Woman* unfolds always showing Sarah in the penumbra, a mysterious figure only imperfectly drawn, and most frustrating to women readers, much more the product of the mental—or literary—fantasy of a man than a real human being. Sue's unexpected *volte face* at the end of *Jude the Obscure,* when she adjures her ideas in order to go back to her first husband, has often been denounced by the critics as little consistent with her temperament, as essentially contrived. Yet, apart from conforming to the fashion of "New Woman" fiction, it shows in practice the full extent of her unpredictability and, like Sarah's unexpected disappearance from the Endicott Family Hotel, has to remain unjustified.

If we are to place *The French Lieutenant's Woman* somewhere in the history of English fiction, it is here, after Hardy, that it naturally comes. After the happy ending of "The Distracted Preacher" that Hardy wrote in April 1879, we find a note he added in May 1912 which may help us to understand why Hardy remains in so many senses a direct forerunner of the fiction of John Fowles. The note reads:

> The ending of this story with the marriage of Lizzy and the minister was almost *de rigueur* in the English magazine at the time of writing. But at this late date, thirty years after, it may not be amiss to give the ending that would have been preferred by the writer to the convention above. Moreover it corresponds more closely with the true incidents of which the tale is a vague and flickering shadow. Lizzy did not, in fact, marry the minister, but much to her credit in the author's opinion—stuck to Jim the smuggler, and emigrated with him after their marriage, an expatrial step forced upon him by his adventurous antecedents. They both died in Wisconsin between 1870 and 1860. (Hardy, *The Wessex Tales,* p. 153)

Hardy yields here to the temptation of breaking the Victorian convention to give us a less happy but more "real" and "historically truthful" version of his tale. This is exactly what John Fowles does in the second ending of *The French Lieutenant's Woman,* and for the same basic reason, with the only difference that, since Hardy was a Victorian, his second ending is as neatly closed as the first.

By rejecting an ending which conforms to the logic of events, in order to give his readers a more "truthful" ending organized according to the logic of coherence, Hardy proves to be, besides the thematic forerunner of Fowles's, the sharer of his intuition that breaking the rules of one convention is both necessary and profitable.

4

Daniel Martin

After *The French Lieutenant's Woman* John Fowles took eight years to publish his next novel, *Daniel Martin* (1977), a book of great complexity and one the author himself has tended to value more highly than the preceding ones.

From the thematic point of view *Daniel Martin* may be read as one more variation on the central theme in all John Fowles's fiction, namely, the achievement of maturity, a new understanding of life, acquired through the experience of love. That this is so in *Daniel Martin* is clear from the first sentence of the novel, which stands alone after George Seferis's epigraph, like Conchis's "waiting room" notice on the threshold of Bourani, encapsulating in gnomic form the whole aim of the hero's quest: "Whole sight, or all the rest is desolation" (p. 7).

The hero, Daniel Martin, must achieve "whole sight" if he wants to escape from the desolation of contemporary life, the existentialist void, T. S. Eliot's waste land of hollow men. In *The Collector* Miranda unsuccessfully tried to help her Caliban mature as a human being. In *The Magus* Conchis lured the purblind and reluctant Nicholas to follow a route carefully pointed out for him by the wise old man, while in *The French Lieutenant's Woman* Charles Smithson's maturation was ironically achieved after a chance encounter with a woman manipulator, who was pursuing her own particular aims. In *Daniel Martin,* however, "whole sight" is consciously sought by the hero himself, while the role of wise old man figure in this novel, Herr Professor Otto Kirnberger, whom the hero encounters towards the end of his quest, is to confirm the route taken rather than to point out the way.

Daniel Martin, the promising playwright turned wealthy but sterile screenwriter by a series of wrong choices made in his early adulthood, realizes, when he is already in his late forties, the utter meaninglessness of his life. By traditional social standards he has been extremely fortunate: he rides the crest of the wave of popularity as a screenwriter in Hollywood. He enjoys the love of a clever and beautiful film star much younger than himself. He has the money and the freedom to do whatever he pleases. He is intelligent and cultivated, a genuine "aristos," but he feels a growing uneasiness as he comes to realize that he is wasting his talents in the film business:

> You write, Interior, medium shot, girl and man on a couch, night. Then you walk out. Let someone else be Jenny and Dan. Someone else tell them what to do. Photograph them. You never really stake yourself. Let it be no one else. Just you. . . . That's all, Jenny. I don't really want to start a new career. Just a way of saying I'm sick of screenplays. (pp. 20–21)

A crudely realistic art, the film is incapable of rendering the real self. If Daniel Martin wants to know himself, to be "no one else. Just you," he must reject screenwriting and try a new medium. Jenny, his lover, proposes the novel:

> "Then write a novel," he sniffs. "Why not."
> "I wouldn't know where to begin."
> "Here." (p. 21)

Following Jenny's suggestion, Daniel selects for the opening chapter of his future novel the very conversation he is having with her at the moment. In order to help Dan reconstruct this conversation, Jenny even promises to write her own version:

> "Then I'll try and write some of it down for you. Tomorrow between takes. Just the gist. . . . Or a version of it, anyway." (p. 23)

For the following chapter of his intended novel, Daniel will have to rely on the creative powers of the novel itself:

> "This *is* the first chapter."
> "And the next?"
> "Something will happen. Like a window opening. No, a door. Like a door in a wall." (p. 22)

No sooner has Jenny uttered these words than the telephone rings, bringing to actuality a past Daniel had believed long buried and forgotten: "Then a voice; and unbelievably, as in a fiction, the door in the wall opens" (p. 24). The voice is that of his ex-wife, Nell, and the message—the imminent death by cancer of Anthony, Dan's best friend from whom he has been estranged for more than twenty years—has the effect of bringing Dan's past to the surface again. Nell's long-distance call urging Dan to return to England to the bedside of Anthony confirms Jenny's hint that literature can create reality, while from the mythological point of view, it constitutes Dan's "call for adventure," the invitation for the hero to start his mythical quest, a dangerous journey, both attractive and frightening, doing what he obscurely wanted was intimately bound up with doing what he obscurely hated. He even tried it out: "I missed my flight (or I nearly missed my flight), owing to a traffic hold-up on the San Diego free-way"—and did not like the sound and feel of it one bit. (p. 73)

Like the traditional mythical hero confronted with the beginning of his quest, Daniel Martin must fight between the compulsion to undertake his journey of individuation and the temptation to lag behind, in the comfortable anonymity of the maternal womb:

"If you run away, Jenny, you can't find your way back. That's all I meant. Trying to . . . it's only a pipe-dream. Trying to crawl back inside the womb. Turn the clock back." (pp. 21–22)

In Carol Barnum's words ("John Fowles's *Daniel Martin:* A Vision of Whole Sight," p. 67), "Like all potential questers (Daniel Martin) fears the difficult journey, particularly the aspect of 'trying to crawl back inside the womb,' which Joseph Campbell calls 'the belly of the whale' motif of the hero's quest."

Placed in a position remarkably similar to that of Nicholas Urfe in *The Magus* (1977), Daniel Martin's reaction as he leaves California is expressed with the same kind of spatial imagery Nicholas employed when he landed in Phraxos:

It was like a journey into space. I [Nicholas Urfe] was standing on Mars, knee-deep in thyme, under a sky that seemed never to have known dust or cloud. (p. 49)

I [Daniel Martin] was not really flying to New York, and home; but into an empty space. (p. 85)

But unlike Nicholas, whose process of maturation will take place in an exotic and openly mythical island in the Aegean, Daniel's "fateful region of both treasures and danger, (of) unimaginable torments (and) impossible delight" (Campbell, *The Hero* . . . , p. 58) is England itself, an England whose values Daniel Martin had rejected in favor of the false values of America, which is throughout presented in terms of a "waste land."

The "opening of the door in the wall," then, leads Dan to a confrontation with and reinterpretation of his past. The flight from California through New York to London, with its crossing of several time zones, literally involves a dislocation of Dan's time schemes which works as an apt metaphor for the mental journey the hero will be forced to undertake in the course of his mythical quest. That this is so is clear from the title of chapter 13, "Forwards Backwards," which deals with Dan's first day in London after his arrival. In the morning, lying awake in bed, "I felt the next stage of the long-journey disorientation: I had never left London, California was a dream" (p. 143). Once within the mythical realm, the hero must perform a task of formidable difficulty. Being a writer, Dan intuits that in order to come to terms with himself, he must recreate his past by writing an autobiographical novel for, in contrast to the film that he finds too crudely realistic, the medium the novel employs, the word, is imprecise enough to be able to recreate reality only analogically:

> Images are inherently fascistic because they overstamp the truth, however dim and blurred, of the real past experience . . . the word is the most imprecise of signs. . . . What I was trying to tell Jenny in Hollywood was that I would murder my past if I tried to evoke it on camera; and it is precisely because I can't really evoke it in words, can only hope to awaken some analogous experience in other memories and sensitivities, that it must be written. (p. 100)

In *The Magus* Nicholas was made to participate in the "metatheater" as a way of educating himself; he also had to listen to a series of cautionary tales and to solve puzzles and riddles. But this cannot be compared to the difficulty of the task allotted to Daniel Martin. For him John Fowles has reserved the very same task he set himself when he decided to write a novel entitled *Daniel Martin*. Of the difficulty of novel writing, Fowles has said (Gussow, "Talk with John Fowles," p. 84): "The novel is an impossible task. It's a mystery why you keep doing it."

An imaginary character existing only in John Fowles's fictional world, Daniel Martin is paradoxically given the role of creator: in order to mature he must write his autobiographical novel, but his task is an impossible one, not only because of its inherent difficulty, but primarily because, in order to exist as a novel, in order to reach the hands of the readers it must find its way out of the realm of fiction—to which Daniel Martin belongs—into the ontological universe.

Throughout the novel, Daniel Martin will ponder over the difficulty of his allotted task, always postponing it, to the point that when we reach the very last paragraph of the novel we realize with a shock that Daniel Martin hasn't *written* his novel yet:

> That evening, in Oxford, leaning beside Jane in her kitchen while she cooked supper for them, Dan told her with a suitable irony that at least he had found a last sentence for the novel *he was never going to write.* (p. 704, my italics)

Dan's unwritten last sentence is "whole sight, or all the rest is desolation," as "Dan's ill-concealed ghost," John Fowles himself, cannot help but tell us in the omniscient comment with which the novel ends:

> Which is perhaps why, in the end, and in the knowledge that Dan's novel can never be read, lies eternally in the future, his ill-concealed ghost has made that impossible last his own impossible first. (p. 704)

With his characteristic delight in surprising the reader, John Fowles has hidden this vital information till the very end of his novel. If we believe the heterodiegetic narrator's cryptic comment that Dan's "ill-concealed ghost" has made Daniel Martin's "impossible last sentence his own first," two things follow. Firstly, the narrator's careful allusion to Dan's ill-concealed ghost in the third person ("has made") may be taken as an open acknowledgment of identity not only between first-level narrator and hero, but explicitly between author and creation, so that the whole novel turns into a huge hide-and-seek game of identities: John Fowles, a writer in his forties, writes a novel about another writer in his forties called Daniel Martin who, in his turn must write an autobiographical novel, using for his hero the pseudonym "Simon Wolfe," a name picked up at random from the Hollywood directory, but which, as the critics[1] have pointed out, can be rearranged to form the name FOWLES (*S imon WOLFE*). Secondly, by making the first sentence in the John Fowles's novel, "whole sight, or all the rest is desolation," both the ontological author's real beginning and the unwritten intended ending of his character's future novel, *Daniel Martin* acquires a circular structure in which the real and the imaginary, the written and the unwritten, the actual and the potential, merge. Thus, the circularity of the identity between author, narrator, and character is echoed by the circularity of the novel's structure, enhanced as it is by the fact that the chapters are not numbered, but only given an allusive title.

In order to be really himself, Daniel Martin must affirm his personality by writing his autobiographical novel in the third person, but, being a fictional character existing only within somebody else's mind, his novel can reach the hands of the readers only through the mediation of the ontological author. In practice this results in the alternation of first- and second-level narrators and in a varying distance between implied author, narrator, and hero: the novel entitled *Daniel Martin,* narrated by a heterodiegetic narrator in the first degree (Genette, *Figures III,* p. 256), who identifies with the implied author, engulfs within itself another novel about "Simon Wolfe" alternately reported by two homodiegetic narrators: Daniel Martin and Jenny McNeil, who combine their roles of characters in the John Fowles's novel with that of narrators of their own creations.

Although Daniel Martin and Jenny McNeil are both homodiegetic narrators, they belong to two different varieties: besides being the hero in John Fowles's novel, Daniel Martin is also the hero of his narrative, while Jenny plays only a secondary role, both as character and narrator, her three "contributions" having a rather restricted scope. Using Gérard Genette's useful terminology *(Narrative Discourse. An Essay in Method,* p. 246) we can say that Daniel Martin is an *autodiegetic* narrator similar to Gil Blas or Watson, but with a difference: while in the more traditional novels the role of the autodiegetic narrator is always kept distinct, to the point that any change of status is felt by the reader as an infraction of an implicit norm, the more experimental kind of contemporary novel has passed beyond that limit, "and doesn't hesitate to establish between narrator and character(s) a variable or floating relationship, a pronominal vertigo in tune with a freer logic, and a more complex conception of 'personality.' "[2]

Thinking about the way in which he should write his novel Dan comes to realize that he has a particular distaste for the narrative "I":

> He reserved an especially, and symptomatically, dark corner for first-person narration; and the closer the narrative *I* approximated to what one could deduce of the authorial *I*, the more murky this corner grew. The truth was that the objectivity of the camera corresponded to some deep psychological need in him. (p. 72)

Psychological need for objectivity, or perhaps "a fear of judgment" (p. 72) lead Daniel Martin to conclude that if he is to write a novel about himself "anything would be better than to present it in the first person . . . even the absurdity of a mythical Simon Wolfe" (p. 73). And indeed, although Daniel Martin says at the end that his novel will never be written, when we set out to read *Daniel Martin* we find that apparently this is not so, for, up to chapter 36, entitled "Pyramids and Prisons," the first-level narration of the fictional John Fowles alternates with Daniel Martin's own narration about a younger Daniel Martin, from whom he tries to detach himself by sticking to the third person narration. In fact, the first chapter of the novel, entitled "The Harvest," which selects one day in the life of the sixteen-year-old Daniel Martin, is reported by the adult Daniel Martin, as we learn at the chapter's end, which finishes with the screenwriter's signature and directions:

> Close shot.
> D. H. M.
> And underneath: *21 Aug 42*. (p. 16)

Apart from the fact that the chapter is signed by D. H. M. (one can't help wondering what the H. stands for, whether it is meant to evoke another D. H.—Lawrence—Daniel Martin's, and Nicholas Urfe's, favorite writer), there can be little doubt about the identity of the narrator: the whole chapter is full of what we could call "cinematic" devices. Firstly, the use of explicit stage directions like "Down, half masked by leaves. Point of view of the hidden bird . . . Close shot" (p. 16). Secondly, the use of the acoustic and visual for the purpose of helping the reader situate the scene described against a background of war: the Torquay sirens, the cannon explosions and the sight of the German two-engined Heinkel. And thirdly, the narrator's insistence that, for all their concreteness of time and place (the Old Batch field on the 21 August 1942), the events described have a ritualistic and plastic quality which renders them ever-recurrent and atemporal, as changeless as a photograph or a picture. To express this the narrator employs two main devices. The first and simplest is open statement by means of similes, as in:

> And he walks back to where they have gone back to work, but there are many more hands now, *as in a Brueghel*.
>
> Then back under the ash-tree, *as ritual as Holy Communion*. . . . (p. 15, my italics)

The second, a peculiar use of the verbal tenses: indeed, from the narrative preterite with which the chapter begins, the narrator insensibly slips into the gnomic present, and present participle, as in the following description of the rabbit hunt:

> They all gather round the last piece: stookers, children, old men, Babe and his lurcher: a black-and-liver dog with a cowed, much-beaten look, always crouched, neurotic, hyper-alert and Argus-eyed, never a yard from his master's heels. The young woman walks up on swollen ankles, carrying her baby son in her arms, the pram left by the gate. Some have sticks, others pile stones. A ring of excited faces, scrutinizing each tremor in the rectangle of corn: commands, the older men knowing, sternly cautious. Doan'ee fuss, lad, keep back. In the rectangle's heart a stirring of ears, a ripple of shaken stems, like a trout-wave in a stream. A hen pheasant explodes with a rattling whir, brown-speckled jack-in-the-box, down the hill and over Fishacre Lane. Laughter. A small girl screams. A tiny rabbit, not eight inches long, runs out from the upper border, stops bemused, then runs again. The boy who helped stook stands ten yards away grinning as a wild band of children sprawl and tumble after the tiny animal, which doubles, stops, spurts, and finally runs back into the wheat. (p. 13)

Often, too, the narrator alternates these presents and present participles with long paragraphs of verbless sentences, as in description of the meal under the ash tree:

> Then back under the ash-tree, as ritual as Holy Communion, the old pink-and-white check cloth, the bread, the quaint bowl of cream, the pots of raspberry and blackcurrant jam, the chipped white mugs, the two tea-pots, a browny-black with yellow bands, the same brown as the cake with all its hoarded sultanas and currants. Best the illicit scalded cream its deep yellow crust folded into the voluptuous white. No cream since time began could equal it; the harvest hunger, sun, the circle of watching children, the smell of sweat. Byre and meadow and breath of Red Devons. Ambrosia, death, sweet raspberry jam. (pp. 15–16)

The present, present participle, and the verbless sentences combine in the above passages to express timelessness.[3] Intertwined with these the narrator also uses iterative futures and infinitives, as in the following description:

> And the day will endure like this, under the perfect azure sky, stooking and stooking the wheat. Again and again old Luscombe will shred an ear from its haulm and roll the grains

between his heavy palms to husk them; cup his hand and blow the husks away; stare; then take
a grain and bite it in half, the germ with its taste of earth and dust, and then spit it out; and
finally put the remaining grains in his trouser pocket, for the poultry that evening. (p. 9)

Here, verb tenses change from the traditional narrative preterite to the
present and present participle, to the iterative future and infinitive, and to the
verbless sentence. These changes, together with accumulation of visual and
acoustic features, the minute description of objects and gestures, and the insistence on the ritualistic and plastic qualities of the events described, have the
effect of slowing down the pace of the narration, giving it the contrived plastic-
ity and atemporality of a photograph. Consistently enough, at the end of the
chapter, the young Daniel Martin is left frozen, "purged of tenses":

He sits with his back to a beech-trunk, staring down through foliage at the field. Without past
or future, purged of tenses; collecting this day, pregnant with being. (p. 16)

The stylistic characteristics of the chapter, as well as the signature at the chapter's end, allow no doubt about *Daniel Martin*'s authorship, but then, how can
we have access to Daniel Martin's narration and simultaneously believe his
protest at the end of the novel that he has not written his novel yet?

In order to answer this question we must remember the first-level narrator's
statement at the end of the novel, that he had made Dan's "impossible last, his
own impossible first," proposing the first sentence in the novel, "whole sight,
or all the rest is desolation," as both Dan's intended ending and John Fowles's
real beginning. Now, looking again at Daniel Martin's signature of the first
chapter, we find that his initials are followed by the words "and underneath: *21
Aug 42.*" And we may ask ourselves, who has written "and underneath," Daniel
Martin, or John Fowles-as-narrator? If we attribute these words to Daniel Martin, they are clearly redundant, for in order to sign his chapter he would simply
have to write his initials, and put the date underneath straightaway, without
having to indicate where the date should be placed. But if, on the other hand,
Fowles had wanted to report faithfully Daniel Martin's unwritten version of
what happened on 16 August 1942, he might find it necessary to explain that
the date should appear under the initials. That is, if we believe Fowles's statement that he has made Daniel Martin's last sentence his own first, we have to
see "The Harvest" as Fowles's faithful reproduction in his novel *(Daniel Martin)*
of Daniel Martin's intended but as yet unwritten memory of that day in the
summer of 1942, told in Daniel Martin's own cinematographic style, the first
sentence and the last direction ("and underneath") being the only two utterances
directly belonging to the first-level narrator, and thus to the narrative instead of
the diegetic level. Their respective positions at the beginning and the end of the

chapter physically mimic their function of parentheses engulfing Daniel Martin's unwritten memory of the harvest.

Although from the very beginning Daniel Martin is conscious of the necessity of detaching himself from his fictional *alter ego* by giving him a different name and by reporting his story in the third person, he will soon find it very difficult to keep this detachment in practice.

In "The Harvest" he succeeds in reporting the whole chapter in the third person up to the very end, where, unexpectedly, he breaks the convention that requires the narrative level and story level to be separated by allowing his hand to slip into the pocket of his character's trousers to take out a clasp-knife:

> Down, half masked by leaves. Point of view of the hidden bird. *I feel* in *his* pocket and bring out a clasp-knife; plunge the blade in the red earth to clean it of the filth from the two rabbits *he has gutted;* slit, liver, intestines, stench. *He stands and turns and begins to carve his initials* on the beech-tree. Deep incisions in the bark, peeling the grey skin away to the sappy green of living stem. Adieu *my* boyhood and my dream. (p. 16, my italics)

Indeed, one of the most baffling features of *Daniel Martin* is precisely what Genette has called a "pronominal vertigo," an unsteadiness of narrative person which has puzzled the critics, provoking all kinds of reactions: from those who dismiss it with a curt remark, like Bruce Woodcock *(John Fowles and Masculinity,* p. 124), who sees it simply as "a prevarication of pronouns which counterpoints the deviousness of Dan's male persona and his attempts to distance or escape it," to those who have offered quite complex and interesting explanations, like Simon Loveday ("The Style of John Fowles: Tense and Person in the First Chapter of *Daniel Martin,*" pp. 198–204), who offers three alternative interpretations for the change of personal pronoun in the paragraph quoted above. According to him,

> Dan-narrator may simply be recording a moment of empathy with his 1942 self. . . .
> Dan-narrator is in a position to intervene in his own past . . . ("I, Dan-narrator, make my character take out a knife"). . . .
> [Or] we should seek two aspects—narrator and character in *"Dan-then"* (as opposed to *"Dan-now"*). . . . The reflective self cleans the knife, but it was the pre-reflective self who gutted the rabbits. . . . These can only be memories, held in "his" mind but experienced by "me." (pp. 201–2)

Simon Loveday rejects the first two explanations for different reasons, but primarily because neither of them is applicable to the whole novel and he adheres to his third proposal, namely to split the personality of Daniel Martin not only into Dan-narrator (the older Dan, or "Dan-now") and Dan-character (the younger Dan, or "Dan-then"), but further into the "pre-reflective" and the "reflective" selves of Dan-then, thus extending the differences in awareness we traditionally find in autobiographical novels between adult narrator and young character to the younger Daniel Martin. Of this difference in awareness Loveday says:

> I suggested above that we must think in terms of a Dan-narrator and a Dan-character. My first two explanations dealt with these two in terms of "now" and "then" respectively: the narrator "now" recounts what his character did "then." This is the traditional—and satisfying—position of the autobiographical novelist, recounting from the view-point of experience the way in which he became what he is: it is even a technique Dan-character uses in the novel for his accounts of his own past delivered to other characters. But we have seen that it does not fit the novel as a whole. I suggest therefore that we should seek these two aspects—narrator and character—in *"Dan-then."* (ibid., p. 202)

Ingenious though it is, the third hypothesis Loveday proposes fails to provide a convincing *new* explanation applicable, as he intends, to the novel as a whole. Indeed, although Loveday tries to set apart what he calls the splitting of Dan-then into a "pre-reflective" and a "reflective" self from the traditional convention of allotting a deeper degree of awareness to narrator than to character, he provides the reader with no concrete evidence for such a differentiation, and even unconsciously assimilates both, as can be seen from his remark that we "should seek these two aspects—*narrator* and *character*— in *'Dan-then.'*"

Throughout his discussion of the point Loveday insists that any explanation should be applicable to the whole novel, and he rejects the traditional technique of establishing a different degree of awareness between narrator and character as an overall explanation for the shifts in narrative person that take place in *Daniel Martin* precisely because "it does not fit the novel as a whole." Surprisingly enough, however, Loveday does not illustrate his proposed explanation by giving examples of other instances in the novel in which the splitting of Dan-then into a "reflective" and a "pre-reflective" self might take place, but rather forces the reader to "move briefly from analysis of style to analysis of image" (ibid., p. 203), definitely abandoning the line of thought he had been pursuing thus far in order to try a metaphorical and psychological plus a "homeophoric" interpretation, applicable only to the paragraph under discussion.

A perusal of the novel soon shows that the shifts in narrative person often indicate not only empathy of narrator with hero, but can also be explained, in spite of appearances, as clear instances of the traditional convention, typical of the autobiographical novel, of stressing the narrator's omniscience and the young hero's lack of hindsight. A good example of this is to be found in "Gratuitous Act." At the beginning of the chapter, the first-level narrator establishes the present moment by reporting in the third person and in the present tense the arrival of the adult Daniel Martin at New York airport:

The now of then is coming down towards New York over a white landscape; snow, the beginning of the world where winter is real. *Dan sets* his watch to Eastern Standard time. (p. 103, my italics)

As in similar examples, we take it for granted here that the nameless heterodiegetic narrator who opens the chapter referring to the adult Daniel Martin in the third person is the fictional John Fowles; in the following paragraph, however, the third person is dropped, and the role of narrator is handed over to the adult Daniel Martin: *"I doubt* if that bed-sitter scene in the Oxford of 1950 sounds credible now" (p. 103, my italics). Although this change from the third to the first person may shock the reader accustomed to have such shifts of narrative person carefully explained by the narrator's comment and marked by quotations (Dan thought: "I doubt if that . . ."), what we have here is a traditional-enough device. The heterodiegetic narrator relinquishes his role in favor of his character in order to allow him to report his train of thought in his own words: the realization that he is leaving the eternal summer of California and entering a new world "where winter is real" and where his Californian watch has to be readjusted acts as the necessary stimulus that brings about the script-writer's flashback to an episode his younger self had in 1950. Dan's memory is reported in the first person and in the preterite; the adult Daniel Martin refers to his friends Nell, Anthony, Jane, and himself as "us," but immediately seems to remember the need to distance himself from his younger *alter ego,* and insensibly slips from the first into the third person:

Our surrender to existentialism and each other was also, of course, fraught with evil. It defiled the printed text of life; broke codes with a vengeance; and it gave *Dan* a fatal taste of adultery. . . . *We* didn't realize the nonexchangeability of life and art. In reality that day *Dan* did not understand what was happening; that as *he* had been led in, so must *he* be led out. (p. 104, my italics)

Here the role of Dan-now as homodiegetic narrator is clear-cut. His omniscient remark that Dan "in reality did not understand what was happening" sets a sharp contrast between the hero's naïveté and the narrator's greater knowledge, while the slip into the third person in the sentence "and it gave Dan a fatal taste of adultery" underlines the fact that the narrator does not share Dan-then's uneasiness of conscience, that he has learned to outgrow it. A similar kind of omniscience is often expressed in proleptic asides by the narrator, like the following:

But they had hardly begun to kiss—and Dan to feel, *though he was never to know,* that everything was still in the balance—when . . . (p. 105, my italics)

"Gratuitous Act" may be taken as an exemplary chapter in the question of embedded narrative levels. In it the alternation between first and second level narration is first established and then blurred: the heterodiegetic narrator (the fictional John Fowles) reports the older Daniel Martin's flight from California to New York in the third person and in a present tense that stands for 1974. Within this frame, Daniel Martin's flashbacks to episodes lived by his younger self in England in 1950 are alternately reported in the first and the third person but always in the preterite. These changes from the first to the third person may be taken to indicate opposing pulls felt by Dan-now, to identify with or to differentiate himself from his younger self, and whenever this differentiation is stressed it is done through omniscient remarks that express the narrator's experience and the hero's lack of insight.

When Daniel Martin made up his mind to write a novel, he promised himself to use a pseudonym and to stick to the third person. We soon find, however, that he never comes to use the name "Simon Wolfe" and that, as we have seen, he often slips seemingly unawares from third- into first-person narration. Knowing it to be an autobiographical novel we may indeed explain this unsteadiness in narrative person as an irrepressible tendency to identify with his hero—Loveday's rejected first explanation as "a moment of empathy"—but we soon find that Jenny, who is also trying her hand at fiction writing for the first time, seems to share Daniel Martin's difficulty in sticking to the concrete facts and in separating the "real" from the imagined self. In "Games" she promises to write her own fictional account of the conversation between Daniel Martin and herself, referring to Dan as "Simon Wolfe": "This isn't what I promised to write, just before you ran away. But it's still pure fiction. Of course. About Mr. Wolfe. Not you" (p. 37). But then she has difficulty in separating the fictional "Simon Wolfe" from the "flesh and blood" Daniel Martin: "When *you,* I mean *he,* talked of charms . . ." (p. 41, my italics). In Jenny's case the difficulty in separating the real Daniel Martin from "Simon Wolfe" cannot be explained as empathy, for she does not identify with Daniel Martin, nor is she concerned with expressing her omniscience. And we begin to realize that for Jenny—as for Daniel Martin—the main difficulty really lies in keeping separate the "real" from the "fictional" Daniel Martin, a difficulty of the same kind as the one John Fowles also seems to have in "concealing" his ghost behind a "cardboard" John Fowles who in turn has to be concealed behind Daniel Martin. Indeed, the fact that the critic is forced to use the attributes "real" or "flesh and blood," and "cardboard," "unreal" or "fictional," in order to explain the alternate roles of Daniel Martin, points to Daniel Martin's paradoxical double nature: Daniel Martin is "real" with respect to his creation (the younger Daniel Martin or "Simon Wolfe"), but "fictional" with respect to his creator (John Fowles), so, while we speak of the "flesh and blood" Daniel Martin as opposed to the "cardboard" Danny or Simon Wolfe, we have to refer to the "cardboard" Daniel

Martin as the hero in the novel written by John Fowles. But John Fowles himself has a double identity: he is the "real writer" and the "cardboard" narrator who, in his turn, identifies with Daniel Martin.

What is more, from this perspective, even the apparently gratuitous "contributions" written by Jenny MacNeil acquire a structural importance, as they serve to confer on Daniel Martin yet another role, besides those of author, narrator, and character: whenever Daniel Martin sits down to read one of Jenny's "contributions" he turns into a reader of fictions, and one who is included within the text, and so exists only as a part of the written text, making true the deconstructivist contention that nothing exists before or after the written text, that writer and reader are engulfed within the all-enveloping text.

Thus, Daniel Martin's ever-changing identity as author, narrator, character, and reader, metaphorically expressed in his university nickname, "Mr. Specula Speculans," a man of infinitely mirrored faces, functions as an apt metaphor for the novel's radical message that literature engulfs reality, while the structural complexity of the novel, the alternation of narrators and the blurring of the ontological, the narrative and the diegetic levels, the *mise en abyme* structure of the novel within the novel, all point to the basic nature of this reality as complex and many-sided.

When, in "The Harvest," Dan-narrator puts his hand in the pocket of Dan-hero, he not only expresses empathy with the latter, shows the narrator's capacity to intervene in the past, by altering the lived facts according to his whim, or emphasizes the difference in reflection between hero and narrator, but he also proves that it is possible to destroy the convention that requires the narrative level and the story level to be separate. As the hand of the narrator slips into the pocket of his character, the narrative and the diegetic levels merge, character and narrator coalesce, the "flesh and blood" and the "cardboard" Daniel Martin fuse by virtue of a metalepsis into a unique person, both ontological and fictional, acting as the living icon of what is to come: a circular novel, with no beginning or end, of endless potentiality, in which author, narrator, and character are both one and many, both different and the same, simultaneously real and unreal.

The polymorphous nature of reality and of the self thus established, Daniel Martin's semi-jocose remark that he is fed up with the cinema, that he must try novel-writing in order to be "really himself," acquires a new seriousness and importance, for it helps us to understand the real direction in which the novel is moving. Rejecting the first explanation he had given for the shifts in narrative person in the novel, Loveday says,

[These shifts in narrative person] can hardly be a record of *an increasing empathy* if the final eleven chapters, bringing Dan-character as close in time as he ever comes to Dan-narrator and recording the genesis of the novel itself, are uniformly in the third person. We must therefore seek a third explanation. (ibid., p. 202, my italics)

The mistake Loveday makes here is in assuming that the shifts in narrative person are meant to record an *increasing* empathy. As Loveday himself acknowledges, the direction towards which the novel moves in the last eleven chapters is precisely the contrary, that is, from unsteadiness and confusion of narrative persons (expressing the difficulty felt by Daniel Martin and Jenny Neil—and by John Fowles himself—in separating the real from the unreal, the fictional from the ontological) towards the desired steadiness and overall control of the narrative, which will only be achieved after the climactic chapter 32, "In the Orchard of the Blessed." In that chapter, Daniel Martin (and John Fowles with him) asks himself a series of crucial questions about the task of the novelist and is finally able to provide decisive answers to them.

After the burial of Anthony and a brief visit to Compton, Daniel Martin takes Jane and her son Paul to Thorncombe for a weekend before Paul returns to school. After dinner, sitting in front of the fire, Dan tells Jane for the first time his intention to write a novel and later, as he walks by himself in the garden in the middle of the night, the novel begins to acquire definite shape:

He had already, without having admitted it to Jenny, borrowed her proposed name for his putative hero: the ghost of Altadena Drive, the pin-found "Simon Wolfe." He didn't like the name and knew he would never use it, but this instinctive rejection gave it a useful kind of otherness, an objectivity when it came to distinguishing between his actual self and a hypothetical fictional projection of himself. (p. 449)

As the quotation makes clear, Dan accepts the pseudonym Simon Wolfe as a mechanism to detach himself from his fictional projection, but we must not forget that Simon Wolfe and Daniel Martin are one and the same, as the heterodiegetic narrator says explicitly:

Neither *the first nor the third person that he also was* wanted Jane in his arms again. (p. 459, my italics)

This point is important, for it helps to explain why Daniel Martin is suddenly assailed by a major difficulty when he thinks about the characteristics of his fictional hero.

The obstacle was this: he was too fortunate, and this gave him, in his "Simon Wolfe" projection, a feeling of inauthenticity, almost of impotence. . . . In short, he felt himself, both artistically and really, in the age-old humanist trap: of being allowed . . . to enjoy life too much to make a convincing case for any real despair or dissatisfaction. (p. 450)

The realization is unexpected and paradoxical: when Daniel Martin started to think about writing a novel while he was in California, he told Jenny that he wanted to do so because he was feeling unhappy and disappointed with the turn his career had taken, but now, thinking about his real motives again, "he had realized his true dilemma was quite the reverse. He was, if he was honest, under the looking glass of eternity, a good deal less unhappy at what he had failed to be than content to accept his lot" (p. 452).

The discovery that he has no real reason to complain about his life, that in fact his "luck was in" (p. 464), comes to Daniel Martin as a revelation. If he wants to comply with the existential, post-Beckettian canon that prescribes an unhappy, aimless hero for contemporary fiction, he will have to distort his authentic personality, giving Simon Wolfe "disadvantages he did not have" (p. 453) or presenting "a character less self-absorbed, less concentrated on his own perception . . . someone less conscious, in effect" (p. 453). Obviously, neither of the two alternatives is fully satisfying, as the intrusive voice of the omniscient narrator superciliously remarks: "The least thinking reader will have noted a third solution, but it had not occurred to the writer-to-be until this moment" (p. 453). By a miracle of simultaneous thinking that betrays the real identity of the omniscient narrator, the third solution suddenly comes to Daniel Martin's mind as he muses alone in the Edenic garden of his beloved Thorncombe: "To hell with cultural fashion; to hell with élitist guilt; to hell with existentialist nausea; and above all, to hell with the imagined that does not say, not only in, but behind the images, the real" (p. 454).

Daniel Martin's (and John Fowles's) "poetic manifesto" strikingly echoes other words written by Lord Byron against the Romantic canon, nearly a century before:

> It is the fashion of the day to lay great stress upon what they call "Imagination" and "Invention," the two commonest of qualities: an Irish peasant with a little whiskie in his head will imagine and invent more than would furnish forth a modern poem. *(The Works of Lord Byron: Letters and Journals,* vol. V, app. 3, p. 554)

Rejecting, like Byron, cultural fashion, imposed feelings, and prescribed recipes for his novel, Daniel Martin makes one momentous decision: to submit the imagined to the real. As the heterodiegetic narrator comments,

> The most important decision of his life . . . did not arrive—nor do most such decisions in reality—as light came on the road of Damascus, in one blinding certainty; but far more as a tentative hypothesis, a seed, a chink in a door. Still to be doubted, neglected, forgotten through most of the future of these pages. (p. 454)

Daniel Martin's realization that he has no reason to complain about his lot in life and the decision to depict his real self in his novel rather than to invent a more fashionable version of himself may be interpreted as the hero's first step towards maturity: rejecting the inauthentic pose of existential boredom (Urfe's "modish *ennui"*), Daniel Martin honestly recognizes his privileged status, his condition of *aristos*. Interestingly enough, this realization only comes to him when he projects himself in his fictional *alter ego,* when he sees himself reflected in his imaginary hero—something he had strongly intuited when he spoke of the importance of "his training in an adamantly third-person art and angle of vision." As the scriptwriter explained, the cinema also acts as a mirror of reality, but the picture of reality it offers is simplistic and easily pinned down in images and visual symbols. On the other hand, the reality he wants to encapsulate in his novel is complex and difficult to express. It forms an "interweaving of strands" and is made up of

> an obscure amalgam of rain, landscapes, pasts, fertilities, femaleness, all of which could perhaps have been derived from that one wet gravestone, his unknown mother's . . . and which would certainly have been so derived by the verdigrised old sage in bronze whom Dan had passed, with no more than an amused glance, in Dorchester that previous afternoon. (p. 464)

These are the confused elements that make up Daniel Martin's reality: memories of his past, of an English setting with clear mythical overtones, a concrete middle-class background and, as the cryptic reference to the statue of Thomas Hardy makes clear, of a specific literary tradition.

Daniel Martin's rejection of the imagined and artificial in favor of the real could lead us to conclude, mistakenly, that in *Daniel Martin* John Fowles is moving away from experimentation and backwards towards the English literary tradition of realism from which he has consistently been detaching himself since the publication of *The Collector.* Such a conclusion would overlook the heterodiegetic narrator's comment that Daniel Martin's revelation was only "a tentative hypothesis. . . . Still to be doubted, neglected, forgotten" (p. 454). It would also overlook the fact that John Fowles only rejects an empty imagination that does not include the real, in the same way as he rejects the pat realism of the cinema. Indeed, from the structural point of view, *Daniel Martin* may be seen as one more concretization of John Fowles's conception of reality as a polymorphous entity that combines in itself the ontological with the fictional, the real with the unreal, a conception he will develop at further length in *Mantissa* and in *A Maggot,* but which had already been powerfully hinted at in *The Magus.*

Only by grasping the complex, paradoxical double nature of John Fowles's conception of reality can we understand why, when "the door in the wall" opens and the hero starts his dangerous journey, he simultaneously undertakes it in two opposed directions: from the purely physical point of view Daniel Martin advances from his present moment into the future. This journey is reported linearly, strictly following the spatio-temporal coordinates. Whether it is the heterodiegetic narrator who reports Dan's actions or whether it is Dan himself who does so, the narrated events always coincide with Dan's doings during the day: Dan moves from his present into his future step by step, day after day as would any man in the real world. Roughly speaking, this journey starts at the moment he leaves California for New York and London, and includes his later visits to Thorncombe, Compton Place, and Oxford, as well as the trip to Egypt and Palmyra in the company of Jane, ending up with the return to England and Oxford.

Simultaneous with this journey is the mental journey backwards, which also begins with Daniel Martin's present in Hollywood (or more precisely with Nell's long-distance call), and which is made up of scattered flashbacks. The linking agents of these flashbacks are not the spatio-temporal coordinates that molded the physical journey of the hero, but rather the power the mind has to associate events often widely separated in space and time which, however, share a trait in common: an equivalence of meaning through contrast or resemblance. Once the principle of free association of ideas is duly acknowledged, it is easy to see a strict logic behind the apparently disconnected events in Dan's past that make up the hero's mental journey. Rearranged in chronological order, these would include episodes from Dan's early childhood and school years in Thorncombe; his university years in Oxford; the London years of playwriting, marriage to Nell and close friendship with Anthony and Jane, culminating in the trip to Tarquinia; and later, the years of divorce and estrangement from Jane and Anthony, and of abandonment of playwriting and England for screenwriting and California.

The physical and the mental journeys take place simultaneously but they remain widely separated in time and space; each moves in the opposite direction, yet they are closely related, since the events of the physical journey activate associations for the hero that, in their turn, constitute the mental quest. Up to chapter 36, entitled "Pyramids and Prisons," the narration of the physical journey alternates with Jenny's contributions and with the flashbacks that make up Daniel Martin's mental journey.

The superimposition of three different narrative voices (i.e., the heterodiegetic narrator's, Jenny's, and Dan's—be it Dan-now or Dan-then) in the first thirty-five chapters of the novel, together with the unsteadiness of narrative person and of verbal tense, produce a widespread effect of dislocation, of successive false endings and involutions which reflect the overlapping of different narrative and ontological levels and also express the difficulty Daniel Martin has in controlling his free association of ideas.

But then, in the remaining eleven chapters of the novel, from "Pyramids and Prisons" onwards, the voices of the two homodiegetic narrators are not heard and the heterodiegetic narrator takes up the role of reporting, in the third person and in the traditional narrative preterite, Dan and Jane's trip to Egypt and Palmyra, which constitutes the final stage in the hero's physical journey.

By creating a fictional projection of himself, and by placing this projection in a context similar to his own, Daniel Martin hopes to disentangle the strands of the confused amalgam that constitutes his life, and to arrest its movement by giving it a definite, literary form. But in order to create a "real" projection of himself, he must first look at himself in an opaque, distorting mirror:

> He had an apprehension that Jane could help—that the "making him think" was essentially a making him look at himself through her eyes. And through her opacity . . . it struck him that she was also unique in not mirroring him clearly; did not reflect what he saw in the less thinking, less perverse and perhaps less distorted glass of more ordinary minds. She still, as she always had, disturbed images, changed voices, recast scenes. (p. 464)

Jane's "opacity," her capacity to "set riddles one ignores at one's cost" (p. 463)—like Sarah Woodruff's baffling "double nature" and like Alison's "oxymoron quality"—is the tantalizing attribute that can act as "cathalytic, inherently and unconsciously dissolvent of time and all the naturalist tries to put between himself and his total reality" (p. 463).

"In the Orchard of the Blessed" is a climactic chapter, for in it Daniel Martin comes to understand not only the quality of the reality he should strive at reflecting in his novel, but also the fact that this reality can only be based on a true understanding of the self.

By centering on episodes of his life which had decisive importance for his development as a human being, Daniel Martin's flashbacks become the key to his—and our—understanding of his true self. Although chaotically arranged in the novel and co-existing with other levels of narration, these flashbacks are neatly linked to each other by a recurrence of theme and symbolism that shares the truth-telling quality of the Goldberg variations:

> Behind what they [the Goldberg variations] said, lay on both sides an identity, a syncretism, a same key, a thousand things beyond verbalization . . . Langland's famous image, the tower on the toft, "Truthe is therinne." (p. 628)

In this light, it is easy to see how, for all their diversity of content and in spite of their separation in time and space, Daniel Martin's flashbacks are often variations on a single theme which has important symbolic and vital meaning for the hero.

As we have seen, the first chapter of the novel, "The Harvest," with its atemporal evocation of a mythical, Wordsworthian English landscape, stands for Daniel Martin's—and John Fowles's—symbol of the mythical "green world" to which every Englishman unconsciously aspires. On the other hand, the third chapter, "Games," set in the dehumanized world of the Hollywood film business, stands for all that the *hortus conclusus* is not: it is the fake world of imitation antiques and hold-it smiles, Fowles's version of T. S. Eliot's *Waste Land*. Placed in between these two extremes the second chapter, "The Woman in the Reeds," set in the university world of Oxford in 1950, represents the crucial moment in Dan's life when he has to choose between "right feeling" and Jane, between social convention and power.

Thematically, then, these first three chapters contain within themselves the pattern for both the physical and the mental journeys of the hero, while the fourth (fittingly entitled "An Unbiassed View," Jenny McNeil's first "contribution"), offers the reader—and Daniel Martin himself—the possibility of contrasting Dan's opinions about himself with those of somebody else.

Following on the pattern established in "The Harvest" there are in the rest of the novel a series of flashbacks which describe fleeting but climactic moments of awareness and revelation felt by Daniel Martin (and sometimes by Jane). They are similar to what the adult Nicholas Urfe called "points of fulcrum," but with a difference: in *Daniel Martin* these moments often take place in a mythical setting of the *hortus conclusus* type. In "The Sacred Combe" Daniel Martin variously describes this kind of place as "la bonne vaux, the valley of abundance, the sacred combe" and, more generally, as

> a place outside the normal world, intensely private and enclosed, intensely green and fertile, numinous, haunted and haunting, dominated by a sense of magic that is also a sense of a mysterious yet profound parity in all existence . . . the Garden of Eden and the Forest of Arden . . . James Hilton's Shangri-la. (p. 306)

In an interview with Daniel Halpern ("A Sort of Exile in Lyme Regis," p. 35), John Fowles described the basic idea of *The Magus* as "a secret world, whose penetration involved ordeal and whose final reward was self-knowledge." As Kerry McSweeney ("Withering into the Truth: John Fowles and *Daniel Martin*," p. 106) fittingly remarks, this description "is equally true of his subsequent novels and of the title novella of *The Ebony Tower*." Indeed, the *hortus conclusus* theme recurs in the isolated and haunting Victorian mansion of *The Collector*, in Conchis's baffling and alluring Bourani; in the Lyme Regis Undercliff; in the beautiful and disquieting Coëtminais and in the archetypal Cleeve valley in *A Maggot*. They are worlds invariably presented as unreal and unique, of infinite potentiality, and meant to stand in contrast to the restrictive everyday world of outward reality. For all their unreality these places symbolize, as Fowles himself has explained (Onega, "Fowles on Fowles," p. 70), that

> the real for me does not lie where we are now, in other words, in cities. They had a phrase in medieval art, the "hortus conclusus," that is, the garden surrounded by a wall. Very often the

Virgin Mary and the Unicorn would be inside this wall and, you see it in medieval painting, everything outside the pretty little walled garden is chaos.

In *Daniel Martin* the *hortus conclusus* theme reappears but with slight variations from the pattern established in Fowles's previous fiction. First of all, there are several locations, instead of one, that share this mythical quality; and secondly, the enjoyment of such a mythical realm is associated with the essence of "Englishness," a theme tentatively broached by John Fowles for the first time in "On Being English but Not British" (1964), and further developed in *The Tree* (1979).

Although "The Harvest" singles out Thorncombe as the prototypical *hortus conclusus*, the English Forest of Arden, to which the hero must return if he wants to fulfill his potentiality, Tsankawi, and Tarquinia also share its mythical, religious and atemporal quality, as does Kitchener's Island in Egypt, the Devon countryside in general and, by extension, the whole English wilderness. Theorizing about the existence of such places in literature, Daniel Martin says in "In the Sacred Combe":

It is this, the sacred combe and all it stands for, that explains why I was losing patience with my profession; and also, far more profoundly than the earlier reason I gave, *why the cinema has never had patience at all for the English.* (p. 306, my italics)

And he adds,

Since we are so careful only to reveal out true selves in private, the "private" form of the real text must serve us better than the publicity of the seen spectacle. (p. 307)

By attributing his own love of privacy and his own opinions about the cinema to the English in general, Daniel Martin makes himself the representative of his whole nation, thus finding an explanation for his Mr. Specula Speculans personality, in what Bruce Woodcock *(John Fowles and Masculinity,* p. 133) has called "the theme of the English tendency to adopt masks summed up in the Robin Hood myth."

The English love of privacy, materialized in Daniel Martin's love of distorting mirrors and matched by Jane's opacity, explains the meandering course the unwritten novel of his life must take: Daniel Martin must reflect in his novel those moments of extasis, those points of fulcrum that cannot be pinned down by the camera, for by doing so, he will also be recovering the essence of his Englishness. In "The Sacred Combe," "Tsankawi," "Phillida," "Thorncombe," "In the Orchard of the Blessed," and "Rain," *Daniel Martin* will evoke a series of climactic experiences, alternating the traditional narrative preterites with characteristic "evocative" presents. One such episode is the one that describes

Dan and Nancy's first kiss when he was sixteen years old. Referring to the combe, the adult Daniel Martin has just before warned us that "I knew I had entered the Garden of Eden" (p. 399):

> Ten minutes later, having dawdled, stopped, kissed again, gone entwined through the trees to the cliff over the old limekilns, scrambled down, one last kiss above the road, desperate, as if it were their last, a moment's blueness in her eyes, still a doubt, a searching, a tenderness he hasn't seen before: *she leaves.* He watches her run down the lane, then break into a walk, round the bend and out of sight, in the green and gold evening light, towards the farm. Then he slowly drags his bike out of the undergrowth, stunned, ravished, rent with joy. Already distilling it, though not yet in words; that first touch of her mouth, that melting away of all her wiles and tricks, the taste of her, the feel of her, the mystery of her.
>
>   And the lovely guilt, the need to lie, *he took* singing home. (pp. 403–4, my italics)

Interestingly enough, those moments of extasis, those five seconds in which "the entire world melted," are inextricably bound up with two feelings: a sense of sexual satisfaction and "the lovely guilt, the need to lie." The combination of the erotic and the religious, together with a delightful consciousness of guilt and the need to lie, make up the constants not only of those few moments of perfect *jouissance* he enjoys with Nancy Reeds, but also of his behavior with women in general.

With his Devon background, with his rebelliousness fostered by his father's constant schooling in the purest traditions of Englishness, with his romantic sense of deprivation exacerbated by his mother's untimely death, and with his artistic sensibility, Daniel Martin appears, like Nicholas Urfe, as the eternal adolescent, haunted, in Bruce Woodcock's words (ibid., p. 130), by "two key mythical monsters in his unconscious which bar this errant knight's quest for his grail: his father and mother."

Commenting on the crucial episode in Dan's youth when his incipient love affair with Nancy Reeds (one can't help seeing the chosen parallelism between Nancy's family name and "the woman in the reeds") was brutally aborted by his father, Bruce Woodcock (ibid., p. 128) says (quoting the adult Dan's reflections about it):

> Faced by his father's command not to see Nancy again, Dan knew he was "trapped by convention, by respectability, by class, by Christianity, by the ubiquitous wartime creed of discipline and self-restraint as the ultimate goods. But the worst of all was knowing that I had asked for this terrible disaster. I believed in God again that night; he had my father's face and I cried with my loathing of his power" (*D. M.* p. 403). It is a castration crisis which, in the eyes of Lacanian analysis of masculinity, is the point of confirmation of male identity, the point at which the male child takes up his position with the father through fear and a desire to *wield the same power.* (my italics)

The desire to wield power like his father, counterbalanced by the sense of deprivation produced by the loss of his mother, aptly synthesizes the two opposed pulls that condition Daniel Martin's behavior. As happens in Fowles's previous fiction, the idea of exerting power is closely associated with the idea of accepting the trap of convention, respectability, and class consciousness; while the search for the lost mother, expressed in the need of the male protagonists to "collect" conquests, invariably indicates the hero's egocentric dependence, his radical immaturity. The combination of both pulls drives Daniel Martin to remark that "'I love you' is a euphemism for 'I want *to own* you'" (p. 75, my italics). In Bruce Woodcock's opinion, "His form of vanity is to use women to reflect himself. . . . All his relations with women are manipulative attempts to script them into the role of surrogates for the lost mother, to fulfil the deficiencies which Dan's masculine legacy forces on him for all its power" (ibid., p. 131).

Reading Daniel Martin's flashbacks about the different women he has encountered throughout his life, one is amused to find the pattern of the splitting into twins of the earlier fiction now developed *ad infinitum.* First of all, in "The Woman in the Reeds" Dan tells us that Jane and her sister Nell "are known as *The Heavenly Twins,* although they are not twins, but a year, both in age and study, and in many other things, apart" (p. 26). Like Alison, who was half-Australian, half-English, Jane and Nell are partly English and partly American and, like them, Daniel Martin's secretary Andrea, with whom he will have his first serious affair after marrying Nell, has the Lawrencian half-English, half-Polish double nature of Lydia in *The Rainbow.*

Again, in "the fable" of the *ménage à trois* with Miriam and Marjory, strongly reminiscent of Urfe's affair with Jojo, the theme of the twins will reappear in the form of an elaborate parody: Daniel calls them "The Fairy Sisters" and, like the imaginary Japanese geisha of Miles Green's feverish desire in *Mantissa* (not in vain does Daniel Martin toy with the idea of calling them Clio and Thalia [p. 284]), they offer Dan a "perfect" relationship, completely devoid of love:

> I remember it now as a glimpse of an ideal world, perhaps even of a future: not in some odious male chauvinistic sense, the access to two bodies, the indulging in the old haven fantasy, but because it was so free of all the encumbrance, the suppuration, the vile selfishness of romantic love. For two months we made it: without spite, without tears, without possessiveness; with nothing really, but human profit. (p. 283)

This cynical "unpossessive" relationship is of the same kind as the one Dan has tried to force on Jenny, refusing to acknowledge love for her, and treating their relationship as ephemeral. Indeed, for all his efforts at finding objective reasons for putting an end to his liaison with Jenny, it is obvious from the start that Dan, like Urfe or Don Juan, is in constant flight from any form of serious attachment. That this is so is clear from the answer Dan gives to Jenny when she asks him what kind of partners he would choose to share a desert island:

> If one had to pick three partners for an eternal desert island, which sex would they be?
> "Three women."
> "I knew you'd say that."
> "Then you needn't have asked."
> "Balanced men say one man and two women."
> "Certainly better for mixed doubles."
> "What you don't know is that three women means you hate women. You want to see them destroy one another." (p. 283)

Finally, the theme of the twins is associated with Nancy Reeds, Dan's first love, through her twin sisters Mary and Louise and, through her, to Jane herself, who found the woman in the reeds, and who, like Jenny, has the infinite potentiality of the actress, Alison's "oxymoron" double nature:

> She [Jane] was very much two people, one had long ago realized that, much more complicated than Nell. (p. 63)

> His problem (Anthony's) is he can only be himself. You [Dan] and I [Jane] can be other people. (p. 67)

> All this made Jane herself seem younger, or at least younger for her age than she had seemed in England; more and more Dan felt the older persona she had shown there was mainly reserved for him. She gave an impression, when they were alone, and at table, that elsewhere she was acting: this more sober and dutiful was her real, or realistic self. (p. 557)

> She [Jane] gave him [Dan] a scrutiny, a moment, then she silently stretched out a hand and gave his wrist, beneath the sleeve of his coat, a squeeze of encouragement, sympathy, tacit appeal, he didn't know, except that this time it was not meant to say more than affection and friendship. Even if he had wanted to reach and hold the hand there, it left his sleeve too quickly, the gesture once made. Again it was *oxymoronic:* offended him by its tact, its timing, touched him in its seeming to know and remember more than it revealed. (p. 625, my italics)

During the novel, in the sections narrated by Daniel Martin, he will try to present himself as a sensitive, complicated man with artistic aspirations; he will try to demonstrate his genuine good will; and will try to find convincing explanations for his infidelities, attributing much of his uneasiness to existential angst. Again and again he will try to convince the women who love him—and the reader with them—of the fact that "he was a man on a brink about to plunge" (p. 625). But in fact it is Daniel Martin who is driving Jenny to the brink of the abyss. She has started to smoke pot again, and she feels miserable and lonely, as we gather from her desperate third "contribution" and from her telephone calls; as miserable and lonely as Nancy Reeds doubtlessly felt after her enforced separation from Dan. Of Dan's reaction, besides feelings of hatred and fear of his father, we only know that he found easy consolation in his cousin Barbara: "We didn't kiss, except under the mistletoe, but we agreed it would be nice to write to each other, to become pen-pals. I thought of Nancy, and Thorncombe, less and less" (p. 424).

Finally, and most importantly, Dan's ex-secretary, Andrea, an all-enduring, sensitive, and unhappy woman, commits suicide[4] for reasons never clearly explained by Dan, but which produce in him a reluctantly acknowledged sense of guilt:

> It wasn't even a feeling that if our eventual two years together had ended in marriage instead of force of circumstance, or mutual refusal to disrupt our ways of life, then she would never have ended her existence. . . . *It was far more a feeling that she had had the last word about all our private lives,* all our profession, all our age. (p. 169, my italics)

The heavily qualified admittance of guilt ("it wasn't even"), as well as the comic euphemism he uses for what was for him a convenient separation ("force of circumstance"), together with the shocking revelation that what really nagged him was that "she had had the last word about all our private lives" show that, at this stage, the "collecting" qualities of Dan are in full bloom. Indeed, in the sections reported by the heterodiegetic narrator, and in spite of the habitual lack of irony in his narration, early detected by Kerry McSweeney ("Withering . . . ," p. 32), one word that is often repeated is "liar":

> Dan gave her [Jane] a quick look then; but her eyes remained on the carpet.
> "That's news to me, Janey."
> *Liar:* it was long sensed, and feared. (p. 67, my italics)

Dan lies to himself, and lies to the women around him as he lies to the reader, arranging the past, adapting the present, imagining flattering versions for the future, and even (as he does on p. 267) adding a gloss to Jenny's "contribution" in order to undermine its disturbing message. Returning from St. Tropez with Nell, where they had enjoyed a period of truce in their matrimonial disagreement, Dan comes to the conclusion that "what the holiday also proved, alas, was that they could be happy (as at Oxford) only in the unreal, not the real," (p. 158).

Dan will live according to this article of faith until the climactic night in his garden at Thorncombe when he will realize that only reality and self-knowledge are all-important. Once he has found the door to self-knowledge in the distorting mirror of Jane's "opacity," the road to maturity is at hand. The last temptation to wander from this road is Jenny's long-distance call, announcing the arrival of her third "contribution." Jenny tells Dan that nothing in it is real, that "it's all imagination" (p. 467), and then asks Dan to burn it unopened. After Thorncombe and Jane, Jenny's call

> had unhappily emphasized the artificiality of their relationship. As always Thorncombe had already made him retreat into the past, his lost domaine, his other world, and it had not needed her voice to remind him of the new distance between them; almost the distance of *the imagined from the real*. (p. 470, my italics)

At the end of the novel, Dan has returned to Oxford, has recovered Jane and has found a purpose in life by joining the Labor Party; he has also seen a haggard, skinny bitch desperately try to prolong the life of her puppies in miserable conditions, by offering her life in return.[5] Jane's tears at the sight confirm our impression that there is reason to hope, that something has melted in the core of our post-atomic ice age. But, as Bruce Woodcock notes,

> despite this confrontation with the ultimate self-awareness of "those remorseless and aloof Dutch eyes" (the Rembrandt self-portrait), Dan is already rehearsing how to describe his meeting with Jenny to Jane, "while she cooked supper for them." (ibid., p. 668)

Daniel Martin's double-dealing, unremitting to the very end of the novel, the ease with which he gets rid of Jenny and even speaks disparagingly of her to Jane, make the reader doubt the force of the impact received by Dan from Rembrandt's silent message: "No true compassion without will, no true will without compassion" (p. 703).

In *The Magus* and also in *The French Lieutenant's Woman* the heterodiegetic narrators refuse to imagine closed endings for their respective novels, thus acknowledging the freedom of their characters to choose a future for themselves. Rejecting the existentialist code in chapter 32, Daniel Martin, and the narrator-author with him, pronounce themselves free to imagine a clear-cut, neatly closed ending, and a happy one at that. The trip to Egypt and Palmyra structurally functions as this closed ending, a "future-past" imagined by the heterodiegetic narrator that is rooted in the "real" past Daniel Martin has so painfully unburied through his flashbacks. But for all the heterodiegetic narrator's efforts at giving an impression of definite settlement, we must not forget that Daniel Martin, like Urfe after his return to England, still has a lot to learn and experience, as Daniel himself acknowledges: "Standing there before the Rembrandt, he experienced a kind of vertigo: *the distances he had to return*" (p. 703, my italics).

Daniel Martin and Jane are left at Oxford exactly at the point where twenty-six years before they had taken the wrong fork of the road; they are now offered, against all spatio-temporal logic, a second opportunity to retrace their steps. The long, difficult quest of the hero has landed him where he began, but with a priceless boon he has acquired on the way, the knowledge that life "is not finally a matter of skill, of knowledge, of intellect; of good luck or bad, but choosing and learning to feel" (p. 703).

Indeed, we may agree with Ina Ferris's view ("Realist Intention and Mythic Impulse in *Daniel Martin,*" p. 149) that *"Daniel Martin* is a second chance story," or, more accurately, a fictionalization of "the pastoral insight into 'what might have been' [that] turn[s] clearly into the redemptive promise of comic resolution." But to go beyond the mere *promise* of comic resolution to the assurance of a closed, happy ending foreseeing a future of harmony for Dan and Jane is to forget T. S. Eliot's memorable warning in "Burnt Norton," that

> What might have been is an abstraction
> Remaining a perpetual possibility
> Only in a world of speculation.
> What might have been and what has been
> Point to an end, which is always present.
>
> (*Four Quartets,* I, 13)

For all the apparent promise of eternal future harmony with which the novel ends, its structural circularity establishes a vicious circle of infinite possible "variations" in which Daniel Martin's last unwritten sentence becomes John Fowles's last written one. Both the potential and the actual, the written and the unwritten, the ontological and the fictional, "what might have been and what has been point to an end, *which is always present."*

Like the paintings of the primitive Egyptians, both Daniel Martin's unwritten and John Fowles's written novels are full of repetitions, involutions, false endings, and multiple parallelisms. One, as unwritten, can only offer open potential endings; the other, neatly circular, leaves the hero at the end of his quest, with a promise of lasting happiness. Whether we choose to believe that the promise eventually becomes an actuality, or whether we don't, will wholly depend on our own imaginative response, on the kind of ending we ourselves might be ready to accept.

In any case, the explanation Herr Professor Otto Kirnberger provided for Minoan and Egyptian art—comparable, as K. A. Chittick has pointed out ("The Laboratory of Narrative and John Fowles's *Daniel Martin,*" p. 72), to Claude Lévi-Strauss's notion of the artist-*bricoleur*—may help us to understand why this meandering structure, this intertwining of strands, this searched-for equivocation and ambiguity are necessary, and why the fragmentary, "opaque" reflection of reality projected by the novel conveys a kind of truth the cinema cannot pin down:

> Life is very precarious, all its processes are mysterious. Very slowly these men see that in small places it can be controlled. They make many mistakes. But they also see *controlling is knowing,* and that the greatest tool of knowing is the symbol that allows you to represent what is not present before your eyes. (p. 575, my italics)

5

Mantissa

In *Daniel Martin* both the homodiegetic and the heterodiegetic narrators agree that they should turn their backs on literary fashion in order to create an art capable of telling "the real." Accordingly, much of the bulk of *Daniel Martin* is made up of realistic events involving aspects of Daniel Martin's private and social life, to the point that we may provisionally agree with Ina Ferris ("Realist Intention . . . ," p. 146) when she says that "such strategies ally *Daniel Martin* with the realism that produces the nineteenth-century novel of social anatomy in Dickens, Balzac and Tolstoy." Our agreement must be provisional because, as I hope to have shown in my analysis of *Daniel Martin* and as Ferris immediately adds, "Fowles' own effort to participate in the tradition serves rather to underline his distance from it, confirming that social realism is essentially alien to his imagination" (ibid., p. 146).

As in *The French Lieutenant's Woman*, in *Daniel Martin* the realistic elements are constantly undermined by an equally powerful though more subterranean tendency towards unreality and fantasy which efficiently puts into question the surface message of the novel. Misled perhaps by Fowles's own protest that only reality matters for the serious novelist, this ambiguity of the novel's message and status has often been overlooked by the critics who have tended to evaluate only the realistic elements of *Daniel Martin*, be it to praise them or to find fault with them. Thus, after reading *Daniel Martin*, a reality-biased critic like John Gardner ("In Defence of the Real," p. 22) would pronounce John Fowles "the only novelist now writing in English whose works are likely to stand as literary classics—the only writer in English who has the power, range, knowledge, and wisdom of a Tolstoy or James," while critics with a bent for post-Modern experimental writing, like Kerry McSweeny ("Withering . . . ," p. 31) would lament *Daniel Martin's* wealth of realistic effects, considering them as primarily "a source of disappointment."

The widespread reluctance to give the experimental side of *Daniel Martin* its proper due might help to explain the critics' bafflement when confronted with what they consider an unexpected development of John Fowles's art in

Mantissa (1982), without doubt the Fowles novel that has been most thoroughly and pitilessly attacked by its earlier reviewers. Together with the accusation that the novel is not very good or is even plain bad, a second complaint is often lodged by the critics: namely, that *Mantissa's* unashamed experimentalism constitutes a break with the literary line traced by John Fowles in his previous fiction. Robert Campbell's words ("John Fowles. *Mantissa,*" p. 84) may be taken as representative of the kind of rebuke not infrequently heard about *Mantissa:*

> One wonders just how happy Fowles was at the publication of his latest novel. It is certainly a departure from anything he has written before. Unfortunately one of the many ways in which it differs from his other books is that it is not very good. It is sad to find a writer of talent has given up what he is good at and sadder still to have to pay money to find that out.

Repenting or not of having spent money on a book and finding it bad, boring, or entertaining are individual reactions dependent on private criteria of taste and literary training. But describing it as "a departure from anything he has written before" is evidently in need of further qualification. Perhaps Kerry McSweeney's account of Fowles's development ("Withering . . . ," p. 31) is more illuminating when she describes John Fowles as "more an unfolding than a growing artist; each new work is a recapitulation as well as an extension of what has gone before and contributes to a cumulative richness still too little understood to be appreciated."

Again, following a line of thought similar to that of Robert Campbell, Ian Gotts ("Fowles' *Mantissa:* Funfair in Another Village," p. 2) describes *Mantissa* as "a curious digression—even regression—in the direction of the existential metafiction that William Palmer predicted for the writer of the *The French Lieutenant's Woman,*" a remark Gotts himself paradoxically undermines, coming as it does only a few lines after quoting Fowles's statement that he regards his work "much more in terms of a countryside than a path." Commenting on this statement, which Gotts apparently refuses to make his own, the critic says, "Fowles likes to imagine his novels surrounding him rather than receding from him in a temporal structure that Daniel might call 'cramped, linear, and progressive'" (p. 82). The visual image of the writer physically surrounded by his novels that form a landscape of equidistant satellites might be complemented by the addition of a criss-cross of thematic and structural relationships linking every novel with the rest, each new novel containing, in McSweeny's above-quoted words, "a recapitulation as well as an extension of what has gone before."

For all its peculiarities of tone and scope, *Mantissa* should be regarded as one more variation on the same basic themes and assumptions developed by John Fowles in his earlier fiction: rather than constituting a curious regression with respect to *Daniel Martin,* it should be seen as standing in a complementary relation to it, comparable, for example, to the complementarity that exists between *Bleak House* (1852–53) and *Hard Times* (1854). Genuinely concerned with the effects of industrialization in Victorian England, Dickens produced (nearly simultaneously) two novels that envisaged the problem from puzzlingly divergent points of view: in *Bleak House* Dickens drew a picture of the positive effects of industrialization, while in *Hard Times* he concentrated on its bad effects. Nobody would seriously maintain today that Dickens was merely being inconsistent about the Industrial Revolution or that he had lost all sense of literary direction. Rather, confronted with a complex, many-sided phenomenon made up of both positive and negative elements, Dickens had felt it necessary to deal with different aspects of it separately. Similarly, the deviation from realism towards open experimentation discernible as we move from *Daniel Martin* to *Mantissa* might be accounted for not as an inconsistent regression in Fowles's literary development, but rather as a predictable pendular swing from realism towards unrealism, consistent with Fowles's view of reality as complex and many-sided, made up (as he explained as early as *The Magus)* of both the ontologically real and of the imagined, of the actually lived and of what might have been.

In order to substantiate our contention that *Mantissa* stands in a complementary relation to John Fowles's previous fiction it would be as well to place it in its proper context. As Ian Gotts (ibid., pp. 81–82) has pointed out, although first published in 1982

> *Mantissa* was actually begun some twelve years before going into print. . . . Despite references made during revision in the 1980s, [it] was begun in 1970 and is best approached in the context of that period's anxieties about the genre's health: an existential comedy about the problems of the serious contemporary novelist's craft.

According to this, John Fowles must have been writing the first draft of *Mantissa* at the same time as he was both revising *The Magus* and writing *Daniel Martin,* and so one would expect to find in *Mantissa* the same creative impulse that had produced the other two novels. Indeed, in Gotts's description of *Mantissa* as "an existential comedy about the problems of the serious contemporary novelist's craft," the only innovation is the word "comedy," the concerns with existentialism, and with the contemporary novelist's craft being, as we have seen, well-known constants in Fowles's previous fiction in general and providing the specific subject matter for *Daniel Martin* in particular. Explaining his aim in writing *Mantissa* in a recent interview (Onega, "Fowles," p. 66), Fowles said,

> *Mantissa* was meant to be a joke. . . . In America and Britain it was really taken much too seriously. I like the French idea of the "jeu d'esprit," the lighter book. Something you suffer from in America is the belief that your novels must get larger and larger, longer and longer, more and more important, bigger and bigger in every way and this really is blowing up a balloon which you know sooner or later is going to burst. . . . I liked the much more European idea of producing very minor works, something you enjoy doing perhaps . . . and *Mantissa* was really meant to be a comment on the problems of being a writer.

Side by side with the full-length, highly serious and complex approach to "the problems of being a writer" that we encounter in *Daniel Martin,* John Fowles was simultaneously giving vent to his more playful, lighthearted and satiric feelings about the same matter in *Mantissa,* a work that, as he explained in the same interview (p. 66), Fowles would have liked to set apart from his other novels by giving it for publication to a "nice Californian publisher" who unfortunately "was just pushed out" by the large publishing houses with which he is under contract.

John Fowles's intention to have *Mantissa* published by a private printer, and his explanation that it is primarily *un jeu d'esprit* in the European tradition of very light fiction, may suffice to explain its reduced length and scope, while the confession that *Mantissa* was meant to be a joke points to its basically ludic and parodic character. As the puzzling cuckoo in Martin Green's hospital room silently asserts, and as John Fowles himself explained ("Fowles," p. 72), *Mantissa* was cast in the shadow of one particular writer, Flann O'Brien. Of him Fowles said:

> We talked a lot about Joyce and Beckett yesterday, but there is a third Irish novelist who I would put very near their level. . . . Flann O'Brien, I think, was a genius at really absurd humor and that book (*At Swim-Two Birds*) was behind *Mantissa.* If I went in for dedicating books to other writers, I would have dedicated it to Flann O'Brien.

Together with experimentalism, John Fowles rejected in *Daniel Martin* a—to use Beckettian terms—black absurdist view of life, consciously devising a happy ending for his novel that would put an end to the hero's vision of the void. Interestingly enough, in the above-quoted paragraph Fowles uses the word *absurd* in a radically different sense.

The quality of Beckett's work may be synthesized as the purest literary concretization of Sartre's and Kierkegaard's existentialism, a minimalist literature both pathetic and exhilarating reduced to the compulsive expression of one single fact: the consciousness of one's own existence, undermined by the certainty that life is purposeless and ephemeral, and that the writer's task is an impossible one. At the other extreme of the absurdist spectrum, Ionesco's *Bald Soprano* may be taken as the prototype of the kind of absurd John Fowles had in mind when he referred to the "absurd humour" of Flann O'Brien. Ionesco's

world is based on heavy parody and pastiche; it is peopled by cardboard stereo-
types who mimic the behavior patterns of real members of the middle class; they
are silly and talkative and their incessant conversation displays a wealth of
cliché-ridden, ready-made nonsensical vagaries strongly reminiscent of the set,
lifeless dialogues of third-class primers of English.

At Swim-Two Birds partakes of this kind of absurd humor but it is more
than that. It is a remarkable catch-all, combining the strong influence of Joyce
with a smack of Swiftean satire and evincing a striving towards that every-
digressive witticism that Laurence Sterne made his most demolishing tool in
Tristram Shandy. Indeed, we might visualize *At Swim-Two Birds* as the link
between *Tristram Shandy* and contemporary metafiction, as a novel that fore-
shadows the contemporary concern with the dubious status of writer and characters, as a novel that contrives to blur the boundaries between the ontologically
real and the imagined, and that even assumes as a matter of course the now-
revolutionary deconstructive thesis that the text pre-exists the writer, that the
writer's role consists only in an endless rewriting of new variations of pre-
existing stories and character types.

The other point of reference is John Fowles's avowed butt of satire: post-
structuralist and deconstructive theory. To my question in the interview (ibid.,
p. 67) mentioned above, "How consciously did you have Roland Barthes's *Le
plaisir du texte* in mind when you were writing *Mantissa?*," Fowles answered:

> I do not think particularly. Dr. Federman yesterday was giving his views on Derrida, Lacan,
> Barthes. . . . I am exactly like him. I have read quite a lot of them on deconstruction and
> post-structuralism and all the rest of it. . . . In *Mantissa* I was making fun of it, rather crude
> fun probably in places, but I was really expressing the old English view that most of French
> intellectual theory since the war has been elegant nonsense . . . attractive nonsense.

Simplifying a great deal, one could say that the history of contemporary deconstructivism goes back to the publication of Jacques Derrida's *De la grammatologie* (1967), which opens with a critique of Saussure. In *De la grammatologie*
Derrida calls into question the traditional values of sign, word, and writing,
discounting the importance of *voice* ("phone") in favor of *writing* ("écriture")
which, according to Derrida, is the real origin of language, the primordial
activity of differentiation. Following Derrida, Roland Barthes, in "The Death
of the Author" (p. 145), reduces the role of the author to that of mere scriptor,
someone who, in contrast to the traditional writer, "is born simultaneously with
the text, is in no way equipped with a being preceding or exceeding the writing."
Similarly, in *S/Z* (p. 10) Barthes attacks the traditional notion of the reader as
"an innocent subject anterior to the text," concluding that the reader is "already
a plurality of other texts, of codes which are infinite."

Thus both scriptor and reader become an integrated part of the text, and the text, as opposed to the "work" (and "writing" as opposed to "literature") becomes the only test of reality. That is, Barthes and deconstructivism in general argue for the acceptance of the existence of a world of signs without truth or origin, independent and prior to the existence of writers and readers.

With these notions in mind and with the shadow of Flann O'Brien in the background, a reading of *Mantissa* proves extraordinarily rewarding. In *At Swim-Two Birds* a first-person narrator who identifies with the author spends most of his days and nights idly lying in bed and writing the story of a writer called Dermot Trellis, who in turn spends most of the day dozing in bed, drugged by the fictional characters he has either created or hired from another writer, the late Mr. William Tracy. Trellis's best creation is John Furriskey, a character he wants to behave like the worst of villains but who refuses to do so on moral and ethical grounds. This theme of a writer lying in bed and retiring to the "privacy of (his) mind" *(At Swim-Two Birds,* p. 1), alternating between periods of drugged sleep in which he is at the mercy of his characters and periods of wakeful creativity in which he exerts a dictatorial control over them, is taken and "varied" *ad infinitum* by John Fowles in *Mantissa.* The novel is divided into four chapters each constituting a different version of the same fictional situation. Erato, the Muse, sums up the whole structure of the novel when she complains about Miles Green's story: "I know exactly what you're trying to do. I may not be the musical one in my family, but I can recognize a fugal inversion when I see it" (p. 69). The musical metaphor is particularly appropriate when it comes to describing the structure of the novel: fugal inversions, or variations on the story in the first chapter, is all we get in the remaining sections. Again and again a writer called Miles Green alternates between periods of blank amnesia and periods of awareness during which he has to fight a battle for dominance over Erato, the Muse, a baffling female figure simultaneously seen as autonomous from the writer and subject to him; both as a fellow creator in her own right and as a figment of Green's imagination.

At the beginning of *Mantissa* we find Miles Green lying in bed in a mysterious hospital room where he is recovering from a bout of amnesia with the help of a strange form of shock treatment intended to restore his normal brain function. As shapely Dr. Delfie explains to Miles Green, the memory nerve center is closely associated with the center which controls sexual activity, so the recuperation of his powers of memory involves a close examination of his sexual reactions. It is no mere coincidence, then, that his symptoms are an inability to remember even his own sex ("with another painful swift and reducing intuition it realized it was not just an I, but a male I," p. 10), or his own name, his wife's or his children's names, in short, his inability to make use of the basic function of language (naming). Following Nietzsche's ideas, Barthes, in *Le plaisir du texte,* describes reading as a passion, a form of pleasure. Each reader takes his pleasure in a different way, obsessively, hysterically, paranoically, etc. Of these different types the hysterical reader reaches authentic bliss (*jouissance*)—an orgasmic experience beyond mere pleasure, in V. B. Leitch's words:

> For the reader of pleasure the text offers a free play of meaning and sex, opening out toward complete freedom. The polymorphous reader comes to the polymorphous text. The reader and the meaning disseminate sumptuously toward infinity. The disintegration of the reader's self as well as the writer's unfold as the text is set going. . . . This loss of self is an orgasmic happening. (*Deconstruction: An Advanced Introduction*, pp. 113–14)

So, in *Mantissa* Dr. Delfie bases her clinical treatment for the recovery of Miles Green's mental powers on the artificial induction of an orgasm. In other words, the modern scriptor, deprived of an existence prior to the text, lies in a void of silence from which he will only be able to escape through writing, an activity which implies *jouissance*, pleasure, and which requires a source of inspiration, a Muse: Dr. Delfie.

As Dr. Delfie, both with the help of Nurse Cory and through her own determined manipulations, eventually succeeds in inducing a controlled orgasm in Miles Green, we suddenly realize that the orgasm is simultaneously metamorphosing into the delivery of a child:

> "Now, one last effort. I can feel it coming. Good. Good. Splendid. With the hips. Hard as you can. . . . There we are . . . there we are.—Perfect. Perfect. Safe as houses. Keep going, don't stop. Right to the very last syllable. Nurse!"
>
> He was vaguely aware of Nurse Cory moving to the end of the bed—out of his sight, since the energetic doctor, still suspended on her arms, blocked the view.
>
> "One last push. One more. One more. One last one."
>
> There was a little gasp from her, as if she were the one who had really given birth; then an abrupt cessation of movement. A silence. (p. 45)

The aftermath of creative effort is, fittingly, "a silence." In *At Swim-Two Birds* the creative endeavors of Dermot Trellis finally produced an "aesthoautogamus" newborn infant of twenty-five, John Furriskey. In *Mantissa* the child of this double "orgasmic delivery," to give it a name, is, of course, a text which Nurse Cory attentively peruses while Dr. Delfie, herself a participant in the whole process, lies on Miles Green's chest, sharing his silence and exhaustion. After the shock of seeing the erotic reading of Miles Green's induced orgasm abruptly turn into the bathetic delivery of a newborn infant, our sense of reality is further tested: Nurse Cory starts reading the newborn text and, of course, it begins with the very same words with which the novel *Mantissa* begins. All of a sudden, the description of the strange hospital room acquires its full meaning: the darkness outside, the gray domed and quilted ceiling, the pink carpeted floor . . . this description draws a realistic enough image of the inside of Miles Green's skull, even though for the reader the details about the furnishings have gone unnoticed the first time around, proving John Fowles's ability to deceive and take the reader by surprise.

At the end of *Daniel Martin* the reader becomes aware of the circularity of the novel when he finds that the last and the first sentences are the same. In *Mantissa* this circularity is established several times and in several different ways. First of all the opening sentence of the novel recurs at the end of chapter 1 and is then "varied" to a slightly different version at the end of chapter 4:

> It was conscious of a luminous and infinite haze, as if it were floating, godlike, alpha and omega, over a sea of vapour and looking down. (p. 9)

> " 'It was conscious of a luminous and infinite haze, as if it were floating, godlike, alpha and o-me-ga. . . .' " She [Nurse Cory] flashed him a vivacious smile. "Is that how you pronounce it, Mr. Green? It's Green, isn't it?" She did not wait for a reply, but went back to her reading . . . "over a sea of vapour and looking—"
> CRASH! (p. 48)

> The oblivious patient lies on his hospital bed, staring in what must now be seen as his most characteristic position, blindly at the ceiling; conscious only of a luminous and infinite haze, as if he were floating, godlike, alpha and omega (and all between), over a sea of vapour. (p. 192)

Secondly, at the end of chapters 2 and 4 Miles Green again loses consciousness, the first time because Erato knocks him out, the second because he bumps his satyr horns against the wall. And thirdly, Erato and Miles Green endlessly discuss alternatives for the same fictional *datum*, offering each other utterly divergent versions colored by their respective feminism and *machismo*, as each takes up in turn the role of creator.

With the baffling discovery one makes at the end of chapter 1 the general scheme of the novel is completed. Like the protagonist in *At Swim-Two Birds,* or in *Endgame,* Miles Green's area of activity is restricted to the inside of his head. His own existence, the existence of Dr. Delfie and Nurse Cory, of his wife and of Staff Sister totally depend of Green's capacity to create them, to write about them, to weave them into a text. So the novel appears as an endlessly prolongable structure without beginning or end, limited only by the writer's capacity to imagine still one more variation of the situation devised in the first chapter. So, the following chapters are perforce different versions of the same story, rewritings of a unique, polymorphic text, dealing with the only possible topic: the ultimate reality of the text as a source, not a product, of linguistic activity.

In chapter 2, Erato, disguised as a punk and holding an electric guitar instead of a lyre, bursts into Miles Green's room in a rage, accusing him of having distorted her real self by having her impersonate the character of Dr.

Delfie. Appeased by Green's apologies, she abandons her disguise and turns into her classical self, ready to propose her own version of the story. As she starts telling her tale about her encounter with a faunish shepherd, however, her imagination wavers: she was successively sixteen, fifteen, fourteen, twelve, and eleven years old; it was a shepherd to whom she made love once; a faun to whom she made love as many times as the alphabet has letters . . . just as she is incapable of concentrating on one consistent line of development, she is equally incapable of avoiding endless digressions from her story. Her physical appearance is as unstable as her tale: with the greatest of ease she is now a punk, now a Greek goddess, now a twentieth-century sex partner, now a Japanese geisha, or she divides into two, as she simultaneously impersonates Dr. Delfie and Nurse Cory (who turns out to be the Dark Lady of Shakespeare's sonnets).

This splitting of the Muse into Dr. Delfie and Nurse Cory betrays John Fowles's favorite topos of the double nature of woman, an idea that, as we have seen, recurs in his fiction from *The Magus* onwards. Like Lily and Rose, Dr. Delfie and Nurse Cory are complementary projections of the archetypal woman. Dr. Delfie has Lily's delicate milk-white skin that symbolizes a purity more apparent than real, while the fact that Nurse Cory is black reminds the reader of Rose's dark tan, indicative of her provocative and liberated sexuality. In *Mantissa,* then, the archetypal virgin/whore dichotomy of woman is ironized and played upon: Dr. Delfie is refined and elegantly classical, a member of the English upper class, but like Alison she is only partially English, in this case, with Italian and Jewish ancestry, while Nurse Cory is a West Indian beauty with eyes "exactly the same colour as the doctor's" (p. 21). Indeed, rather than by the color of her skin, Nurse Cory is distinguishable from Dr. Delfie only because she is "a suspicion prouder and bolder. Even more sweetly impudent and provocative" (p. 164). Nurse Cory and Dr. Delfie are the complementary projections of Erato, the Muse, whose body "somehow contrives, all at the same time, to be both demure and provocative, classical and modern, individual and Eve like, tender and unforgetting, present and past, real and dreamed, soft and . . ." (p. 72).

So Erato enjoys the paradoxical oxymoron quality of Alison and by extension of every "real" woman in the fiction of John Fowles. She is also as endlessly transformable as the innumerable potential characters in the mind of the writer, but she is also, throughout, a Greek muse, Miles Green's inspiration and, as such, has opinions which differ from his: "I wish I'd never let you talk me into being a black girl now" (p. 164).

In this duality, Erato's potential adaptability to the wishes of the writer and her waywardness, her reluctance to follow the author's whim without giving her opinion, we catch a glimpse of one of Fowles's major concerns, already present in *The French Lieutenant's Woman:* the question of whether the omniscient author is really free to make use of his characters at will or whether he should submit to verisimilitude and consistency in the depiction of character. Erato stresses the same point again when she attacks Miles Green—as author—for using the third person to refer to Miles Green the character in his erotic tale:

> "It's not my fault that I'm the programmed slave of whatever stupid mood you've created. . . . To say nothing of *your* character. I notice there's not been a single word about his exceedingly dubious status. I wonder who's pulling *his* strings?"
> "I am. I'm me. Don't be ridiculous."
> She gives him a sarcastic little smile, and looks away. "God, you're so naïve." (pp. 87–88, emphasis in the original)

What Erato is implying is that the author as such cannot be wholly separated from his characters. Miles Green the character in an autobiographical tale is theoretically different from Miles Green the author who has written the tale, but, of course, Miles Green, as author, is only a tool in the hands of John Fowles, the author of a tale about an author called Miles Green who writes a tale about the writing of a tale. With this involuted structure, strongly reminiscent of the structure of *Daniel Martin,* Fowles takes up again the problematic he seriously tackled in the earlier novel, expressing the impossibility the author has of getting away from the all-enveloping text: the author acquires his identity as a result of his activity as a writer of novels and so cessation of this activity will reduce him to silence, to nothingness, "as merciful silence descends at last on the grey room" (p. 192).

Thus, the modern writer is faced with only two alternatives: he can choose silence and extinction or devote his life and energies to endlessly rewriting the same text. The boundaries of the text being the border between the rational and the irrational, the intelligible and the unintelligible, the writer tends to strip his tale of unnecessary linguistic material, aiming at the realm of the unwritable:

> "If we could only find some absolutely impossible. . . ."
> "Unwritable. . . ."
> "Unfinishable. . . ."
> "Unimaginable. . . ."
> "Endlessly revisable. . . ."
> "Text without words. . . ."
> "We could both be real selves at last." (p. 159)

Miles Green's aim is to write a version in which Erato's role is reduced to that of a Japanese geisha, who speaks only a little English: "With her, any dialogue but that of the flesh is magnificently impossible" (p. 186). The Japanese geisha is, of course, the prototype of the ever-compliant character, "his infinitely compliant woman, true wax at last, dutiful, uncomplaining, admiring, and above all peerlessly dumb" (p. 186).

Thus, following Barthes, Miles Green dreams of an erotic fictional world where the author can use his characters at will, and where the action is reduced to pleasure, after the suppression of the "boring stretches between the sexy bits" (p. 159). But, of course, this *jouissance* can only be achieved through the harmonious blending of Erato and Miles Green, the perfect communion of author and Muse, a communion which can only be reached if he relinquishes his prerogative of omniscience: compared with the first artificial orgasm devised by Miles Green in the first version of the story, the orgasm reached on the carpet of the hospital room in the second version, represents the short-lived climax of that mutual understanding which produces the real work of art:

> "Oh darling."
> "My darling."
> "Darling."
> "Darling."
> "Darling."
> "Oh my darling." (p. 151)

No sooner have they reached this climax of understanding than the mental walls of Green's hospital room collapse, and a series of people, "nurses male and female, cleaners, partners, doctors, specialists, staff of all kinds" (p. 153) are allowed to contemplate the intimate scene, that is to say, to share their *jouissance*. But, of course, the effect is fleeting, a mere truce in the endless battle for dominance. Subdued only temporarily, Erato soon recovers her autonomy, turning Miles Green into a satyr and pronouncing his illness "a severe case of satyriasis" (p. 188). Throughout the book one function of the battle of wits between Muse and writer has been to denounce Miles Green's "fuckin' chauvinist pig['s]" ideas (p. 53) and to expose his inability to see that "the world's full of highly pertinent male-female situations whose fictional exploration does subtend a viable sociological function" (p. 88).

The Muse's words echo and parody Daniel Martin's "poetic manifesto." In Miles Green, then, John Fowles is satirizing the kind of novelist Daniel Martin despises: a writer satisfied with the onanistic display of his male fantasies and incapable of devising a faithful mirror of nature that would convey a morally edifying and sociologically useful message. The slaps and blows directed at Miles Green's head by the Muse, as well as her acrid fustigations of his self-indulgent chauvinism may be read as clear hints that Fowles rejects an art that does not reach beyond itself. However, the paradoxical nature of Erato, her waywardness and latent eroticism, her unreliability and inconsistency, her militant feminism and flagrant stupidity as described by the resentful Miles Green, together with the too crude and heavy lampooning to which the amnesic writer is subjected, makes it difficult for the reader—and much more so, perhaps, if the reader is a woman—to avoid feeling that there is an ambiguity in the novel's message, that the irony is double and that the denunciation of Green's chauvinism affirms rather than denies the masculine position under attack. Remarking on how overdone and embarrassing Green's self-deprecation often appears, Bruce Woodcock *(Male Mythologies,* p. 147) says, "The extreme self-parody suggests an accompanying extreme of defensiveness over this most touchy area of male power. Flirtatiously, *Mantissa* offers a choice as to whether we consider it a text of subversive erotic play *à la Barthes* or a text of phallic reinforcement."

John Fowles has repeatedly said that in *Mantissa* he just wanted to make fun of post-structuralist and deconstructive theory. In order to do so, he equated creativity with sex, turning the writer's desire to exert omniscient control over his characters into a battle for sexual dominance over the Muse. Although the sexual metaphor literally follows Roland Barthes's concept of *jouissance,* this is a kind of metaphor that suits Fowles's imagination perfectly, as the writer himself conceded in a much quoted remark (Stolley, *"The French Lieutenant's Woman's* Man. Novelist John Fowles," p. 58): "My imagination is highly erotic. . . . I think about almost everything in terms of erotic situations."

Miles Green's quasi-pornographic fantasies bring to mind the claustrophobic sadism of *The Collector:* they recall the voyeuristic shock therapy undergone by Nicholas Urfe in *The Magus* and the sickeningly restrained eroticism of Charles in *The French Lieutenant's Woman,* and they recast the *ménage à trois* situation enjoyed by Daniel Martin with the Fairy Sisters, which is "varied" by Mr. B., Dick, and Rebecca in *A Maggot.* Bruce Woodcock (ibid., p. 152), commenting on *Mantissa,* aptly summed up the ingredients that are to be found, not only in this novel, but in all Fowles's novels: "All the elements of Fowles' sexual imagination that we might anticipate are there: the *ménage à trois;* the man subjected to two powerful women; the room cut off from the rest of the world; the archetypal enigmatic female encountering the uncertain male."

Beneath the parody and the joking tone and beneath the denunciation of male chauvinism, the doubt remains as to whether those ideas that are ostensibly under attack in *Mantissa* are in fact being reinforced. In a similar way, the mockery of Green's incapacity to escape the vicious circle of his imagination, with which Fowles wants to denounce experimentalism for its own sake, admits another, curiously opposed, interpretation. While Fowles's parody of deconstructive tenets expresses his contempt for post-structuralist and deconstructivist theory (explicitly avowed in interviews), this same parody evinces such a thorough knowledge of these theories, and such a concern with the issues they raise, that one is tempted to see there, too, an attempt to come to terms with the overwhelming realization that the contemporary writer comes at the end of a very long and great tradition of writing, what Harold Bloom called the "anxiety of influence" produced by the knowledge that everything has already been tried, invented and refined.[1]

Answering a question about the structure of his novels in the A.E.D.E.A.N. interview (ibid., p. 63), John Fowles said:

> Many clever people linguistically cannot write novels because you really have to be two people, one has to be innocent and really slightly self-hypnotized and the other has to be very stern and a kind of professor of himself. I like, in the actual business of writing, this feeling that you do not know where you are going. . . .

The interesting thing about Fowles's rambling method is that, for all his lack of a preconceived plan, all his novels without exception show a neatly designed structure[2] and in them his wanderings always land him back in the very same place: no matter whether he allows his imagination unrestricted freedom, as he did in *The Magus;* or whether he forces himself to write realistically, as he did in *Daniel Martin;* or whether he consciously endeavors to parody those things he believes he should reject, as in *Mantissa,* the result is, astonishingly, always the same: a fiction that breaks through the intentional limits imposed in order to affirm its incontrovertible truth that reality is complex and many-sided, made up of the imagined and the really lived, of what is and what might have been.

Secluded in the domed and quilted room of his own brain, Miles Green, a naïve contemporary *miles gloriosus,* boastfully and chauvinistically tries to assert omniscient control over his created world, only to find himself exhausted and trapped within the monothematic sexist world of his own imagination. Paradoxically and, many would say, fortunately, John Fowles's endeavors to affirm his rational conviction that he should write realistically and that he should infuse a certain ideology and moral lesson into his fiction serve the contrary purpose of showing how fettered he is within the boundaries of his creative mind, for, do what he will, his novels once and again assert their own, invariable message that creativity is all-important, that "right feeling" and socialist teaching can only aspire to be accessories of the finished, autonomous and self-sufficient work of art.

After the climactic sexual encounter of Miles Green and Erato on the carpet of the hospital room, the whole world is offered the opportunity to participate in their moment of perfect *jouissance* by peeping into the room. The walls, however, soon lose their newly acquired transparency. As they become solid again, all the watchers, except Staff Sister, are excluded from the (aesthetic) vision of the accomplished work of art. Caught by surprise, Staff Sister stumbles forward and is trapped within the walls of Green's brain. Like the author, the Muse, and the characters, the narrow-minded literary critic with a bent for moralizing belongs, as she does, in the quilted and domed room of the author's imagination. Interestingly enough, her version of what is going on in Miles Green's hospital room is utterly different from the versions given by Erato or

Miles Green. Her version, like Erato's and Miles Green's versions of the story—
and our own—are just subjective interpretations of one polymorphous text
which admits numberless interpretations of varying validity. Whether Green's
version, or Erato's, or Staff Sister's, or our own, are more (or less) accurate
"misreadings" of one polymorphous text (Fowles's novel), there is no way of
telling.

We may take this hint and apply it to the criticism of *Mantissa* itself. The
fact that this novel has provoked so many different interpretations by the critics,
some vigorously denied by the author, is the best proof that, for all its unique-
ness and self-assertive autonomy, the literary text, like reality itself, can never
be wholly pinned down and that one of the freedoms it allows is the individual
freedom to "misread" it, to adjust its message to the idiosyncrasy of the individual imagination, including that of John Fowles.

6

A Maggot

In a recent interview with James R. Baker ("An Interview with John Fowles," p. 668), John Fowles once again expressed his conviction that "all novelists are neurotics and schizophrenics" and that good novels cannot be written "from your rational old-fashioned, humanist self. You have to be erratic, a victim of hazard." Nowhere is this theory of Fowles's made more explicit than in *A Maggot* (1985), the writer's latest novel and one in which he seems determined to carry to the limit the game of polarizations between reality and unreality which he started to play more than twenty years earlier, in *The Magus*.

A historical novel at first sight, *A Maggot* is situated in 1736 "in a sort of dozing solstitial standstill . . . at a time of reaction from the intemperate extremisms of the previous century, yet already hatching the seeds . . . of the world-upheaval to come" (p. 16). One aim of *A Maggot*, then, seems to be the re-creation of the atmosphere of that "strange doldrum of time, place and spirit" (p. 16), Swift's, Pope's, and Walpole's England. Another, we will soon find, is the testing of the literary conventions coined and developed in the period that saw the rise of the novel.

When the English novel emerged in the first half of the eighteenth century, it did so by fighting its way out of history and out of other literary genres. Acknowledgment of its fictionality would lead to confusion with the romance, thus threatening the novel with devaluation of its moral capacity, a fact that would preclude the recognition of social utility for the new genre. In order to assuage this danger a series of reality-enhancing mechanisms quickly developed: the writer assumed the role of "editor" and professed the historical genuineness of the material gathered either directly from the mouth of the protagonist of the events narrated, or transcribed from the latter's "true" letters or memories. Thus, for instance, *The Life and Strange Surprizing Adventures of Robinson Crusoe, of York, Mariner* are "written by himself"; *The Fortunes and Misfortunes of the Famous Moll Flanders* are "written from her own memorandum," and Roxana's progressive corruption is described as her own "confession," transcribed by a "Writer" and prefaced by an "Editor."

At the same time, all kinds of plausible and not-so-plausible explanations are given about the way in which the manuscript reached the hands of the editor. The aloof monk who finds a mysterious age-old manuscript in a remote convent is, as is well known, a frequent, stereotyped convention of mid-eighteenth-century Gothic fiction that still lingers, though avowedly in a somewhat altered, more rationalist version, in Hawthorne's *The Scarlet Letter.*

Conventions like the letter, the memoir, and the confession, printed with a prologue and an epilogue by the editor, were primarily aimed at hiding the fictionality of the novel, and at bringing it closer to history, thus showing the battle started in the Renaissance between Aristotelian defenders and Platonic detractors of "poesie" to be still very much alive. In this connection, Richardson's insistence on the exemplary value of his characters and on the fact that the letters "are written according to Nature, avoiding all romantic flights, improbable surprises, and irrational machinery" (prologue to the second volume of Pamela, p. v), constitutes a classical example.

In *A Maggot* John Fowles openly draws on all these well-known eighteenth-century literary conventions, in the same way he had drawn on Victorian narrative conventions in *The French Lieutenant's Woman.* So he brackets the novel with a Prologue and an Epilogue which he signs *in propria persona,* and then creates a hetero-extradiegetic narrator who identifies with the twentieth-century author of Prologue and Epilogue. This narrator, who assumes the all-knowing and detached objectivity of a historian, calls to mind the pedantic narrator of *The French Lieutenant's Woman.* He is overbearing and historically accurate and, like his predecessor in the earlier novel, seems to enjoy his heavily didactic role of commentator on the social and political life of early eighteenth-century England to the point of ignoring the fact that he is often blatantly anachronistic.

However, in keeping with the eighteenth-century convention of objectivity that reduces the roles of implied author and/or narrator to those of editor and/or finder of genuine material, our narrator-historian refuses to tell his tale in his own words, and prefers to disclose its numerous mysteries by handing over to the reader, without ever trying to interpret them, a series of genuine-looking documents: letters; a number of historical chronicles taken from *The Gentleman's Magazine,* covering the same span of time as the action of the main plot (that is, from April 30, 1736 till February 29, 1737); and the Examinations and Depositions of several witnesses to the events that ended up in the disappearance of a mysterious Lord's son and the death of his deaf-mute servant.

Asked by James R. Baker (ibid., p. 664) about the reasons he had had for including genuine historical chronicles in his novel, John Fowles answered,

> I put *The Gentleman's Magazine* extracts in, I hope, out of a kind of honesty—to remind people what the real language of that time, the printed language, really sounded and looked

like. I've felt this about other people's historical novels: you look up something in a historical text, check it against the novel, and you suddenly remember what the language really sounded like. I thought I would go a step further this time and give the reader a taste of the real thing.

According to this statement, the historical chronicles interspersed in the novel are not meant, as we would have expected, to function as a reality-enhancing mechanism but, on the contrary, as a *foil* to set off the differences between "the real thing" and Fowles's fictional creation. Similarly, the seemingly reality-affirming device of writing a Prologue and an Epilogue somehow fails to meet the traditional reader's expectation for, as Julian Moynahan observes,

> We expect prologues and epilogues to be places where a writer stands by his work, clears up problems, levels with the reader; yet this prologue and epilogue are studiedly evasive. ("Fly Casting," p. 47)

The "evasiveness" of which Moynahan complains refers, it seems, to the author's downright refusal to try and enhance the reality of his created world for, instead of fostering the historicity of the facts narrated, as an eighteenth-century editor would have done, John Fowles relentlessly undermines the reader's "willing suspension of disbelief" very much in the same way in which he had destroyed in chapter 13 of *The French Lieutenant's Woman* the carefully built illusion of reality created so far. Thus, for instance, John Fowles tells us in the Prologue that he doesn't even know the exact date of birth of Ann Lee, the real historical woman with whose birth the novel ends, insisting that "I have given that child her historical name; but I would not have this seen as a historical novel. It is a maggot" (p. 6).

A little earlier the author had explained to the reader two different meanings of the term "maggot." One is "the larval stage of a winged creature" (p. 15), which he compares to "the written text." The other is "whim or quirk," a sudden desire or idea that will soon pass. Thus, this second meaning of "maggot" evokes the banality, futility, and avowed minimalism expressed by the title of the author's preceding novel, *Mantissa*.

Angered by the "evasiveness" of the author's Prologue and Epilogue, Julian Moynahan rejects Fowles's "bobbing and weaving, the pretense of explaining things while continuing to play games" (ibid., p. 47), and he lamely ends his review of *A Maggot* with a platitudinous lament: "I become convinced that Fowles has failed to write a serious book. As he says, it is a maggot" (ibid., p. 49).

One "seriously" wonders whether serious here means "realistically biased," "mirthless," "morally edifying," or a combination of the three. Indeed, it is shocking—and I suppose discouraging for John Fowles—to find certain critics making the same kind of complaints over and over again after the publication of every new novel. Their complaints prove that they have chosen to ignore the constant message each one of the novels contains. *A Maggot* cannot meet the requirements of Julian Moynahan for the same reason that *The French Lieutenant's Woman* failed to meet those of other reality-biased critics; that is, because neither is *A Maggot* an eighteenth-century historical novel, nor is *The French Lieutenant's Woman* a Victorian romance, and this, simply, because they have been written in the twentieth century.

It seems necessary, then, to stress once again the essentially parodic nature of John Fowles's use of traditional novelistic conventions. As soon as this is realized, the author's statement that his novel is not a historical novel, but just "a maggot," acquires its real sense, for with it Fowles is openly standing by his work, presenting it to the reader as what it is and expressing his conviction that, even after *Mantissa,* it is possible to give the screw still another turn even if, in order to do so, "the hypothesis," in Walter Miller, Jr.'s words, "seems to be that readers will tolerate more teasing, and more indeterminacy as to plot and character, than is usually expected of them" ("Chariots and Goddesses, or What?" p. 11).

However, the fact that so many critics insist on biting the bait of realism proves how carefully Fowles displays his realistic traps. Indeed, from the structural point of view, *A Maggot* deserves to be ranked with a *A Tale of a Tub.* Purportedly a faithful report of a legal inquiry *à la* Defoe, aimed at throwing light on the mysterious disappearance of an aristocrat who hides his identity under a most stridently Richardsonian *Mr. B.,* the novel is best described as an all-inclusive patchwork, made up of both fictional and historical material, stitched together by the wonderfully accurate imitation of diverse eighteenth-century styles; so accurate indeed that the Historical Chronicles—supposedly reproduced in order to act as foils for contrast with them—in practice work in both directions, establishing differences but also psychologically reinforcing the illusion of realism of the created world.

Thus, significantly, we have a fiction that affirms its realism even against the open protests of fictionality of its creator, to the point that it leads critics to blame John Fowles for trying to write a historical novel without even knowing the exact date of birth of Ann Lee, ignoring Fowles's protests that that wasn't his aim at all. The irony is more poignant when one compares the reluctance to believe Fowles's open statements with the reaction of mistrust generated in the reader by the eager protests of writers like Swift or Defoe about the historicity of the adventures undertaken by heroes like Gulliver or Crusoe.

In the A.E.D.E.A.N. interview (ibid., p. 61) John Fowles explained how not only *The French Lieutenant's Woman* and *The Collector,* but also *Mantissa* and *Daniel Martin,* developed out of tiny images, "very like cinema stills, just as say good Buñuel stills or Eisenstein stills, just as they can evoke the whole film even though there is only one frame, one picture . . . and that seems to have some effect on me."

In the interview Fowles didn't say whether the same was applicable to *A Maggot,* but he does refer to one such "good Buñuel still" in the Prologue of this novel, when he relates the second meaning of "maggot" to his obsession "for several years before its writing [with] a small group of travellers, faceless, without apparent motive, [who] went . . . towards an event" (p. 5). It is with a description of this vision that the novel begins. In the first line the "forlorn little group of travellers is placed in the late and last afternoon of an April long ago" (p. 7). They "cross a remote upland in the far south-west of England [following] a peaty track [that] traverses a waste of dead, heather and ling" (p. 7).

The compelling image brims over with literary allusions. In one stroke the reader is inevitably led to produce a series of quasi-simultaneous associations: firstly, with the merry cavalcade riding towards the shrine of Sir Thomas à Becket under the "soote showers" of an even remoter April. This mental association is immediately qualified, however, by the inevitable evocation of the tragic Hardian heath and also by T. S. Eliot's unforgettable reminder that "April is the cruellest month" in the waste land. So, from the start, *A Maggot* affirms its polysemic value, presenting itself as a twentieth-century novel capable of absorbing and recasting not only the inheritance of the eighteenth-century pseudo-historical novel, but the bulk of the Western literary tradition as a whole.

The complexity of the apparently simple image out of which the whole novel develops foretells the kind of complexity the reader will encounter throughout the rest of the novel. The vision of five faceless travellers silently following a peaty track across the waste land is a clear enough indication for the knowing reader that John Fowles has once again written another variation on his unique theme. But the fact that the riders are five instead of one poses the first difficulty, for, faceless and enveloped in a misty haze as they are, it is impossible to know who is the one among them who bears the mark of the hero.

As they come out of the haze, however, the reader is allowed to contemplate them physically; two men, one in his twenties, the other past middle-age, seem to lead the group. Behind them a young manservant and a pretty maid on the same mare, and finally a braggart bodyguard, who has just come to meet them. They do not exchange a word but "ride as if lost in their own separate worlds" (p. 8).

As they approach the town of C–, the mythical nature of the territory they are entering is heavily stressed. Noisy guardians of the first threshold, a family of ravens cry out "with deep and ominous voices, complaining of this intrusion into their domain" (p. 8). Soon after, the landscape becomes post-atomic. A wood of leafless trees traversed by a slippery track bordering a ravine are all indications that the riders are trespassing on forbidden territory:

> They arrive at what is almost a ravine, sloping faces of half-buried rock, an awkward scramble even on foot. The leading rider seems not to notice it, though his horse hesitates nervously, picking its way. One of its hind feet slips, for a moment it seems it must fall, and trap its rider. But somehow it, and the lurching man, keep balance. They go a little slower, negotiate one more slip and scramble with a clatter of frantic hooves, then come to more level ground. The horse gives a little snorting whinny. The man rides on, without even a glance back to see how the others fare. (pp. 9–10)

The young gentleman who leads the way is the first one to climb the ravine. He doesn't seem to partake of the fear his horse and the other travellers experience as the track becomes more steep and slippery, and he is the only one who does not dismount. The feat accomplished by them all, the landscape starts to metamorphose: the maid picks up a little bunch of sweet-violets, the first ones that they have seen along their way, and then, quite unexpectedly, she breaks the ominous silence with a "melancholy old folk-air, *Daphne*" (p. 12). Immediately, a mistle-thrush echoes her song "from far across the valley, barely audible, as fragmented as the muffled girl's voice" (p. 12), and then,

> Through the bare branches ahead, there is a gleam of luminous gold. . . . Now the sound of rushing water dominates. They ride for a little way close above a fast and furious moorland stream and greener vegetation: more violets, wood-sorrel, first ferns, nests of primroses, emerald young rushes and grass (p. 12).

Once the abyss is surmounted and the waste land left behind, the thrush, as in "Burnt Norton" *(Four Quartets,* I, 13–14), entices the travellers to open the door of the primeval garden:

> Other echoes
> Inhabit the garden. Shall we follow?
> Quick, said the bird, find them, find them,
> Round the corner. Through the first gate,
> Into our first world, shall we follow
> The deception of the thrush? Into our first world.

As the valley stretches in front of the travellers, three or four flocks become visible, watched over by as many silent shepherds, "monolythic [*sic*] figures in cloaks of brown frieze, like primitive bishops with their crooks. One had two children beside him. Their sheep, Exmoor Horns, were smaller and scraggier than modern sheep, and tight-coated" (p. 13). In this paragraph the description of flocks and shepherds by the omniscient narrator sets up two opposed patterns of expectation in the reader: on the one hand, the emblematic sheep and the fact that the shepherds are compared to monolithic figures, bishops of a primitive religion, work to reinforce our intuition that the travellers are entering a primeval garden. On the other hand, the blatantly anachronistic accuracy with which the narrator-cum-historiographer points to the racial characteristics of the common Devon eighteenth-century sheep works to the contrary effect, undermining the mythical resonances.

Again and again the narrator combines commonsensical and accurate descriptions like this one with hints of a much more metaphysical character; thus, for instance, he tells us how the two shepherd children await the travellers at the side of the road, "with strangely intent eyes, watching *beings from fable, not reality,* approach" (pp. 13–14, my italics) and he explains how, instead of giving them the money they beg, "the young woman raised her left hand and took a pinch of spray of violets, then threw them at the small girl" (p. 14). But subsequently the narrator cuts off the possible symbolism of the flower baptism with an ironic comment: "[The violets] fell across the child's arm, over her bent crown of *no doubt lice-ridden hair,* then to the ground" (p. 14, my italics).

Likewise, after describing the valley in paradisiacal terms the narrator reminds the twentieth-century reader that

> the period had no sympathy with unregulated or primordial nature. It was aggressive wilderness, an ugly and all-invasive reminder of the Fall, of man's eternal exile from the Garden of Eden; and particularly aggressive to a nation of profit-haunted puritans, on the threshold of an age of commerce, in its flagrant uselessness. The time . . . remained essentially hostile to wild nature, seeing it only as something to be tamed, classified, utilized, exploited. (p. 15)

By stressing the opposition between the twentieth-century, post-romantic acceptance of unregulated Nature as expression of the exuberant abundance of the Edenic garden, with the eighteenth-century, rationalist interpretation of this same abundance as the expression of chaos, and as such of the most dreadful evidence of the existence of evil, the narrator is warning us of the relativity of any kind of univocal interpretation of the wilderness, and pointing at its all-inclusive and paradoxical double nature, made up of both the *bons vaux* and of the waste land, at once both luxuriantly paradisiacal and chaotically infernal.

So, from the start, the narrator plays with the twentieth-century reader's background, evoking in him a series of mythical and literary connotations which he subsequently undermines with the warning that, if he wants to recreate the experience, feelings, and thoughts of the eighteenth-century characters, the twentieth-century reader will have to adapt to the *Weltanschauung* of the preceding age, and to remember that often his own interpretation would never have occurred to "a nation of profit-haunted puritans, on the threshold of an age of commerce" (p. 15). Translated into Fowlesian terms, one could say that the differences in *Weltanschauungen* between the twentieth-century, post-romantic reader and the eighteenth-century, profit-haunted mercantile Puritan drawn by the narrator are similar to those drawn by John Fowles between the cultivated *aristos* and the literal-minded, kleptomaniacal collector.

Asked by James R. Baker (ibid., p. 664) why he so often set his characters in these "seemingly inert troughs of history," just before change occurs, John Fowles answered:

> I suppose because I'm more interested in beginnings than endings . . . What fascinates me is the time of early proclaimers of something that later becomes clear and established. . . . In *A Maggot*, yes, in the 1730s and '40s, certainly you do begin to sniff the French Revolution coming, the American War of Independence, the Romantic movement (pp. 665–66).

The author's explanation qualifies the narrator's, throwing light on the latter's remark that "this particular last day of April falls in a year very nearly equidistant from 1689, the culmination of the English Revolution, and 1789, the start of the French" (p. 16).

From one perspective, then, Walpole's England can be seen literally as what it appears to be: "some strange doldrum of time, place and spirit" (pp. 15–16). From another, however, it can be seen as one of those fascinating times "of early proclaimers of revolutionary ideas, later to become clear and established." From the perspective of "those two better-class travellers (Mr. B. and Mr. Brown) riding that day into the town" (p. 15), the period is becalming and dull; but from the backward perspective and better knowledge of history enjoyed by John Fowles or by any twentieth-century historian, the period becomes fascinating and pregnant with significance.

The narrator's double-edged style, his insistence on the different mentalities of the different centuries and on the unavoidable subjectivity of human interpretation, figuratively express Carl Jung's concept of "historical stratification." In his "Foreword to White's *God and the Unconscious*" (pp. 309–10), Jung synthesizes the psychological evolution of man through history in three great stages: metaphysical, rationalist, and psychological:

> [While] the eighteenth-century rationalist can operate only with rational concepts, which must on no account savour of metaphysics, for the latter are taboo . . . , it would be an anachronism, i.e., a regression for the man of the twentieth century to solve his conflicts either rationalistically or metaphysically. Therefore, for better or worse, he has built himself a psychology.

Apparently, the historical stratification of human mental evolution is simultaneously traceable in the polymorphic nature of the journey undertaken by the mysterious travellers. While from the eighteenth-century, rationalist point of view, the journey is an ontologically real trip on horseback from London to Devon, from a metaphysical perspective the journey becomes a mythical hero's quest: the travellers have crossed a first threshold, traversed in silence the waste land, risked their lives across the abyss and finally encountered the door to the primeval garden. Now, from the point of view of the twentieth-century reader, the parallelism of the imagery employed by the narrator to describe the arrival of the travellers at their destination with the first section of "Burnt Norton" enhances not only its mythical component but also points to the fact that the journey is primarily a *psychological* journey backwards, aimed at the recovery of that fourth dimension of time, "what might have been":

> Footfalls echo in the memory
> Down the passage which we did not take
> Towards the door we never opened
> Into the rose-garden. My words echo
> Thus, in your mind
> But to what purpose
> Disturbing the dust on a bowl of rose-leaves
> I do not know.
>
> *(Four Quartets,* I, 13)

The point is important, for it may help the reader to understand the novel's many apparent paradoxes and ambiguities, as well as the puzzling contradictory style of the narrator. As in *Daniel Martin,* the physical and the psychological journeys in *A Maggot* complement and oppose each other, the first journey apparently moving forward and working to enhance the realism of the events narrated; the second one moving backwards and working to the contrary effect. But in *A Maggot,* the fact that the hypothesis for the psychological journey seems to be the recreation of "what might have been" according to five, instead of one, characters, multiplies its dimension, opening up a whole range of different possibilities.

Paid by an anonymous lord, Henry Ayscough, a cunning and efficient barrister, has painstakingly accumulated all kinds of available evidence about the journey undertaken by the Lord's heir which ended up in his disappearance and in the death of his manservant. This evidence, recorded in a series of Letters and of Examinations and Depositions, are handed over to the reader, together with nine Historical Chronicles from *The Gentleman's Magazine.* Although it is evident that the narrator-historian often intrudes omnisciently with his asides and comments, his remarks regularly throw light on the socio-historical, cultural, and religious background of early eighteenth-century England, but do not add any conclusive information about the journey itself. Structurally, this means that the reader is offered the "genuine" material exactly as it was gathered by Henry Ayscough from the mouths of the different witnesses, that is, scattered, fragmentary, redundant, often contradictory, and containing both factual and imaginary evidence.

Giving proof of a recklessly practical and rational Tory mentality, Henry Ayscough sets himself precisely to the task of unearthing the "truth" of *what actually happened* that May 1, 1736, separating it from *what might have happened,* ignorant as he perforce was of T. S. Eliot's warning that

What might have been and what has been
Point to an end, which is always present.

(ibid., p. 13)

Once the reader is ready to accept the fact that an inquiry into the past involves
not only, as Ayscough believed, an assessment of what happened, but also of
what might have happened, of both the factual and of the speculatively possible,
of the ontologically real and of the psychological, the incessant "bobbing and
weaving" acquire their *raison d'être*. As the novel progresses we see the symbolism of the "facelessness" of the characters expand to its utmost consequences. In spite of all the seemingly factual evidence gathered from the ostler
and the maid of The Black Hart Inn, we soon discover, for instance, that neither
of these travellers is what he seems to be. Mr. Brown, the elderly middle-class
merchant who appears as the uncle of the younger gentleman, turns out to be
an actor called Francis Lacy, who has been hired by his supposed nephew when
he was in London, performing Fielding's *Pasquin* (p. 117). Likewise, the
Plautinian bodyguard, Sergeant Timothy Farthing, is a minor actor called David
Jones, who had once played "a blundering braggart, a drunken sergeant in Mr.
Farquhar's *The Recruiting Officer*" (p. 137), and who had since then lost a series
of jobs as scrivener's clerk, window polisher, chairman and door keeper at
Drury Lane, due to his glib tongue and his continuous state of drunkenness. The
pretty maid called Louise is soon recognized by Farthing as a reckless prostitute
known as Fanny or "The Quaker Maid," but really called Rebecca Lee, née
Hocknell. Known to be the most debauched *"meretricum regina initiarum lenis"*
(p. 188), she also possesses some acting ability, for "she had as well been
actress or whore" (p. 156), her special attraction being her ability to play
innocence, "Prude, modest sister, Miss Fresh-from-the-Country, Miss Timid
Don't-Tempt-me, Miss Simple" (p. 158), etc.

The young gentleman, alternately called Mr. Bartholomew, Mr. B., Mr.
Smith, or "Philocomoedia," is neither the supposed nephew of Mr. Brown, nor
the youngest son of a baronet, but the heir of an anonymous lord, and the one
who has hired the rest and given them roles. At first sight, only the deaf-mute
servant Dick Thurlow is what he seems to be, the faithful and inseparable
servant of his nameless lord, but we soon find that their relationship is also
dubious. First of all, Dick looks at his master with "no sign of respect," but
rather "it is such a look as a husband and wife, or sibling, might give" and
when they stand "in their silence, in each other's looking," they do so "as in a
mirror" (p. 45).

As Henry Ayscough himself later explains, Mr. B. and Dick were born "on
the very same hour of the very same day" in the former's father's state, and
"they were suckled at the same breast, [they were] therefore foster-brothers"
(p. 170). Reared together and keeping each other constant company, it even

seemed at times that Dick was "himself the master, knew as much as he" (p. 170). More than that, like other twins in Fowles's earlier fiction, Mr. B and Dick Thurlow enjoy a striking complementarity. Both "were one mind, one will, one appetite" to the point that if Mr. B. "die, he dies the next instant" (p. 171). However, they were also somehow jealous of each other for, while Dick seemed to feel "anger against the fate that has made him what he is" (p. 170), Mr. B. knows that "albeit Dick was ignorant in so many things, he had in recompense a kind of wisdom. . . . He had the senses of an animal, and could see things we cannot" (p. 171).

The suspected impotent, physically unattractive Lord is of superior intelligence, and the highly-sexed athlete with vacant blue eyes has a strangely inscrutable face

> which does not reveal whether its expressionlessness is that of an illiterate stupidity, an ignorant acceptance of destiny not far removed from that of the two horses he is holding; or whether it hides something deeper, some resentment of grace. (p. 11)

This perfectly fits the pattern of opposites that makes up the hero's personality in Jungian terms. Mr. B.'s physical deficiencies indicate his condition of higher (or conscious) half; Dick's beastliness and his identification with the horses, his condition of lower (or unconscious) half of the self. The fact that they were born at the same time, and in the same place, that they were suckled by the same mother, and even perhaps had been fathered by the same man, as well as the strong hint that perhaps the children were changed in their cradles, that Dick was the Lord and Mr. B. the servant, all work to the effect of underlining the fact that they are one and the same.

As Carl Jung explained ("Symbols of the Mother and of Rebirth," pp. 207-72), the quest for individuation of the hero is a psychological struggle in which he has to fight first against the father, who represents the spiritual side of man, and whose archetypal function consists in the repression of the instinctual, and so threatens to destroy the hero's unconscious; and secondly with the mother for, dominated as he is by her, the hero must find his regeneration by entering once more the maternal womb, even at the risk of committing incest; and yet he must do so without falling into the temptation of lingering there forever, as the maternal womb offers a perilous shelter for the regressive libido, threatening to drown the conscious self. Only by confronting and coping with both dangers can the hero attain the inaccessible treasure, his own individuation, or, in mythical terms, his rebirth to immortality for, mythically, the victory of the son is expressed as the concession by the father of his own divine nature.

Once again, in widely different cultures, under widely different forms, this myth reappears with its strikingly homogeneous stages. The hero and his horse undertake a heroic quest towards the sacred wood where the maternal womb is encountered in the form of a mysterious cave. Invariably, the rider stands for the conscious. The horse, symbol as he is of the unconscious, often represents, as does Dick Thurlow, the *concuspiscencia effrenata* (Jung, "The Battle for Deliverance from the Mother," p. 280), the most violent sexual appetites. But he is also endowed with the numinous instinctual power to lead the way to the *locus amoenus* that encloses the *anima*.

The psychological interpretation of the journey undertaken by Mr. B. and his fellow-travellers helps us to understand why Mr. B. needed Rebecca for the journey and also why she has a paradoxical double nature, for Rebecca's oxymoronic qualities are those of the *anima*. Alternately presented as whore and as virgin, she represents yet another split of the hero's personality, simultaneously repressed by Mr. B., the ego's conscious side, and lusted after by Dick, the ego's instinctual half.

The triangular relationship of Rebecca (anima), Mr. B. (conscious), and Dick (unconscious) is figuratively expressed when Mr. B. cuts short Farthing's gossip about Dick and Rebecca lying in bed together, with the sarcastic question "May Man not lie with his own wife?" (p. 44), just before the narrator describes the mysterious relationship of Mr. B. and Dick as that of "husband and wife, or siblings" (p. 45); while the complementarity of the three is best expressed in their allotted sexual roles, with Dick and Rebecca the active couple and Mr. B. the *voyeur*.

Thus, from a psychological perspective, the journey becomes a hero's quest for a new totality of the self, which must be achieved through his acceptance of the *coincidentia oppositorum*, the reconciliation of his conscious, his unconscious, and his anima potentialities, in the global perception of the self as such.

Assailed by Francis Lacy's curiosity, Mr. B., half seriously, half jokingly, offers the actor several possible explanations about his real identity and about the real aim of their journey. According to these, Mr. B. could be:

1. *A political insurgent:* "Perhaps I am one of those seditious northern Jacks? another Bolingbroke? . . . I go to plot with some emissary of James Stuart" (p. 42).

2. *A Dr. Faustus:* "Necromantical, think you not? I am here to creep into the woods and meet some disciple of the Witch of Endor. To exchange my eternal soul against the secrets of the other world" (p. 42).

3. *A fanciful dreamer:* "What I am upon may be a wild goose chase, a foolish dream" (p. 43).

4. *An unfree literary character:* "I am born with a fixed destiny. I am, as you might be, offered a part in a history, and I am not forgiven for refusing to play it" (p. 43).

Furthermore, in common with Maurice Conchis in *The Magus,* Mr. B. seems to have the protean power to metamorphose physically, appearing successively as a pantaloon figure "from some *fête galante* by Watteau" (p. 53); as "an anachronistic skinhead," and even more improbably, as "Buddhist monk, praeternaturally equable and contained" (p. 55). Alternatively brutal and kind with Rebecca, Mr. B. enjoys the baffling oxymoronic quality, also shared by her, to appear as both devilish and celestial, "as if he was not one man, but two" (p. 254).

The purpose of their journey is as shadowy as the identities of the characters. According to one version, Mr. B. has thought out a scheme to disobey his father and elope with the woman he loves, after having rescued her from the remote place in Devon where she is being kept by her family. According to another, Mr. B. travels to his wealthy aunt in Bidesford, in order to secure his inheritance. A third version presents Mr. B. as suffering from impotence, the purpose of the journey, then, being to try some miraculous water reputed to cure this kind of ailment. A fourth version presents Mr. B. obsessed with esoteric knowledge. According to this version, Mr. B. would be traveling to the mythic circle of Stonehenge in order to recover through obscure calculation the long-lost power of the ancients to communicate with external beings, whether fiendish, celestial, or simply extraterrestrial.

The first version is the one Mr. B. uses to convince Mr. Francis Lacy to play the role of uncle for him. Now, the elopement of a young couple of high class, who risk their inheritance by defying their respective fathers in order to affirm their romantic attachment, constitutes a traditional plot of eighteenth-century romance and one so stereotyped that Henry Ayscough cannot but suspect the actor's readiness to believe it:

Q. *Facile credimus quod volumus.* You swallowed this cock-and-bull whole, it seems?
....
A. I was merely, as he put it, to safeconduct him to the threshold. (pp. 132–33)

The second version is more realistic, although as stale as the first one by literary standards. The dutiful nephew who pays due homage to the wealthy dowager and asks her pardon for his youthful dissipation draws on the common eighteenth-century notion of man as unregenerate Adam and, as such, constitutes a classical commonplace of eighteenth-century edifying prose.

A "Mr. B." who suffers from impotence can be seen as a joking reference to *Pamela* in the line of *Joseph Andrews,* while the fourth version presents Mr. B. as a Dr. Faustus intent on applying his knowledge "to practice more than heavenly power permits" (Marlowe, *Dr. Faustus,* Epilogue, 1, 27). This fourth version, which admits a double interpretation of Mr. B. as a demonic or angelic agent, has an eighteenth-century counterpart in the Gothic novel, that striking literary phenomenon expressing the culmination of a century of philosophical speculation on the causes of good and evil.[1]

The four different versions offered by Mr. B. himself about the journey's aim have two things in common: one is the fact that they are all more or less recognizably literary; the other, that they all refer, as do the hypotheses about Mr. B.'s real identity, to some form of disobedience or frustration: the hero (1) disobeys his father (or his king); (2) repents his past libertinism; (3) feels castrated (or unfree); or (4) challenges divine rule, in order to know more.

Once it is realized that both the versions about the real aim of the journey and about Mr. B.'s identity are simply more or less fanciful literary "variations" on one unique theme—*some form of disobedience or frustration*—it is possible to accept the word of Mr. B. when, pressed by Lacy, he formally says:

> "I give you my word, Lacy. You know *I am a disobedient son. . . .*"
> "*I seek a meeting with someone.* That much is true." (p. 26, my italics)

The someone Mr. B. seeks is, as he explains a little later, some obscure female being: "I go to meet one I desire to know, and respect, as much as I would a bride—or my Muse indeed, were I a poet" (p. 42).

Mr. B.'s cryptic statement that he goes to meet someone he respects as much as a bride or a Muse fosters the psychological and the literary interpretations. From the psychological point of view, there is little doubt that Mr. B. is trying to instigate a meeting with the mother capable of bringing about his spiritual rebirth. The incestuous union with the mother becomes, in literary terms, the climactic meeting with the Muse, the source of inspiration.

With the help of Henry Ayscough's patient research the reader is soon able to know how Mr. B. had thought of succeeding in his enterprise. Thanks to a letter written by Mr. Nicholas Saunders, successor of Sir Isaac Newton *in Catedrâ Lucasianâ* (pp. 192–95), we discover that Mr. B. has been a distinguished scholar at Christ's College, Cambridge, where he had become acquainted with the *Liber Abaci* of Leonardo da Pisa, a learned Italian monk "of many centuries ago" (p. 146), who had tried to calculate the mathematical proportion to be found everywhere in nature by "the adding of each last two figures to make the next, to wit one, two, three, five, eight, thirteen, one and twenty, thus forward as you may will" (p. 146).

This sequence, called by da Pisa *phyllotaxis* (p. 194), was based "on a secret of the Greeks, who did discover a perfect proportion . . . to be of one to one and six tenths" (p. 146). Mr. B. believed with da Pisa that this proportion was traceable "everywhere in nature . . . indeed even discernible in the motions of the planets and the arrangements of the stars in the heavens (and so thought) that a chronology of the future might be established from the aforesaid sequence" (pp. 194–95).

The reference to "the Greeks" brings to mind the mathematical speculations about the origin of the universe of Pythagoras and his school, and of Plato, also discernible in St. John's Gospel and in the Gnostic conception of the Trinity.

According to Pythagoras, "one," the absolute unity, is unknowable and cannot be numbered, so that "two" is the first number, knowable as "the other." "One" and "the other" form an opposition which is solved in "three," the first uneven and perfect number, because it has a beginning, a middle, and an end. As Jung ("A Psychological Approach to the Dogma of the Trinity," p. 119) remarks, three "appears as a suitable synonym for a process of development in time, and thus forms a parallel to the self-revelation of the Deity as the absolute One unfolded into Three, [the] intellectual idea of the equilateral triangle [thus becoming] a conceptual model for the logical image of the Trinity."

Plato accepts the Pythagorean conception of a triadic formula for the God-image in philosophical terms, but then devises in the *Timaeus* an account of the actual process of creation of the world as the combination, not of three elements, but of four, arranged as two separate pairs of opposites in a *quaternario*.

Da Pisa's numerical sequence one, two, three, five, etc., brings to mind Plato's question at the beginning of the *Timaeus:* "One, two three—but . . . where is the fourth?" As Carl Jung ("A Psychological Approach . . . ," p. 164) observes, Plato's question synthesizes the platonic dilemma, also observable in Goethe's *Faust,* between the philosophical trinitarian conception of the God-image and the actual process of the creation of the world in a *quaternario,* the quaternity being "an archetype of almost universal occurrence . . . there are four element, four prime qualities, four colours, four castes, four ways of spiritual development in Buddhism, etc. So, too, there are four aspects of psychological orientation" (ibid., p. 167).

The universal archetype of the quaternity, which remained a natural phenomenon among the Pythagoreans, acquired the tinge of heresy in the philosophical speculation of medieval Christianity, as it was felt that, since the principle that ruled the world was a trinity, the quaternity must therefore be "of the devil" (ibid., p. 177). For Plato, the "fourth" element, *physis,* signifies "realization," i.e., entry into an essentially different condition, that of worldly materiality, which is the diametrical opposite of spirit. The Assumption into heaven of the Blessed Virgin Mary in *body* and soul indicates, according to Jung a medieval attempt not only to recognize the divinity of the *Theotokos,* but also to legitimate the quaternity, including matter in the metaphysical realm. Thus matter, Mother Earth, comes to represent the *concreteness* of God's thoughts and is, therefore, the very thing that makes individuation possible.

Man's connection with physis, with the material world and its demands, is the cause of his anomalous position: on the one hand, he has the capacity for enlightenment, on the other he is in thrall to the Lord of this world . . . On account of his sinlessness, Christ on the contrary lives in the Platonic realm of pure ideas whither only man's thought can reach, but not he himself in his totality. Man is, in truth, the bridge spanning the gulf between "this world"—the realm of the dark Tricephalus—and the heavenly Trinity. That is why, even in the days of unqualified belief in the Trinity, there was always a quest for the lost fourth, from the time of the Neopythagoreans down to Goethe's *Faust*. Although these seekers thought of themselves as Christians, they were really Christians only on the side, devoting their lives to a work whose purpose it was to redeem the "four-horned serpent," the fallen Lucifer, and to free the *anima mundi* imprisoned in matter. What in their view lay hidden in matter was the *lumen luminum*, the *Sapientia Dei*, and their work was a "gift of the Holy Spirit." (ibid., pp. 177–78)

So, from the point of view of eighteenth-century scholarship, Mr. B.'s mathematical speculations in search of the hidden proportion traceable everywhere in nature and treasured by the ancients that built Stonehenge has to be understood as the alchemical quest for the "lost four," that is, for the *lapis philosophorum;* for the *Sapientia Dei* hidden in matter, capable of synthesizing right and left, black and white, matter and spirit.

Believing with John Locke that "we mortals are locked as at Newgate . . . within the chains and bars of our senses" (p. 149), Mr. B. acutely feels a kind of existentialist angst *avant la lettre* as he perceives himself incapable of breaking loose from the notion of his own span of life as the accumulation of past, present, and future. Consequently, freedom for him implies the apprehension of time in God's own terms as "one eternally now" (p. 149). Mr. B.'s mathematical speculations are, therefore, aimed at the transcendence of the number three which, as we have seen, appears as a synonym for the process of development in time, and at the rediscovery of the mathematical equation capable of transmuting time into "the dance of the Gogs and Magogs," that universal movement of the spheres expressed in Stonehenge's *Chorum Giganteum* (p. 149).

According to alchemical tradition, Mr. B.'s mysterious wooden chest contains a series of leatherbound books and sheaves of paper full of "numbers and signs that were no alphabet letters [written] among figures. [One such figure] was a great circle, and another with three sides, and marks like the moon" (p. 83). In the chest there was also "a great clock of brass, without its case . . . a mizmaze of wheels" (p. 84). "Alchemical symbolism," Jung tells us,

has produced, aside from the personal figures, a whole series of non-human forms, geometrical configurations like the sphere, circle, square, and octagon, or chemical symbols like the Philosopher's Stone, the ruby, the diamond, quicksilver, gold, water, fire, and spirit (in the sense of volatile substance). . . . These symbols express the non-human character of the totality of the self, as was reported long ago when, at Pentecost, the spirit descended on the disciples in tongues of fire. ("A Psychological Approach . . . ," pp. 185–86)

In keeping with alchemical symbolization, Mr. B.'s clocks and wheels express, then, the nonhuman nature of the totality of the self, to be achieved by himself in his sought-after encounter with the *spiritus mundi,* the Mother Earth. The form in which this totality is perceived by the self, Jung explains (ibid. p. 185), "has a numinous character, it is an overwhelming psychic experience, that can take the form of religious conversion, illumination, emotional shock, mystical experience" (ibid., pp. 183–84), and is equivalent, in Christian terms, to the descent of the Holy Ghost. The self thus illuminated becomes the *Anthropos,* the Cosmic Man.

It is in order to promote this illumination that Mr. B. arranges the journey to Stonehenge. Farthing and Francis Lacy are only hired "to safeconduct him to the threshold" (p. 133). Once the threshold is reached both are dismissed and Mr. B. proceeds to the forlorn cave in the Devon wilderness, a man in a mortal struggle with his undiscovered *anima* and with his instinctual unconscious, in search of his "lost four." This is the real aim of Mr. B.'s quest, no matter whether we describe it in alchemical, Christian, metaphysical, or psychological terms as the search for the philosopher's stone, the acquisition of the *Sapientia Dei,* the meeting with the Goddess, the individuation of the self, or in any other way.

Consequently, once the terminological fog is dissipated, it is possible to reduce Mr. B.'s journey to its basic stages, which neatly follow Jung's scheme (ibid., p. 175) of the quaternity:

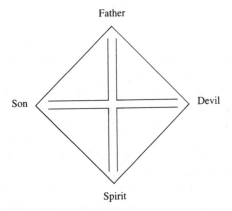

In mythological terms, the will to be different and contrary is characteristically evil, just as disobedience was the hallmark of original sin. That is why the Son revolting against the Father has a "light" side and a "dark" emanation and contains in himself both the principles of good and evil. The conflict created by the duality of the Son must resolve itself in the fourth principle (Spirit), capable of restoring the unity of the first in its full development. With these notions in mind, Mr. B.'s journey may be visualized as follows:

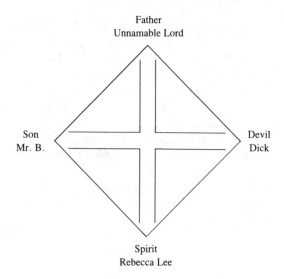

Jung's scheme gives sense to the fact that Mr. B.'s father is an "Unnamable Lord" like God himself. It also explains the otherwise puzzling satanic and celestial duality of Mr. B; his interchangeability with Dick, his dark emanation; and his need of Rebecca for the achievement of his sought-after individuation. Finally, it also explains why the events that take place first at Stonehenge and then within Dolling's Cave are reported by David Jones as satanic experiences and by Rebecca Lee as encounters with celestial beings.

After the arrival of the five travelers at Amesbury on the 26th of April, Mr. B. shows great interest in visiting Stonehenge. They all go and see it in the course of the day, and then retire to bed. A little before midnight, however, David Jones sees Mr. B., Dick, and Rebecca stealthily abandon the inn again. What Jones takes at first to be the solemnization of a clandestine wedding soon turns into a much more mysterious and disquieting affair. According to the version Rebecca later gives to Jones, Mr. B. had convinced her to go to Stonehenge in order to participate in a heathen ritual, intended to restore his sexual capacity. According to this version, Mr. B. had obliged the reluctant Rebecca to lie upon a great sacrificial stone, with her petticoat raised in the posture of love. Then

> there was all of a sudden a great rush or hurtle close in the night above, as of some great falcon that passed. And as a flash of lightning . . . and tho' but in this great flash, she did see a figure that stood above her on a stone pillar as a statue might . . . that seemed of a great and dark-cloaked blackamoor, which did gaze most greedily down upon her, like he was that falcon whose wings she heard, his cloak still aflutter from his falling, and so he would in an instant spring down upon her, as a bird upon its prey. . . . A moment or two after the lightning, there came a strange gust of air upon her, as from a furnace (which) did carry a most rank and foul stench as of roasting carrion upon it. (pp. 252–53)

To Henry Ayscough's question "Who thought she this figure was, this buzzard blackamoor?" Jones conclusively answers:

> A. The king of Hell, sir, the Prince of Darkness.
> Q. Satan himself, the Devil?
> A. Yes, sir. (p. 253)

The vision of the falcon turned blackamoor with his vampire-like cloak aflutter, greedily gazing down on Rebecca and ready to jump on her, constitutes a wonderfully pictorial description of the embodiment of *concupiscentia effrenata,* in the tradition of the eighteenth-century Gothic fiction. In keeping with this literary tradition, heralded by Richardson, Rebecca falls into a swoon similar to the ones suffered by Pamela whenever Mr. B. tried to assault her sexually, thus preventing herself (and the reader) from knowing with certainty what really happened to her, whether she was sexually abused either by the ghastly apparition or by Mr. Bartholomew, after he had miraculously recovered his sexual prowess, or whether, as happened to Pamela, her losing of consciousness acts as an unexpected safeguard of her virtue.

For all its indeterminacy, it is clear, however, that, according to the version given by Rebecca to David Jones, she endured some sort of demonic experience. This is eventually denied by Rebecca herself, in her Examination and Deposition, where she says that she was not made to lie on the sacrificial stone, but rather to kneel on it, Mr. B. and Dick kneeling beside her. Soon afterwards, she heard a great rush as of wings or of a great roaring wind, which suddenly stopped, and then,

> there crept upon the air such a smell I cannot say, as of new-mown meadows and summer flowers, that was most sweet . . . then again . . . a light . . . as of a sun . . . so bright I no

> sooner looked to it than I must look down bedazzled, why, near blind of it; and there I saw, who stood not fifteen paces from where we knelt, among the stones, a young man and an old, that gazed upon us. . . . They stood, and looked on us. The younger man a little nearer, the older behind. And the younger stood with his finger pointed up, as if towards the light, yet methought his eyes did rest upon me. (p. 325)

Again, as was the case with the report of the Stonehenge events, David Jones will give Henry Ayscough a demonic version of what happened in Dolling's Cave, gathered by him from Rebecca's lips the very same evening of the first of May. According to this version, Mr. B. offered Rebecca as a bride to the devil himself, who appeared in the cave in the shape of the Stonehenge blackamoor, this time escorted by three hideous witches, one young and two old. Forced back upon the ground, and offered to the devil stark naked, Rebecca fell into a swoon as she had done at Stonehenge, but not before seeing Mr. B. and Dick participate in the blood-curdling black wedding with the witches, performing all kind of abominations among themselves.

Obliged by one of the hags to take a potion, Rebecca finally falls asleep and has a dream in which she sees the face of the devil metamorphose into that of Mr. B., and immediately afterwards, she observes various hangings with different scenes of slaughter and brutality acted "as on a stage" (p. 262), the sight of which produces in Rebecca a great longing for Christ, the Redeemer. In one of these hangings she sees the "fair corpse of a young lady being gnawed by a seethe of maggots as it lay, unburied, and one which was monstrous large, out of all nature" (p. 266). Horrified by the vision, she prays and begs God's pardon for her past behavior.

This "satanic" version is denied by Rebecca during her Examination and Deposition in the same way in which she had denied the satanic version of what happened at Stonehenge, offering instead a diametrically divergent, "celestial" version of what had happened in the cave.

According to this version, Mr. B., Dick and Rebecca were received at the entrance of the cave by a most beautiful young lady dressed in silver, of somewhat Jewish features and of slightly masculine demeanor, who led them into the cave as if they were her guests. Instead of the monstrously large maggot gnawing the corpse of the young lady of her dream in the satanic version, Rebecca now sees an enormous maggot-like floating balloon which she describes as "white as snow and bearing on its sides and belly a wheel with figures, in a line" (p. 359). Immediately afterwards, to match the three hideous witches, the young lady in silver divides herself into three identical women.

Discussing in "Psychology and Religion" (p. 68) the vision of Guillaume de Digulleville *(Guillaume de Digulleville, Trois romans-poèmes du XIVe siècle)*, written by Joseph Delacotte, a fifteenth-century French abbot, Jung analyzes the explanation of the symbol of the Trinity the angel gives to Guillaume as the combination of three colors in one: "The almighty King who puts three colours in one, cannot he also make one substance to be three?" (ibid., p. 69). Neatly following this archetypal symbolism,[2] the three women Rebecca sees become distinguishable only through the different colors of the posies they hold:

> The oldest bore a posy of flowers of darkest purple, near to black; and the youngest . . . of purest white; and her mother flowers of red, like blood. Else were all three as peas in a pod, spite of their ages. (p. 365)

And then,

> by some strange feat . . . they were joined as one with her, or seemed to melt thus inside of her; . . . and the one woman, she of the grey hair, the mother, left to stand there where were three. (p. 366)

This grey-haired mother subsequently calls Rebecca by her name and presents her with "her posy of the three hues of flowers, like it was her private favour she gave" (p. 367).

Led to the interior of the maggot by the "mother," Rebecca is offered a series of fantastic visions she compares to "some good magic, as in a dream" (p. 371). In them she sees a happy land she calls June Eternal, which she explicitly identifies with Heaven (p. 375). On a green meadow she meets two men and a woman, all robed in white. The two men are the same men that appeared before her at Stonehenge, the woman, by a strange power of ubiquity, is the same one who stands at Rebecca's side in the maggot. Rebecca intuitively realizes that the older man and woman "and the young man were of one family" (p. 378) and, a little later, she discovers that the young man has a twin, who is lying nearby, asleep:

> These two men were one, the only one, the man of men: our Lord Jesus Christ, who died for us, yet was resurrected. . . . Undeserving sinner I may be, there was I brought certain, most certain, within the presence of the Father and the Son. [And she was] she without whom God the Father could not have made His works, whom some would call the Holy Spirit. She is *Holy Mother Wisdom.* (p. 379, my italics)

Rebecca's passionate description of her vision of Heaven and of a Holy Trinity made up of a Father, a Son and his Dark Emanation, and a female Holy Spirit divisible into three, is received by the orthodox Christian and conservative rationalist, Henry Ayscough, with suspicion and incredulity. This conception of the Trinity, defended by eighteenth-century Shakers, as the narrator-historian suggests, has it roots in a much older tradition of Christianity, as Jung points out:

The mother quality was originally an attribute of the Holy Ghost, an the latter was known as Sophia-Sapientia by certain early Christians. This feminine quality could not be completely eradicated; it still adheres to the symbol of the Holy Ghost, the *columba spiritus sancti.* ("Psychology and Religion," p. 73)

Thus, again, Jung's authority confirms the archetypal character of the novel's symbolization, a fact Walter Miller, Jr. underlines when he says:

The fascinating central motif in the novel is the numinous female triad linked to a mysterious fourth—three witches and Satan (the Lord transformed), or a female Holy Trinity joined by a harlot. The idea of goddess triads was spread everywhere by the Indo-European migration thousands of years ago. Classically, we have the Fates, the Norns, the Furies. Mr. Fowles does not mention it, but the British Isles have been haunted since pre-Christian times by various versions of the old Celtic Morrigan triad: the phantom Queen, She-Who-Brings-Panic and the Raven of Battle. ("Chariots . . . ," p. 11)

So, for the twentieth-century reader, the dreamlike experience undergone by Rebecca in both versions has the neatness of a recurrent archetype which, at the psychological level, perfectly fits the Jungian scheme reproduced above. The joining of a Holy Trinity with a dark or profane fourth, expressed in the passing of the three-colored posy of flowers to Rebecca, is, as Miller also reminds us, "a powerful event in the life of the collective psyche" (ibid., p. 11).

Describing Mr. B.'s reaction after the satanic events that took place at Stonehenge, David Jones says that Mr. B. had been very much pleased with Rebecca, had embraced her gratefully "as she might be a sister or a wife" and had told her "Thou art a brave girl. I am well content with thee" (p. 253). In the celestial version offered later by Rebecca, Mr. B. likewise showed himself very much pleased. He "took [Rebecca's] hands and pressed them, as one who is grateful, and looked [her] in the eyes, . . . and said, you are she I have sought," then turned to Dick and embraced him "not as a master and man, but as brothers might upon some happy outcome to their affairs" (p. 328).

In a similar way, the otherwise utterly divergent versions of David Jones and of Rebecca about what happened in the cave significantly coincide when they come to report the effect produced in the latter by both the satanic and the celestial experiences. Indeed, the vision of the horrifying maggots gnawing the corpse of the young lady, as well as the sight of a little girl Rebecca identifies with herself, roasting in the fire, produce in the prostitute the same kind of religious conversion that her vision of Heaven and of the Holy Trinity in the celestial version had brought about.

Whether satanic or celestial, then, the outcome of the obscure preliminary ritual that took place at Stonehenge seemed to please Mr. B., exactly as he was pleased in both the demonic and the heavenly versions of the events that took place within the cave. The same events were described as producing in Rebecca the same numinous effect. Mr. B.'s happiness and Rebecca's conversion in both versions match the double nature of the Son and is the best proof we have that, as Walter Miller, Jr., unfailingly detects, "the equivalence of the infernal and the celestial versions of the scene in the cave conforms to Jung's psychology, and *both versions of the cave scene are true*" (ibid., p.11, my italics).

Only by accepting both versions as true can we find a clue to the mysterious disappearance of Mr. B. within the cave and to the subsequent death of his manservant. In the satanic version of what happened in the cave, Rebecca falls asleep and has a vision of the Devil dressed in black and she realizes that, for all their differences in looks and of complexion, "yet somehow she knew they were both the one" (p. 261). Similarly, in her celestial version of the parallel dream, Rebecca sees Mr. B. metamorphose physically, becoming "one with He I had seen in the meadow in June Eternal, that does forgive all sins, and to all despair bring peace" (p. 383). This is the last time Mr. B. is seen, for in both versions he subsequently disappears. And each time Rebecca explicitly says that Mr. B. has gone to Heaven or to Hell.

For the rationalist Ayscough, Mr. B.'s disappearance can only be explained as murder. For days his assistants comb the surroundings and interior of the cave in search of Mr. B.'s corpse, and they are terribly puzzled when the corpse is not to be found. For those twentieth-century readers who insist, like Ayscough, on finding a rationalist solution to the riddle, John Fowles offers a possible reading of the white floating maggot, with its panels of twinkling lights and its television screens, and of the silver garments of the ladies, according to which the maggot would simply be a spaceship, and the ladies in silver some kind of astronauts from outer space, who had managed to break the barriers of space and time with their more advanced technology, and to establish some kind of communication with Mr. B., thanks to his mathematical speculations. According to this version, Mr. B. would have been literally invited to fly into the future, to some remote galaxy.

One possible objection to these interpretations, however, is the fact that neither Ayscough's rationalist explanation nor the science fiction solution can convincingly account for either the religious conversion of Rebecca or for the death of Dick, and would only be acceptable if the satanic version were to be discarded. So, in order to find an all-inclusive explanation of what really happened at Dolling's Cave, we must again resort to the psychological interpretation.

As Mr. B., Dick, and Rebecca separate from Lacy and Jones two-and-a-half miles above the ford upon the Bidesford road, the mythical nature of the realm they are entering is again suggested in the combination of the paradisiacal valley and of the infernal ravine that characterizes the Cleeve, so called "after its cleft and woody sides, that make it more ravine than vale" (p. 279). A steep, meandering shepherd path takes the daring travellers to the heart of this forlorn, heavily forested, and rocky country, marked by a stream that falls "from higher crosses of the road," forming a natural basin of drinking water. It is right at the end of this path that the long sought-for cavern-mouth gapes, opening into apparently abysmal darkness.

Called Dolling's or Dollin's Cave, after a rogue who lived there with his gang "in the manner of Robin Hood" (p. 280) three generations before, the cave was regularly used by gypsies in the winter and by shepherds in the summer, but seems to have been known to man since prehistoric times (as the menhir that stands beside the drinking-pool clearly indicates). The habitation of the cave by shepherds and gypsies figuratively expresses its association with good and evil, which is further extended through the legend attached to the implantation of the huge standing rock as the outcome of a fight between a brave, righteous shepherd and Satan himself. Finally, the ambivalent quality of the cave is again reinforced by the paradoxical nature of Dolling's gang, simultaneously associable with evil, through their outlaw activities, and with good, through their identification with the green world of Robin Hood.

The heavily forested valley, the narrow cleft, the springwater, and the connotation of the name of the cave with "doll" all point to the female nature of the place; while the shape of the cave itself described by Rich'd Pygge as "somewhat the shape of an egg" (p. 281) conclusively indicates its condition of *mandala*. The mandala, Jung tells us (ibid., p. 72), symbolizes "the feminine element, of the earth, the body, and matter in general, which were yet, in the form of Mary's womb, the sacred abode of the Deity and the indispensable instrument for the divine work of redemption" and, as a symbol of totality, expresses the only solution to the devastating conflict between matter and spirit originated by the rebellion of the Son against the Father. As Jung explains (ibid., p. 57),

> The goal of psychological, as of biological, development is self-realization, or individuation. But since man knows himself only as an ego, and the self, as a totality, is indescribable and indistinguishable from a God-image, self-realization—to put it in religious or metaphysical terms—amounts to God's incarnation . . . and because individuation is an heroic and often tragic task, the most difficult of all, it involves suffering. . . . The drama of the archetypal life of Christ described in symbolic images the events of the conscious life—as well as the life that transcends consciousness—of a man who has been transformed by his higher destiny.

With Jung's words in mind, the events that take place in Dolling's Cave on that 1 May 1736 acquire overall significance. Mr. B., the Christ figure at war with the Father, allows his instinctual half, Dick Thurlow, to lead him and Rebecca, his anima, to the womb of the Mother Earth. There he must find a new totality of the self by assimilating his instinctual animality and by acknowledging his female facet, knowing that this fight involves agonizing suffering but also the hope of rebirth, as Rebecca's ritual bath in the pool, her beautiful white dress, and her coronation as Queen of May indicate. It is in this sense that the huge floating maggot acquires a new meaning as a somewhat futuristic version of "the belly of the whale," while its satanic counterpart, the large gnawing maggot, stands for the coiled serpent, which symbolizes the danger of annihilation of the conscious, if the unconscious yields to the temptation of lingering forever in the darkness of the maternal womb.

Thus, the large gnawing maggot and the white celestial maggot synthesize the dual quality of the events that took place within the cave. Like Dylan Thomas's "long friends," these maggots are simultaneously repulsive and attractive, because they symbolize death and rebirth. In the myth, the maggot eats the king; the fish, the maggot; the fisherman, the fish, and so on forever and ever, creating the cosmic circle of life and death.[3]

In order to achieve its individuation, the ego must sacrifice its unconscious, obliging it to find its way to the surface again. In Christian terms this sacrifice, which amounts to the assimilation of the instinctual, is expressed with the symbol of God's crucifixion which, in an altered form, recasts, as Zöckler *(The Cross of Christ,* p. 241) long ago pointed out, the symbol of Adam's spiritual suicide brought about by the paradisiacal apple tree. Psychologically, this tree of life is a symbolic equivalent of the Mother, to whom the Son sacrifices his life, thus activating the archetypal idea of regeneration by re-entrance in the maternal womb, without falling into the danger of committing incest. Psychologically, then, the sacrifice of the Cross is a happy event, for it expresses the transformation of the shadow to the symbolic equivalent of the Mother, thus making possible the rebirth of the Son as God himself.

After the events in the cave, Mr. B. disappears and is searched for, exactly as Christ was searched for by his disciples. Henry Ayscough's inquiry about the whereabouts of Mr. B., reminiscent of the disciples' search for Christ, admits only one possible answer: "Why seek ye the living among the dead? He is not here" (Luke 24: 5f).

The same can be said of Dick's death. Following the mythical, religious, and psychological archetype with remarkable neatness, Dick comes out of the cave in utter discomfiture, in order to go to the heart of the Cleeve, to hang himself from a tree. There, with characteristic accuracy, John Fowles presents us with his corpse hanging from the tree of life, simultaneously dead and life-giving, as the little posy of violets apparently growing out of his mouth indubitably indicates:

> 'Twas a tuft torn up by its roots, stuffed in the poor man's mouth before he took his last leap, and still bloomed as green as on a bank. 'Twas taken as witchcraft, sir, by many. But the more learned say the plant took sustenance from the flesh, finding it soil at heart. (p. 73)

In mythical, religious, and psychological terms the self-inflicted death of the hero is not a sin, but on the contrary, the incontestable proof that the war between man and his shadow has been won by man, for only through self-torture and death can man achieve his individuation, can he be reborn as God himself.

Once the symbolic meaning of Dick's death and of Mr. B.'s disappearance is thoroughly grasped, the events that follow acquire an unavoidable logic, adjusting themselves to make up the whole design of the puzzle. In the satanic version, Rebecca's numinous experience is presented, in keeping with the old conception of *unio mystica* (Jung, "The Battle for Deliverance from the Mother," p. 287), as sexual intercourse. In the celestial version, her numinous experience is described as contact with the *lumen lumini,* with the *sapientia Dei* of Holy Mother Wisdom. In both versions, the numinous experience amounts to a *renovatio,* Jung's fourth form of rebirth or *Wiedergeburt* ("Concerning Rebirth," p. 114). Due to it, Rebecca loses both her physical and her spiritual barrenness, and undergoes an essential transformation, i.e., a rebirth as an individual.

Rebecca's daughter has been physically begotten by Dick (and by Satan), but has been spiritually fathered by Mr. B. (and Christ). Thus, the son becomes in turn father, and Rebecca acquires the category of *Theotokos,* of mother of a new Redeemer, who already has in her seed the essence of good and evil. In this sense, the birth of Ann Lee signifies the beginning of a new cycle, as she again breaks the newly achieved unity of her father, and places herself in the position of the rebellious daughter who must undertake a new process of individuation. Rebecca implicitly points to the cyclical nature of the archetype when she insists that her daughter is not Christ proper, but simply a witness whose role will be to pave the way for the Second Coming of a Christ she thinks of as a woman, in keeping with Shaker belief.

When Mr. B. explained to Francis Lacy the aim of his journey to Devon, he said literally that he was a disobedient son in search of a woman whom he compared to his bride and to his source of inspiration. After that, Mr. B. once and again tested the credulity of his fellow travellers by telling them a series of tales about the real aim of his journey. These tales can be described, as we have seen, as fanciful literary variations on a unique theme, which echo different eighteenth-century literary traditions. The fact that Mr. B. is capable of creating these literary variations himself, as well as his insistence that he has been offered a part in a history and is not forgiven for refusing to play it, qualifies the realistic as well as the psychological interpretations, adding to them a further perspective. Explaining to Francis Lacy his belief in predestination, Mr. B.

likened mankind to an audience in a playhouse who were not actors, and had no notion that they acted to fixed and written lines, and even less that behind the actors lay an author and a manager [and that] we were like the personages in a tale or novel that had no knowledge they were such; and thought ourselves most real, not seeing we were made of imperfect words and ideas, and to serve other ends. (pp. 149–50)

The comparison of mankind to an audience in a playhouse, taken, no doubt, by Francis Lacy and by Henry Ayscough, as simply a rhetorical license of Mr. B.'s, also admits, however, a more literal interpretation. Literally, Mr. B. selected two players and a prostitute reputed for her acting ability, removed them from the London theatre and the brothel where they respectively worked, and hired them to interpret still another role in *comoedia vitae* (p. 22). For himself Mr. B. reserved the role of manager, of baffling "impresario" like the dubious bearded fellow in *The French Lieutenant's Woman,* and even of *The Magus,* as his protean capacity to metamorphose and his decision to burn his books (as Conchis did) clearly indicate; but manager and magus with a difference, for Mr B. knows (as the other characters do not) that even behind himself there is still another manager and that he, like the rest, is "made of imperfect words and ideas, and to serve other ends."

So, to the realistic, to the mythical, and to the psychological levels, a fourth, literary, level has to be added, in which the revolt of the Son against the Father becomes the character's refusal to play the role allotted to him by the author. No matter whether we consider Mr. B. in realistic terms as the son of a Lord who has disappeared and has to be found, or as a Cambridge scholar involved in alchemical research, or as a mythical hero undertaking his heroic quest, or as a psychologically split ego who must cure his neurosis and find a new totality of the self; what he primarily is, is a literary character who has been asked to play all these roles within a fictional universe and who, for all the apparent freedom he seemed to have in devising the roles of the other characters, was conscious at heart of his radical bondage and of the fact that, for all his rebelliousness, he must comply and serve other ends, John Fowles's ends, no doubt.

From this perspective, Mr. B.'s final disappearance has to be interpreted (like that of the Tory M. P., John Marcus Fielding, in "The Enigma" *(The Ebony Tower,* pp. 185–239), as the rebellious character's affirmation of his freedom; that is, as a desperate attempt at disobeying "the unreal literary rules" ("The Enigma," p. 232) created for him by the author, by stepping out of the history, thus simultaneously killing himself as a character and becoming "the *Deus absconditus,* the God who went missing" ("The Enigma," p. 235).

Conclusion

In the introduction, I summarized the different trends at work in the contemporary English novel from the fifties onwards, tracing the steady evolution from the "angry" reaction against experimentalism in the 1950s to a new form of experimentation best described as an overriding concern with the nature of fiction and reality. This concern has led in recent decades to a new kind of experimental writing, characterized by its self-conscious and systematic concern with its own status as an artifact and with the relationships between fiction and reality.

This general scheme is perfectly applicable to the literary evolution of John Fowles, who, with his double training in English realism and French experimentalism, seems as concerned with writing about the real as he is determined to test and undermine the received conventions of literary realism.

The tension created by this double, paradoxical endeavor finds complex but consistent expression in his novels. John Fowles's stylistic versatility, his remarkable capacity to create different styles according to the different requirements of the subject matter of each novel, combined with his thorough knowledge of history, work to produce an overriding effect of realism; while his repeated parodying of well-worn literary traditions and his breaking all rules of literary decorum work to produce the contrary effect of highlighting the literary nature of the world created.

Kerry McSweeney's description ("Withering . . . ," p. 31) of John Fowles as "more an unfolding than a growing artist" points to a most important characteristic of the writer, for it underlines Fowles's unflinching tendency to take up the same topics in every novel, testing the thematic, the stylistic, and also the structural implications a bit further each time.

From the thematic point of view, every novel deals in one way or another with Fowles's major concern: human freedom, focused from two major perspectives. From the point of view of man in isolation, freedom is presented as a process of individuation of the self; from the point of view of man in relation to society, as a power-bondage relationship.

Following Heraclitus's theory of the Many *(hoi polloi)*, the masses, the untaught, and the Few *(hoi aristoi)*, the elect, the chosen and civilized, Fowles explains in *The Aristos* his belief that the status of the Few is a privileged one they have got through mere good luck, both socially and genetically. Consequently, for him, being an *aristos* means not so much that you are entitled to exert power on the less privileged, but rather that you are in "a state of responsibility" (p. 10) with respect to the masses.

In *The Collector*, Frederick Clegg, the representative of the Many, is a collector; Miranda, the prototypical *aristos*, an art student. In every novel by John Fowles, collecting and creating turn into activities symbolic of two basic attitudes to life to be found simultaneously in every balanced man: the collector is *l'homme moyen sensuel*, the intrinsic materialist, a man who only lives to satisfy his senses, watching, touching, possessing. So the collector is the least imaginative of men, for in order to exist he must tangibly possess the objects that obsess him, while the creator rejects this material reality and uses his imagination to create his own subjective alternatives to it.

From *The Magus* onwards, the immature *aristos* is invariably described as a collector: Nicholas d'Urfé collects "girlfriends" and the young Conchis birdsounds; Charles Smithson, ammonites; Daniel Martin and his friend Anthony, orchids. Consequently, "learning" for them always implies the rejection of their collecting activities. Those who are unable to overcome this tendency, like Frederick Clegg in *The Collector* or Alphonse de Deukans in *The Magus*, are unbalanced or even mentally deranged—as unbalanced as, at the other extreme of the spectrum, Miles Green, the hero of *Mantissa*, a writer reduced to his mental activity of creating literary worlds, and suffering from total amnesia with regard to the material universe.

The struggle between collectors and creators; the teaching of the young by the mature *aristos;* and the use and abuse of power, are all subjects John Fowles touches on and develops along different lines in his novels. Whether the hero is confronted with a Prospero-like figure, a magus who either exerts power over him (or her) in order to teach him, as is the case with Nicholas Urfe with Conchis, or with Miranda with G. P.; or who confirms the route taken, as does Herr Professor Otto Kirnberger with Daniel Martin; whether he has to face, like Charles Smithson, or like Miles Green, a mysterious woman, pursuing her own, unimaginable ends; or whether he has to revolt against his father, as does Mr. Bartholomew, the result of the confrontation always takes the form of *anagnorisis*, a cathartic discovery of the utter isolation of man and of the remoteness of God. At this stage, the hero suffers an agonizing phase of deterministic despair, as he apprehends the existentialist void or its equivalent. But as soon as he masters his angst, and accepts the void, he is seized by *une joie de vivre*, a *delirium vivens*, the passion to exist that comes together with the realization that man is radically free to choose even death, as Conchis or Dick

Thurlow do. This realization of personal freedom, which is presented in psychological terms, brings about the hero's "individuation" and often follows the discovery of the polymorphous nature of reality.

The assumption that man must seek his freedom in order to mature and that reality is complex and many-sided, made up not only of the ontologically real but also of the imagined, not only of the actual, but also of the potentially possible, not only of what is or was, but also of what might have been, are perhaps the two basic messages John Fowles wants us to distill from his novels. These messages are to be found not only at the thematic level, but are also echoed and reflected structurally.

From the structural point of view, each novel works to affirm the polymorphous nature of reality by different means: by presenting two or more opposed, utterly divergent but also complementary worlds enjoying the same status; by the alternation of narrative voices; the shifts of time and space; the multiplication of realistic, mythical, psychological, and literary versions of the same events; and through the parodic use of well-known literary conventions. Indeed, from *The Collector* onwards, each novel consciously assumes and parodies one—or more—traditional novel-writing conventions, but as we move from *The Collector* to *A Maggot* we also move from a fiction that is predominantly realistic to a much more boldly experimental and specifically metafictional kind of fiction, for, even though in *Daniel Martin* Fowles seemed determined to adhere to the canons of realism, the novel naturally moves to the metafictional pole, affirming, along with the other novels, the importance of the psychological and of the literary aspects of reality.

In *The Collector,* John Fowles offers us two complementary versions of the events—Frederick Clegg's "objective" first-person account counterbalanced and undermined by Miranda's much more literary version recorded in her diary—and forces us to accept them as part of a unique whole by interrupting Clegg's narrative midway in order to have us read Miranda's diary, a diary Miranda has hidden under the mattress of her bed in the prison-cellar where it is likely to remain for ages after her death, unless Clegg himself finds it, and allows us access to it through his mind and eyes.

In the last entry of her diary, Miranda lapses from the preterite into the present tense. Being a metadiscourse within the main one, Miranda's present is included within Clegg's story time, so that the time of her narrative and the time of her story coincide in her present, though with reference to Clegg's narration they have taken place in the past. When Clegg's diegesis and narration overlap in the present, however, his present can only be measured with reference to our own present. Thus, when narrative and story time coincide at the end of the novel we realize with a pang that we are not dealing with the confession of a remote crime, but with the account of some horribly near experience that shows signs of intending to stretch into the future, threatening not only Marian, the next victim, but also the reader. The compression of narrative and story time in a pregnant present is a device John Fowles uses again in the following novels. With it he structurally expresses his existentialist conception of time as a succession of "nows," which precludes knowledge of the future.

In *The Collector,* Miranda intuits that it is possible to destroy her awful reality by striving to create a fictional alternative to it with her diary. In *The Magus* this alternative world is a reality so tangible that the hero, Nicholas Urfe, is able to bodily cross its boundaries and physically enter its realm. Again, the structure of the novel neatly echoes its message.

Structurally, the novel *The Magus* may be said to follow a circular development involving three major stages: from London to Phraxos and back to London again. At the narrative level, the overall structure of *The Magus,* like that of *The Collector,* can be seen as linear, by virtue of the discourse narrated by Nicholas Urfe. Within this linear development, the central episodes corresponding to his visits to Bourani disrupt the linear development by the introduction of a second narrator: at Bourani Nicholas sometimes hands over the narrative role to Maurice Conchis, who in his turn narrates his own life-story to Nicholas Urfe.

Conchis's narration, like Miranda's, is to be considered as a metadiscourse engulfed by the primary narration, although the stories Conchis narrates refer to episodes of his own life and so must be viewed as retrospective heterodiegetic digressions, that is, as digressive anachronies related only analogically to the diegesis. At the end of the novel, a third narrator identifiable with the implied author omnisciently comments in two metalepses on the moral of the whole novel, thus adding to the discourse and the metadiscourse a third, ontological level.

Unlike the mythical hero, Nicholas Urfe undergoes at Bourani a series of trials exclusively intended to test and improve his perception of reality. If Nicholas is to mature, he must learn to distrust his senses and to foster his imagination. So the quality of the hero's quest is wholly fictional and psychological, and is carried out by means of three major literary tests: first, he has to participate in the metatheater, an allegorical masque consisting of two devices— portrait-like staging of iconic scenes by secondary actors, and performance of the *Three Hearts* story by Urfe himself and the twin sisters. Secondly, he hears the narration of Conchis's life-story; and thirdly he is made to listen to a series of tales with a moral, such as "The Tale of the Swiss and the Goats" or "The Tale of the Prince and the Magician."

From a thematic point of view, the situation Urfe has lived with Alison in England, the situation he is living with Lily at Bourani, and the situation Conchis describes when he narrates his life-story bear clear-cut analogies, so much so that both the metadiscourse and the metatheater may be considered as inverted *mises en abyme* of the primary discourse. Indeed, the function of the masque at Bourani is to enact materially the morals encapsulated in the iconic tales and in Conchis's life-story, in order to provide a concrete realization of the theoretical lessons imparted by them. Thus, for example, after Conchis has spoken of his long-deceased fiancée, Lily appears at the villa. Quite accurately, Nicholas himself interprets the incidents as devices "designated to deceive all his senses" (p. 143). As we learn later, Lily's role in the masque is meant to convince Urfe of the fact that it is possible to touch a woman who only exists in his imagination.

Structurally, then, if we take the main story (Alison and Nicholas) to represent the material, and the masque (Lily and Nicholas), the psychological aspects of reality, and Conchis's story (Lily and Conchis), the inverted mirror image of the first, we may understand *The Magus* as one tale containing three variations of the same story told from complementary perspectives which, when mixed, offer a polymorphous unique whole of a literary character. The fact that it is so difficult to separate these three theoretically different "variations" in practice points to one important structural characteristic of the novel: namely that the *mises en abyme* it contains are not "concentrating" but, on the contrary, are *mises en abyme éclatées,* that is, *mises en abyme* whose elements appear scattered and intertwined with the elements of the main story and with the elements of each other, forming an inextricable unity.

At the very end of the novel, the narrator-author, breaking the rules of narrative decorum, takes over the narration to comment in a gnomic present on the insecure future of the hero. As he had already done in *The Collector,* John Fowles suddenly removes the gap between narrative and story time, to leave his hero and heroine in a *frozen present.* Alison and Nicholas frozen in an eternal present is John Fowles's verbal icon for the final truth he has tried to develop through the whole novel, namely that, for the contemporary existentialist hero, the aim of the quest is the quest itself.

Thus, in *The Magus,* the changes of intro-homodiegetic narrators and the metaleptic intrusions of the extra-heterodiegetic narrator-author work to confirm the thematic assertion that reality is polymorphous and that the boundaries between fiction and nonfiction are easily crossed and so, by implication, wholly artificial.

In *The French Lieutenant's Woman* John Fowles carries the game a step further, denying even the existence of these fragile barriers. In this novel, the contemporary "real" world of the twentieth-century heterodiegetic narrator is meant to set a contrast to the "fictional" Victorian world of the diegesis. In order to accommodate his narration to the Victorian convention, the narrator assumes the role of omniscience and sustains it with minor frame-breaks up to the beginning of chapter 13, where his answer to the rhetorical question which closes chapter 12, "Where is Sarah. Out of what shadows does she come?" (p. 84), acts as a major frame-break, shattering to its foundations the illusion of realism created so far: "I do not know. The story I'm telling is all imagination" (p. 85).

After this first major frame-break, the narrator toys with the convention: he corrects himself, confesses his ignorance about certain matters, admits that he is inventing them, and blurs the boundaries between fiction and reality by including historical figures like Hitler or Dante Gabriel Rossetti within the diegesis. Finally, he even allows himself to appear in the story in the flesh, first facing Charles Smithson in a train, and later on tossing a coin to help himself decide which of the two endings he has selected for his novel he will narrate first.

In this example, as in many others to be found throughout the novel, the narrator uses the Victorian convention of the omniscient narrator parodically. Robert Burden ("The Novel Interrogates Itself . . . ," p. 135) has defined parody as "a mode of imitation in subversive form," while pastiche is defined as "a nonsubversive form of imitation." These definitions of parody and pastiche may explain the major frame-breaks in the novels of John Fowles as well as the overriding use of traditional conventions: the "confession" and "diary" conventions in *The Collector;* the pattern of the mythical hero's quest in *The Magus,* in *Daniel Martin,* and in *A Maggot;* the Victorian convention of omniscience, and the thematic indebtedness to Victorian romance in *The French Lieutenant's Woman.* They also may explain the use of seemingly eighteenth-or nineteenth-century styles; the telling of tales; the literal quotations; the wealth of literary allusions, both to past and to contemporary literature: the echoes of Shakespeare, of Richardson and Defoe, of Jane Austen and Hardy, of T. S. Eliot and, in a word, every possible sort of imitation, enhancing the fictionality of the worlds created and expressing conscious indebtedness to the bulk of the Western literary tradition as a whole.

The inclusion of the implied author and of historical figures and events in the diegesis of *The French Lieutenant's Woman* are meant to blur the boundaries between fictional and ontological reality. The narration of three different endings (one imagined by Charles Smithson, and two others selected by the narrator) function to enhance the existentialist conviction that the future of man is not predetermined, but depends on successive acts of the will.

As in *The French Lieutenant's Woman,* in *Daniel Martin* a basic contrast is drawn between two worlds. In the later novel, the English world of Daniel's childhood and university years in the 1940s and 1950s is set in contrast with the American, movie-star world of his mature age in the 1970s. But, again, the English world endlessly transforms itself, as the adult narrator recalls particular episodes of it. To match the ever-changing nature of his past, the voice of the narrator simultaneously changes: he tells the story of his childhood and youth at Thorncombe and Oxford in the third person and in the preterite, but lapses into the first person and the present tense whenever he digresses about his recent past or present, and even sometimes in the middle of his reported memories. At the same time, he pretends to be writing an autobiographical novel about a fictional character called Simon Wolfe, while his girlfriend, Jenny McNeil, writes her own divergent and complementary version of the same story.

Following the pattern of *The Magus,* Daniel Martin undertakes a climactic journey at two different levels. On the one hand, the journey is an ontologically real trip from California through New York to England, and then Egypt and Palmyra, ending up in England again. On the other, it is a psychological quest for individuation, made up of Daniel Martin's flashbacks to his childhood and early adulthood in England. When, at the end of the novel, Daniel Martin and Jane are left at Oxford, exactly at the point where they had taken the wrong fork of the road twenty-six years before, the psychological and the ontological journeys fuse into each other in an all-enveloping "now," similar to the pregnant "nows" reached at the end of *The Collector,* of *The Magus,* and of *The French Lieutenant's Woman.*

In *A Maggot* the contrast of opposed and complementary worlds is set between the twentieth-century world of the heterodiegetic narrator-cum-chronicler and the eighteenth-century world of the fictional mother of Ann Lee, the historical founder of the Shakers. If the Gothic historical romance and the Victorian multiplot novel provide the patterns for parody in *The French Lieutenant's Woman, A Maggot* combines echoes of eighteenth-century edifying prose; of the sentimental and of the gothic novel, as of the genuine judicial reports made by Defoe and other early journalists on the confessions of convicts at Newgate. In the novel, the confessions are interspersed with diverse eighteenth-century genuinely historical chronicles from *The Gentleman's Magazine,* which further show John Fowles's relish in the use not only of parody but also of deliberate pastiche, and which again warns us against the temptation to separate the ontological from the fictional.

Although in *A Maggot* the eighteenth-century world is described with remarkable wealth and accuracy of detail, the novel simultaneously affirms its radical twentieth-century character. Matching the ontological, the psychological, and the literary layers described for *The Magus,* which find their counterpart in the simultaneous movement backwards and forwards of the ontological and of the psychological hero's quest in *Daniel Martin, A Maggot* offers the reader a rationalist, a metaphysical, and a psychological version of the events narrated which, although apparently existing in order to cancel each other out, actually work to affirm the possibility of their co-existence on a fourth, all-enveloping literary level.

The polymorphous nature of reality thus stated, it is easy to see that it not only affects the material and the psychological universe of the protagonists, but the protagonists themselves: in Fowles's novels, every man or woman contains within him or herself a number of divergent and complementary potentialities which must be discovered, comprehended, and fostered. Daniel Martin's infinite mirrored faces express his condition of creator, like Conchis's and Mr. B.'s ever-changing identities; and, from *The Magus* onwards, every heroine of John Fowles has in herself a duality of character that continuously baffles the hero: Alison's oxymoronic quality is expressed as the splitting into twin characters (Lily and Rose) in the metatheater; as their names indicate in the Victorian convention, Lily is spiritual and virginal, Rose down-to-earth and sexually aggressive.

This archetypal dichotomy of woman will reappear in "The Ebony Tower," where the Mouse stands for the ideal and the Freak for the real; in *The French Lieutenant's Woman,* where Sarah is alternatively seen as an innocent, virginal maiden, and as a succuba; in *Daniel Martin,* in the parodically Victorian "Heavenly Twins" Nell and Jane; in the "Fairy Sisters" Marjory and Miriam; and in Nancy Reed's twin sisters Mary and Louise; in *Mantissa,* in the splitting of the muse into Dr. Delfie a Nurse Cory; and in *A Maggot,* where Rebecca Hocknell, also known as Fanny and Louise, a barren prostitute, mysteriously transforms herself into a pious visionary and the mother of a religious reformer.

Summing up the ideas discussed so far, we can say that if for Miranda the material reality had to be obliterated by a conscious effort of the imagination; if for Nicholas Urfe it was possible to walk in and out of the fictional world at will; and if for the narrator of *The French Lieutenant's Woman* these barriers did not seem to exist, for Daniel Martin the Cartesian proposition has become "I create, I am: all the rest is dream, though concrete and executed" (p. 236).

It is no wonder, then, that in the following novel, *Mantissa,* John Fowles should write a novel about the writing of a novel by a writer whose notion of reality is restricted to the workings of his mind. Doing away with ontological reality as a whole, *Mantissa* offers the reader a psychological reality in which space is restricted to the inside of Martin Green's skull, and time to a present devoid of past or future, exclusively filled by the obsessive skirmishes of muse and writer about the only possibly topic: how to write still one more variation of a unique, all-enveloping and life-generating text.

With the publication of *Mantissa* the contest inaugurated with *The Collector* between fact and fiction, between the tangible and the imaginary or, in Fowles's terms, between the English realistic pull and the French experimental temptation, is finally resolved in favor of metafiction. The publication of *A Maggot,* one year later, with its display of historical data and its wealth of realistic detail, apparently a pendular swing backwards from experimentalism into realism, similar to the one attempted in *Daniel Martin,* constitutes nevertheless—like *Daniel Martin* itself—a most radical study in the difficulty of separating the mental from the actual, "what might have been" from "what has been," the real from the unreal, and so thoroughly confirms Fowles's steady course in the direction of metafiction.

Although published after *The Collector, The Magus* is, as is well known, the first novel written by John Fowles. For years the writer had trouble with this novel, rewriting it once and again. One reason for Fowles's dissatisfaction with it might be attributed to the enormous scope and range of this novel, which may be said to sum up his whole vision of the world. So many and so important are the ideas Fowles compressed in this novel that he has spent twenty more years developing aspects of them in his subsequent fiction. When, for example, Daniel Martin exultantly cries "I create, I am" and decides to accommodate his life to this dictum, he is only discovering something Nicholas Urfe had already intuited when he affirmed, "Not *cogito,* but *scribo, pingo, ergo sum*" (p. 58). And when in *A Maggot* Mr. B. burns his books in order to direct the actors he himself has hired, he is only putting into practice, of his own accord, the lesson Maurice Conchis wanted Urfe to take in; namely, that in order to mature, man has to become his own *magus.* The fact that Nicholas needed somebody to open his eyes, whereas Mr. B. did not, proves that after a long, painful process of refinement John Fowles's unique hero has reached the kind of superior understanding about the human condition that is sought for by all religions and which implies, in Buddhist terms, the rejection of *"lilas,* the pursuit of triviality" *(The Magus,* p. 306).

At a surface level, the word "maggot," like the word "mantissa," may be said to evoke precisely the kind of triviality expressed by the Buddhist concept of *lilas.* At a deeper level, however, "the maggot" symbolizes, as we have seen, the cyclical movement of life and death which, visualized in the *mandala,* sums up, in archetypal terms, the basic pattern of the self's struggle into being.

Explaining the meaning of "maggot" in the preface of the novel, John Fowles said that he had written it "out of obsession with a theme" (p. 5). We might take the author's statement literally for, as I hope to have shown in my analysis of the novels, not only *A Maggot* but every one of the six full-length novels so far written by John Fowles depicts, beneath the profusion of contradictory data, alternative versions, and literary references, a major concern with one single theme, iconically expressed in the archetypal meaning of the word "maggot"—namely, the essence and purpose of human existence.

Being a twentieth-century agnostic, John Fowles time and again has expressed his need for human transcendence in the only terms available: through the kind of archetypal symbolism that Jung presented as the contemporary alternative to pre-rationalist myth and religion. The archetypal quality of Mr. B.'s journey is what confers on him his representative character.

His struggle for individuation synthesizes the never-ending striving not only of every John Fowles's hero, but of every man. The fact that this striving is presented as cyclical and progressive (that is, as endlessly yielding Christ-figures like Ann Lee, ready to take up the amelioration of mankind at the point where it was left in the preceding cycle), may be taken as evidence that John

Fowles has finally reached beyond the hopelessness of existentialism in order to affirm a certain faith in a capacity for progressive improvement, not only of the individual, but of the human species at large.

However, undermining this hope, the doubt still remains as to whether Mr. B. stands for every man or whether John Fowles still holds the existentialist belief that general truths are mere illusions, that each individual has to work out his own salvation for himself, for, encapsulated in his own particularity, he is utterly alone. Or again, expressed in John Fowles's own terms, whether man is really free to aspire to and eventually to achieve the divine status of the Father, or whether his freedom is only an illusion made to appear temporarily real within a wholly unreal, literary world, ironically created by the power of John Fowles's magic wand.

Appendix

Fowles on Fowles

John Fowles Interviewed by Susana Onega

It is not every day that we have the opportunity to listen to a writer speaking about his work. This act is, then, in itself a very special occasion, which becomes a real event when the writer in question is one of the greatest living English novelists and one who, like his male protagonists, values his privacy so much.

Readers of his novels have often stressed his protean quality, his astounding capacity to create different styles according to the different requirements of the subject matter of each novel; they have also often drawn attention to his fertile imagination, and his unusual ability to blend personal experience with fantasy, giving his novels a mythical scope. By virtue of his art, the countries he describes in his novels, whether exotic, like Greece or Egypt, or familiar, like England or the United States, invariably acquire a special quality, the timeless, changeless beauty and power of the land of romance or myth.

The best justification I can find for having temporarily drawn him away from his garden in Dorset and his work is the hope that the love he has always felt for the eastern Mediterranean countries may extend to include Spain, despite the hazards of walking down Las Ramblas on a Sunday afternoon. And, who knows, such a prosaic place as the scene of a national conference may some day be immortalized as the setting for some deeply engaging plot.

Ladies and gentlemen, it is an extraordinary pleasure and honor for me to introduce to you Mr. John Fowles and to give him our warmest welcome.

I have lots of questions I would like to ask you, as, I expect, many people in the audience have. I shall start with a question of my own but anyone who wants should feel free to take part at any moment.

In an interview published in *Counterpoint* in 1968 you placed Frederick Clegg, the protagonist of *The Collector,* at the end of the line of "angry young

This interview originally appeared in Actas del X Congreso Nacional de A.E.D.E.A.N., 1988, pp. 57–76.

men" which starts with *Lucky Jim*. Have you ever thought of yourself as a member of "The Movement"?

John Fowles: Could I please start by saying that if we had been in China I should get up now and clap you back. It is lovely for any novelist, even something of a hermit or a recluse like myself, to see such an audience as this. I have been in Spain before but it is very pleasant to be back again, after a long interval in my case.

Angry young men. I was never really an Angry Young Man myself and I do not think I could be put into that movement. If we are talking about it in general, I am grateful that it did happen. The typical novelist, I suppose, of that movement was Alan Sillitoe, of whom I spoke rather badly in one of my novels, but that was because of the needs of the novel. It was not really my personal opinion. The Movement had an important effect in the English theater and the English cinema; it was really a kind of "cleaning" of English art in general, and a valuable one, working-class in its inspiration and with a tiredness for all the old classical ways of English thinking about the arts. It was like a kind of minor fire in a house and it burnt some rooms which needed burning. I come from a small town in Dorset which had a bad fire a hundred years ago. The fire is now regarded as a blessing; it completely destroyed the abominable poor quarter of the town. Things that are tragedies in one way can be very beneficial in another.

The trouble with the Angry Young Men is that unfortunately, because I am really a socialist of a kind by conviction, there is a richness in the middle classes and the middle-class field of life, for the novelist especially, that confining yourself to the working-class view of life, the proletarian one, rather restricts. This was the case with Alan Sillitoe, for example; another English novelist, David Storey, is another case. They tended to get themselves into a corner and found they lacked a richness of subject. This I regard as less political than biological; it is just for me that, perhaps unfairly, the middle classes lead richer, wider lives. This will not satisfy any Marxists or Communists who are here today but the Angry Young Men are for me a historical movement. It performed a useful function but now it is over. It is not a phrase you hear any more in contemporary discussions of English literature.

Susana Onega: In an interview with Lorna Sage you talked about a tension in your work, an opposed pull between the English, realistic tradition, and your French, experimental background. What are the basic ideas you have accepted from each and to what extent have they conditioned your literary evolution?

John Fowles: When I was much younger I taught in a French university for a year and I was supposed to teach English there. Now I was a disaster as a lecturer at that university because I really knew nothing about English literature. I did know a little, I had been to Oxford and had studied French literature and I knew French novels and that country historically quite well, but when I suddenly had to get up and start talking about Shelley, Keats, Byron, and Rupert

Brooke, whatever was on the French syllabus in the English Faculty, I was absolutely at sea. I ought never to have been appointed. In fact, at the end of that year the university said goodbye to me with no regrets at all.

I then went to Greece, and the school in Greece where I taught also said goodbye to me at the end of my stay there—in other words, I was sacked, or fired. That was for rather different reasons but I think, in general, it is quite good for novelists to have failures like that early in life. What you have to do if you are to be a novelist is *not* to be a teacher.

There is a theory in England that if you want to be a novelist—and it is even stronger in the United States—that all would-be writers go "on campus." They go to university and they do not earn their living from books, they earn it from some job they have in a university. I think teaching is a very bad thing for a creative writer to do, if we are talking about it as a career, and whenever young novelists in England say, "What advice have you got?," I always say, "Anything, but don't be a teacher." It is curious because obviously teaching a language with its literature and writing might seem to be parallel and close activities, but in some ways teaching literature is a very bad basis for actually writing or creating literature. This is why you do not get many professors of literature who are really good writers in a creative sense. There have been one or two. We have two famous professors of English in England at the moment who are also good writers. One is Malcolm Bradbury and the other is David Lodge, but they are exceptions to the rule. There have been one or two in America, too. Lionel Trilling in America was a famous critic and teacher of English as well as a novelist, but on the whole you do not learn to write books by being good at analyzing them and explaining them. That may seem strange to you, but, believe me, it is true.

Susana Onega: Do you think every novelist, even the most experimental one, should write only about things and places he has firsthand knowledge of? Or to put it another way, do you think that real life experience is as necessary as genius?

John Fowles: I think for the young writer it is important. I am greatly in favor because I am an internationalist by spirit. I think it is very important for young writers, I would say for all young people really, to travel. I traveled a lot when I was young, but I am now at an age when I have a little bit of that complacent syndrome, I have seen everything and I have read everything. This is a danger when you get to my age. I am sixty years old at the moment. You think you have travelled everywhere and you will get no new experiences, but this is not true, as I have just learnt in Spain *[S. O.: Yes, Las Ramblas, unfortunately]*. It is really more than that. I am at the moment thinking, no more than tossing around in my mind, an idea for a new novel and I find coming to Spain lovely and fertile for the writer. All feeds in, objects you see suddenly attract you and you think, "My goodness, I could use that!" or "That's something I must remember." So, this is why I am always persecuting my very kind hosts here about strange words I see, or habits. Novelists are magpies and steal objects if they can. We really have to be magpies, and amass masses of information we will never put in our books and perhaps will never use. If you have a novelist's mind it is rather like owning a junk room in a house or an old *brocante,* an old second-hand dealer's. In some way you have got to have this room full of old furniture, in our case events and characters, characters you have never developed. Then suddenly one day you feel there will be a place for such and such a character or event. This, I think, is one important way we really are very very different from professors, teachers of English. I feel I am a sheep among goats here in Zaragoza, or a goat among sheep. A novelist is truly very different from an expert on literature. We do not have to have ordered minds, we do not have to know Derrida or Barthes or the great theorists backwards, we have very loose ideas, a mass of mixed information that is really of no use to us or anybody else, but we have to carry round our minds stuffed with these facts. You have to have a private treasury, a house which is full of objects or memories that one day may be useful, may be useful, you may use them, or they may disappear and sink out of sight. It is by writing like this that we get an important response with that other person the reader. The novelist does not have a relationship with readers, in the plural. We have to remember it is always with one reader and that reader you have to tickle as you "tickle" a trout, you have to evoke a world, to tease their emotions. You are appealing in most novels, I think, to the corresponding junk-room nature of the reader's mind from your own. It is not by theory, by logic, by order, as a rule, that you establish this communion with this one reader who is your brother or sister in the experience of reading a book.

Susana Onega: You have often explained that some of your novels developed from a single image: The French Lieutenant's Woman, *for example, developed from the image of a woman standing on the quay at Lyme Regis, and looking out over a rough sea; or* The Collector, *from a piece of news in the papers about the kidnapping of a young woman who was held prisoner in an air-raid shelter in London. Did any of the other novels also originate in a similar way?*

John Fowles: It used to happen to me by something like a cinema "still." I used to get one vision. In another novel, one of my favorite novels in fact, *Daniel Martin,* I did have an image that in the novel is at the very end of the book. It was of a woman standing in a desert somewhere. I did not at that time even know where it was. She seemed to be weeping, to be lost, a moment of total desolation. It is from tiny images like that, very like cinema stills, say good Buñuel stills or Eisenstein stills, the way they can evoke the whole film even though there is only one frame, one picture . . . and that seems to have some effect on me. I do not think this is true of many novelists . . . it is just a peculiarity of my own. I am a visual person in other ways, I would normally much rather go to an art gallery than sit on a literary discussion. Pictures have always spoken to me, in emotional terms anyway, and I think that is all I can answer.

Susana Onega: In The French Lieutenant's Woman *the narrator protests that he cannot control his characters, and that once created, they are free to choose what they do; if you agree with your narrator, the obvious conclusion is that you do not have a preconceived plan when you start writing a novel, that you haven't decided the ending beforehand. Is that right?*

John Fowles: Yes. Again please remember this is one person speaking to you and that you must not take this as applying to all novelists. I know others do write to carefully preconceived, prepared plans, and if you read books on how to write a novel, usually they will say, "Make a careful plan and keep to it." I am completely different. I am, I suppose, a wanderer or a rambler. *The Rambler* was a famous eighteenth-century periodical in England and the title has always attracted me. The wanderer, the person who strolls and deviates through life. I always think the notion of the fork in the road is very important when you are creating narrative, because you are continually coming to forks. Now, if you write to an elaborate, prepared plan, the choice is taken out of your hands, your plan says you must take this fork to the right, you must take this fork to the left, but I do not like that. I like, in the actual business of writing, this feeling that you do not know where you are going. You have in this to know deep principles or feelings that guide you very loosely, but on the actual page you often do not know when a scene is going to end, how it is going to end, or, if you end it in one way, is it going to change the future of the book. This, you see, is a state of uncertainty, or in terms of the modern physics, indeterminacy. . . . You are never quite sure where the concrete facts and characters that the narrative develops in a book are going to lead. You sometimes have extraordinary mornings and these are the only times in my life when I would, very modestly, claim a genius. That is when ideas flow in on you with such force that very often you cannot write them down, they come so fast, in my case often fragments of dialogue, so fast that you literally cannot write them down. They are very rare, these moments; you pray for them, you can't create them in any way, they just come; and I have noticed, rather oddly, usually when you are feeling ill and depressed. I do not know whether you know the French religious philosopher Pascal, but Pascal once had a religious experience like this which he could never describe. He just had to say "Fire! Fire! Fire!" He means "I was flooded with fire and it was beyond description." Very occasionally you have these feelings, almost visions, when you see the whole book. You see all sorts of developments and these moments give you an extraordinary feeling of euphoria, of happiness. Very often later on, when you look at things you have scribbled down frantically, you realize they were nonsense, but usually you get one or two grains, sometimes much more, that are important in your book. This is another distinction between creative writers, poets, and teachers of literature. These are not rational moments, they are much more shamanistic. A shaman, if you remember, in Stone Age and earlier times, was a kind of tribal magician, a tribal priest. Somebody in England at the moment, a writer called Nicholas Humphreys, who is really a zoologist, he studies animal behavior, has recently written a book suggesting that playwrights, poets, novelists can all be associated with the notion of the shaman speaking both to and for the tribe.

Susana Onega: But if this is so, how do you explain the structural perfection of your novels?

John Fowles: I do not think they are perfect.

Susana Onega: Yes, for instance, the symmetrical embedding of Miranda's and Clegg's complementary narrations in The Collector. *This cannot happen by chance. Or can it?*

John Fowles: Well, perhaps I could answer rather obliquely. There are two stages in writing a novel; there are many stages but there are two broad ones. One is the slightly shamanistic first draft. To say that one is inspired by the muses, as they used to in the eighteenth century, is ridiculous, but this is an area where you have to suppress the teacher, the censor, the critical part of you. Many very clever people linguistically cannot write novels because you have to learn to be two people. One has to be innocent, self-hypnotized, and the other has to be very stern and objective, a kind of professor of himself. I once had a letter from America from an American student who said, "Dear Mr. Fowles, I understand you are something of an expert on the fiction of John Fowles." Now that amused and interested me, because he obviously thought there must be two different people. One was a kind of unofficial professor of John Fowles and there was this other chap, Mr. Fowles, who he had to write to. But that schizophrenia he had, you need yourself. In that second period or self you have to be very stern, you have to have your blue pencil in hand. The old rule in English is, if you are going through a page of your own prose, the first thing you strike out is what you think is the best sentence in it. There is some sense in that. You very often get so attracted by one single phrase or sentence that you cannot see it is distorting the whole page, or even a chapter. The best solution is often to drop it.

Susana Onega: Thank you. And the open endings of The Magus *and of* The French Lieutenant's Woman *aren't meant to echo the thesis of the novels that the existentialist hero's quest is the quest itself?*

John Fowles: Yes, I was when I was younger, when I was well below half of my present age, we all were in England at that time . . . we were on our knees before Camus and Sartre and French existentialism. It was not because we truly understood it but we had a kind of notion, a dream of what it was about. Most of us were victims of it. I quite like that philosophy as a structure in a novel and in a sense I still use it. I would not say now that I am any longer an existentialist in the social sense, the cultural sense. I am really much more interested, in terms of the modern novel, in what fiction is about. I read quite recently most of Italo Calvino, the Italian novelist. That had a considerable effect on me because I felt he was doing what I am trying to do, or what I have tried to do. We writers are of course always slightly jealous and envious of each other and we can stab each other in the back very often, but there are some writers with whom you feel a brotherhood, a fraternal or even sisterly feeling, and Calvino is one of those. I feel great sympathy for Márquez, too, for Borges, the whole South American influence on the current European novel. I think this is for me the major influence on fiction today. It is much more important than that of Beckett or the black novel, the absurdist novel, and also the existentialist novels, Sartre's theater and so on. I really feel that has passed, that is gone.

Susana Onega: In The Collector, The Magus, *and* The French Lieutenant's Woman *the heroes are invariably left in a "frozen present," but this is not so in* Daniel Martin. *Would you say that the happy ending at the end of this novel expresses your jump beyond existentialism?*

John Fowles: Well, this is slightly difficult. When I was writing that book I had got very fed up, very displeased with the whole black, absurdist strain in European literature. I do sincerely admire Beckett as a writer, but I suppose Beckett would be the obvious representative of that, Ionesco and so on. I suddenly felt, "This novel I am going to end happily," and believe me, in our age it is a difficult thing to force yourself to do because the whole drift of modern intellectual European life is that life is hell, it is absurd, it is tragic, there are no happy endings. God knows it has been tragic in a very literal sense, but I somehow thought I would like to end the book happily, just as the Victorian novelists did. The Victorian novelists often tied themselves in knots so that they could have a happy ending, but I felt I would like to try that in a modern British novel. *Daniel Martin* was very much against Britain because, like all good English writers, I hate many aspects of my country. It seemed right somehow that at least it should end happily when I had said so many things against Britain, and America also, incidentally. It was a very anti–Anglo-Saxon book.

Susana Onega: The hero, Daniel Martin, finally decides to give up script-writing in order to write a novel, after he has succeeded in recovering the love of Jane: are love and creativity the two antidotes against the void?

John Fowles: Well, love, obviously, I should have thought. But creativity, you see, is so unkind. I mean, we can talk about how good democracy enhances many things, but, as I know from the manuscripts I get from other would-be writers, very often they are very handicapped. They have defects of body, or of mind, or of career, they have had to leave school early or whatever it is. Clearly life is cruel, you can only say, "I have sympathy for your problem." But when it comes to actually judging the novel, I am afraid aesthetic justice is without feeling. You have to say, "You can't write" or "This is badly written" or "This is a cliché." Only the Marxists allow clichés, political in their case, to count. Really, I do not know how you deal with this, but there are points when you have to say to people, "You can't write," "You can't think," or even more important, "You can't imagine," because this is a part of the human mind we know very little about: why some people can imagine vividly and why some people can organize that imagination, because creation does need a certain amount of organization. Why some people can do these things and also learn to suppress themselves, because novelists cannot do everything they like. You soon learn when you write novels that you are in a prison. I do not deny for a moment I am in a prison when I am writing a book, but it is really like being in a prison that is perhaps six-by-four and you think, "How could I make it a little bit larger?," perhaps seven-by-five. In other words, you try to create a little bit of freedom, as a prisoner might do in prison circumstances. It can be intolerable when you are writing a novel, when you know you are in this cell, you do not know how to get out of it. Occasionally the escape attempts are what makes the novel, you have got yourself into a kind of fixed code, a fixed theorem, like a geometrical theorem, and it is escaping from that which, I think, often produces remarkable books. Beckett is a good example of trying to get out of the prison we are all in.

Susana Onega: At a given point in the novel, Daniel Martin says: "I create, I am. All the rest is dream, though concrete and executed." Would you say that Mantissa *fictionalizes this statement?*

John Fowles: Mantissa *was meant to be a joke. It was first going to be published by a Californian private printer—he prints very nice books—but unfortunately I was under contract with large British and American publishers. They turned cruel on me, they said, "No, we want this," and this nice little Californian publisher was just pushed out by these large publishing houses. In America and Britain it was really taken much too seriously. I like the French idea of the *jeu d'esprit*, the lighter book. Something you suffer from in America is this belief that your novels must get larger and larger, longer and longer, more and more important, bigger and bigger in every way. This is blowing up a balloon of hot air. I liked the much more European idea of producing very minor works, something you enjoy doing perhaps, do not spend a great deal of time on and that you will not go to the stake for. You will not be martyred for this book. *Mantissa* was really meant to be a comment, no more, on the problems of being a writer. I have always had a kind of belief in the muses. Of course there is not a muse of the novel, but I chose Erato, the muse of lyric love poetry in ancient Greece. The notion that she was locked up with a would-be novelist and of course they really hate each other.

You get this kind of problem when you are writing, or at least I get it, because I am a man often very attached to women characters. You just do not

know when you are writing dialogue—dialogue is the most difficult part, technically, of any novel—you do not know what they are going to say. I had a famous
case in *The French Lieutenant's Woman.* I remember spending a whole day, I
needed one sentence that Sarah, the heroine of *The French Lieutenant's Woman,*
was saying. I tried sentence after sentence, all in the wastepaper basket—and
then I realized she was actually saying, inasmuch as a literary character can be
real, "I don't say anything at this point." She was saying, "Your mistake is
thinking that dialogue here is necessary. It isn't necessary," and so, that is how
it is in the book. She is silent. This relationship you have with main characters
is slightly like the dialogue I put in *Mantissa:* they often seem to be fighting
you. They say, "I'm not going to walk down this road," I'm not going to be
burgled," whatever it is. In a strange way you have to listen to this. It is a little
bit as it is with schoolchildren. Occasionally you have to smack them and say,
"No! You're going to do what I tell you to do!" but, like schoolchildren,
occasionally they are telling you something which you had better listen to if you
are going to be a good teacher.

    Susana Onega: What was your real aim in writing Mantissa? *How con-
sciously did you have Roland Barthes's* Le plaisir du texte *in mind when you
were writing it?*

    John Fowles: I do not think particularly. Dr. Federman yesterday was
giving his views on Derrida, Lacan, Barthes. . . . I am exactly like him. I have
read quite a lot of them on deconstruction and post-structuralism and all the rest
of it. I really do not understand what it is all about. I speak French and I read
French quite well but I am afraid most of it is absolutely over my head. A much
more scholarly English novelist than myself is Iris Murdoch. I heard her saying
only the other day that she regarded it as philosophical nonsense, very largely.
Of course it can be very elegantly expressed; especially Roland Barthes I think
is a good writer, but I am really very doubtful whether all of that has had much
influence on me. In *Mantissa* I was making fun of it, rather crude fun in places.
But I was really expressing the old English view that most of French intellectual
theory since the war has been elegant nonsense . . . attractive nonsense. This is
the old business of the practical English never understanding the very rhetorical
and clever French. France and England are undoubtedly the two countries in
Europe that are furthest apart, although they are so near geographically. The
English are much nearer to Spain, Italy, Greece, than England and France will
ever be.

    Susana Onega: Mantissa *also brings to mind the deconstructivist theory
that there is a unique, all-enveloping written text, a text that is prior to the
writer himself. This reduces the role of the writer to a mere "scriptor," somebody whose only task is to endlessly rewrite this unique and polymorphous text.
Would it be right to say that, for all their thematic and stylistic differences, all
your novels are simply "variations" of the same novel?*

John Fowles: Yes, in one sense. I have often said I have only written about one woman in my life. I mean, I feel that. I do not put it in the novels but I feel when writing that the heroine of one novel is the same woman as the heroine of another novel. They may be different enough in outward characteristics but they are for me a family—just one woman, basically. Novels, where they come from in your mind, whether they come from some prior unconscious text, I think I would really not like to say. I am not sure. I think also we are touching on an area where it is dangerous for the novelist to be too clever. It is like the old story of your watch being slow and you take it to bits to improve the time—and of course you have finally no watch any more. By trying to repair it you have lost it. Usually, when I am asked this kind of question, I say I would rather let others judge, as they certainly have in the past. I think this is a job for the critics. They can say that I have certain characteristics of fictional literary behavior and structure and so on. It is not for me to discover that I am a poor conditioned guinea pig or rabbit. It is safer that I keep that at a distance.

Susana Onega: Most of your novels seem to have been written with a view to parodying well-worn literary traditions: the "confession" and epistolary technique, in The Collector, *for example; the historical romance, in* The French Lieutenant's Woman; *or the "Examinations and Depositions" of convicts in* A Maggot, *which strongly echo the reports made by Daniel Defoe at Newgate. Also, in all your novels there is an explicit reference to certain writers of the past, like Shakespeare, Dickens, Thomas Hardy, or T. S. Eliot, and they even include literal quotations from their works. Why do you do this?*

John Fowles: Do you mean in *A Maggot?*

Susana Onega: In general; specifically in A Maggot.

John Fowles: A Maggot is set in the year 1735 and what I did, although the novel itself is fiction, I suddenly thought one day, I have never liked historical novels—why I have written two I am not quite sure but in general I am much more interested in real history. I would much rather read the historical texts of the period. It occurred to me that in *A Maggot* it would be nice, because I am imitating eighteenth-century dialogue, to give the reader passages from a well-known magazine of the time called *The Gentleman's Magazine,* which all educated people once read. It is also useful because it does give you many authentic facts of the time, and shows how they were printed. English printing was then different. And an impression of the cruelty of the time, because the English then had a barbarous judicial system. If you stole a handkerchief or a spoon then you would probably be hanged in eighteenth-century London—an awful system. I have also always liked the old trial report, where trials are reported in dialogue alone: purely question, answer, question, answer. That is quite common. It did not start with Defoe by any means but I like it, as a novelist, because it sets you an enormous problem. This is another strange thing that novelists have to do to themselves. They have to set themselves difficult situations. If you use this trial technique—question, answer, question, answer—you lose half your arms, half your weapons as a novelist. There is no description of what people are doing . . . "She smiled," "She lit a cigarette" (not in the eighteenth century!); but anything you can say in an ordinary novel is forbidden by using this technique of the trial report. I like that because it also makes your dialogue much better. You have to express far more through your dialogue than you will in an ordinary conversation. A friend of mine in England is the playwright Harold Pinter, and I think he is the chief exponent of this in English. That is, really cutting down to an incredible degree—that is why he is such a good scriptwriter in films— unnecessary dialogue by making every line of his dialogue really work. Every word of it works, even the silences, in his best plays, work. I really wanted in *A Maggot* to use that difficult power of pure dialogue a little, although he is a playwright and of course I am a novelist. I think that the novel has not caught up with the modern world in the sense of what the novelist can leave out. This is one of the great qualities a novelist must have, knowing what to omit, what to leave out. Many novelists, I am afraid I would accuse the Americans a little bit here, write far too many words. They do not let the reader do any work. You must, you see, get the reader on your side and the way to get people on your side is to give them pleasant work or intriguing, interesting work. Therefore, all that you leave out, all the gaps in your text, are so much fuel for this one-to-one relationship you have with the reader. I am guilty of this fault myself. I look through old texts I have written and think I ought to have left many things out. You realize you are much too fat, you are much too rich always; you can be sparer. I was reading a little bit of Cervantes, *Don Quixote*, the other day. Of course that is historical, but I was tempted even then to pick up my blue pencil. There are whole passages where you think, "Well, he doesn't really need that." He is a great writer and of course it is historical and enjoyable, but from a strictly modern point of view—the same is true of Defoe in England—it is their prolixity, their unnecessary prolixity, that strikes me personally when you re-read them.

Susana Onega: Another recurrent feature in your novels is the existence of two complementary and opposed worlds. One seems to be described in realistic terms, while the other is symbolic and mythical. Invariably the mythical realm is an untrimmed garden, a valley, or a combe. This dichotomy between the city and the green world is a traditional one in literature, but in that delightful little autobiography of yours, The Tree, you describe the green world as something real and at hand, you even use proper names, such as Ware Common or Wistman's Wood. Should we take it that there are no boundaries, then, between the real and the unreal?

John Fowles: Well, the real in the general sense, the real for me does not lie where we are now, in other words, in cities. It lies for me very much in the countryside and in the wild. They had a phrase in medieval art, the "hortus conclusus," that is, the garden surrounded by a wall. Very often the Virgin Mary and the Unicorn would be inside this wall and, you see it in medieval painting, everything outside the pretty little walled garden is chaos. I must not get on to ecology and conservation terms. We have ruined the nature of Europe very largely and of course we are busy ruining it in South America and elsewhere now. Man really hates everything outside the "hortus conclusus," this walled garden. We do not like the wilderness, the chaos. The Church was against it for centuries because it was where sin took place. In England, for instance, it was hated because of the Puritan ethos; because man could not get profit, he could not make money out of the chaos, the wilderness. This has always hurt me very profoundly, that we have this profound schism, the schism between us and wild nature. I loved the countryside on the way here to Zaragoza from Barcelona. That, for me, is a kind of paradise still, bare fields (not enough trees, though), a few shepherds, sheep. I really prefer that, I am afraid, to great congregations of human beings. I do not really like speaking to you like this. I do not like crowds of people. If it were possible, I would rather have had half an hour alone with each of you here because that, for me, is where all the reality is. It is in small groups of human beings, ideally in the "I-thou" two-persons confrontation. I really fear for Europe, its increasing cultural and economic madness, the greater crowds, the greater masses, the appalling tendency all over Europe to go to the big city. I know there are wage reasons and all the rest of it, but I am all for getting back to the country. I am all for depopulation. I should not say this in a Catholic country but I find the world population growth abominable. It is one of the worst problems the world has at the moment.

Susana Onega: Women also seem to have a double nature in your novels: Alison's "oxymoron quality," for example, expressed in the splitting into twins, in The Magus; *Sarah's baffling double nature, alternately innocent and corrupt, like Rebecca Hocknell in* A Maggot, *etc. Are women as complex and polymorphous as reality, or literature?*

John Fowles: I have always found them quite exceptionally difficult to . . . well, "handle" is rather an ambiguous word in English. Let me say, to have relations with. I am not a "feminist" in the fiercely active political sense it is usually used in England and America nowadays, but I have sympathy for the general "anima," the feminine spirit, the feminine intelligence, and I think that all male judgments of the way women go about life are so biased that they are virtually worthless. Man is really being a very prejudiced judge of his own case and of course when judging against women. It is counted very bad taste in England now to talk favorably of women's intuition. The real feminists in England do not like this sentimental talk of female intuition. I am afraid I still have some faith in that. Women cannot, I think, sometimes think as logically or rationally as men can, but thinking logically or rationally often leads you into error. It is by no means certain that the result is any worse in a woman, if you like, muddling her way through to a decision, or feeling her emotional way to a decision, than that of a highly rational man. My impression in Spain is that feminism has not really quite got there to the same extent it has with us. Perhaps that is to come.

Susana Onega: There are so many more things I would love to ask you, but I'm afraid the old tyrant, time, won't allow me more than one question before I hand over the microphone to the audience. Let's make it a naughty question: At the end of Mantissa, *the mental walls of Martin Green's hospital room become solid again, trapping the Staff Sister within them. Assuming that she stands for the prototypical literary critic, do we have any reason to hope that there is, after all, a little corner reserved for her within the creative mind, that she is creative in a way?*

John Fowles: Well, the whole of this book, *Mantissa,* takes place in a cell, but of course the cell is the human brain. It all takes place in the brain. It is supposed to be a lunatic asylum and this is where the hero, or anti-hero, of the book is incarcerated. If I could just say, there is an Irishman—we talked a lot about Joyce and Beckett yesterday, but there is a third Irish novelist who I could put very near their level—I do not know if he is known here, his name is Flann O'Brien. He was a journalist, a very funny, humorous journalist also. He had several pseudonyms. Flann O'Brien, I think, was a genius at really absurd humor and that book was behind *Mantissa.* If I went in for dedicating books to other writers, I would have dedicated it to Flann O'Brien. I suspect his humor is very difficult indeed if you are not Irish. Even the English have a little trouble with it. The Irish are a marvelous literary race. Everyone who is not Irish issues a secret little prayer, "I wish I were Irish." They really have superb writers. We owe them a great deal in England, Wales, and Scotland. Sorry, now I have forgotten the question.

Susana Onega: No, that was a very diplomatic answer. I was asking whether the literary critic has a right to have a corner within the creative mind.

John Fowles: Yes, yes, I think so. If you remember, a part of the muse herself is a critic. Whatever inspires you also usefully criticizes what you are.

Susana Onega: Any questions, please? Could you please keep the questions short?

Question from audience: A lot of critics have spoken about the importance of the literary allusions to Victorian novels, particularly in The French Lieutenant's Woman. *But don't you think that perhaps the literary allusions to the poetry of the age are the key to the novel? I mean, to the development of the characters, such as Charles, for instance. I am referring to the allusions to the poetry of Hardy and Tennyson, the epigraphs at the beginning of each chapter. Don't you think they are the key to the development of the characters in the novel?*

John Fowles: No. The answer is "no" because the novel was already written when I fitted in the epigraphs. I picked them just as in the last novel I wrote, *A Maggot*. It was really to give the general feel of the period. They were all well-known writers. They were people who were like illustrations, almost like literal illustrations from the Victorian period, from something like the humorous magazine *Punch*. Certainly now and again, when I was reading generally, I would think, "That would be a good allusion," and I would note it down. But such allusions certainly did not affect the story at all.

   Question from audience: Just a very simple question. I would like you to explain why there are two different endings in The French Lieutenant's Woman.

   John Fowles: Why did I put a double ending in *The French Lieutenant's Woman?* That was purely personal because I knew the novel required the hero and the heroine to part, to separate, yet I was slightly in love with both of them and I wanted them to come together and be happy. This is very familiar when you are writing a novel. You like two characters and you want them to come together and you want a happy ending; but some twentieth-century part of you, who is really the victim of black, absurdist art in a way, says they must split, they must separate. All that happened to me was that I thought, "Why don't I put both endings?" In a way it is so like life. Life also has forks. Very small matters sometimes do bring people together or separate them. We cannot control the present, let alone the future. It was simply that I had the idea that it would be interesting to use both possible ends and leave it to the reader to decide. Lazy readers do not like this; they want clear and definite endings. Many readers, you see, write to me and say, "Did they get together?" or, "Please will you write an addition to the novel?" With *The Collector* I have had that last, especially from South America. They obviously like the idea of English kidnappers of attractive young women. That was the reason, quite simply. A personal problem of my own, which then I thrust onto the reader.

   Susana Onega: Any other questions?

   Question from audience: A very short question. You have said that novelists are sick, obsessive creatures. What about the "Bluebeard syndrome" and the "Camelot syndrome"? How do they relate in your novels?

   John Fowles: I can assure you we are very far from normal creatures. *The Collector* story obsessed me, because by chance a girl was truly kidnapped in South London. This was told in a minor news item, which not only I saw but curiously enough one of the French *nouveaux romanciers*, Simone Jacquemard. She wrote a novel also about it, much more metaphysical and abstract than mine. It was a strange case and I suspect quite a lot of novelists who happened to see it were struck by it. A young man captured a girl and he put her in an air-raid shelter, he made her undress to her underclothes and he told her to dig a hole through to Australia; a hole through the entire Earth in this tiny air-raid shelter, not much bigger than this table. The curious fact is he did not molest her sexually at all. I do not know all the details of the real case but I have the impression that something about the girl had made her a willing victim and the man was obviously mad. The girl did not seem to make any attempt to escape and of course this has become a well-known syndrome now of the relationship that develops between kidnapper and kidnapped. For some extraordinary reason they almost fall in love, certainly into mutual respect, in some of these more outrageous cases. I also saw the Bluebeard in Bartók's opera, *Bluebeard's Castle*. I was very fond of Bartók's music at the time and it had not occurred to me, the Bluebeard connection. I did not really use it in the novel very much, but it had an effect when I was writing it. And of course Miranda and *The Tempest* parallel. That was an obvious twist, really, a symbolic twist.

Susana Onega: Thank you. Any other questions?

Question from audience: A short question. Do you actually enjoy writing? There are writers who feel a need to write but do not enjoy the business of writing. Do you find it pleasurable?

John Fowles: Do I enjoy life?

Susana Onega: No, do you enjoy writing?

John Fowles: Oh yes, I am sorry. I thought you were asking if I enjoyed life. I was going to say that no writer really enjoys life. It is an impossibility. We enjoy it occasionally but writing novels you have to be a moody person, you have to be up and down, gullible one moment, cynical the next. So that is answered. Writing, very largely, is an "up" moment. Some writing is just boring. It is like digging a long trench or making a road; in other words it is largely mechanical . . . I suppose "bureaucratic" would be a better word for it. First draft writing, when you are first writing, even a simple piece, is always a pleasure because words are so complicated, there are so many ways to handle them. You can feel happy with just a single page or a paragraph, if you are lucky you have solved some little problem, you have made something shorter, you have made it crisper, you have made it more poetic, whatever it is. I cannot imagine not being a writer. I was once on a T.V. program in America with Truman Capote . . . I will not say "God bless him." I foolishly said that even if I would never be published I would still go on writing just because the activity of writing was for me miraculous, marvelous in the old sense. He mocked me; he said he wrote only for money. The only near parallel I know to it is what I feel in nature watching plants, birds occasionally, but writing is really on a level of its own. I am not in the least a religious person, but it is the nearest you get to religious experience, that shaman thing, speaking for the tribe. So the answer is "Yes." If you do not enjoy writing, do not be a novelist. It is also essential that you love it because a lot of it is so long, so time-consuming; and it is very psyche-draining, that is, it drains your psyche, your private soul. After you have finished a novel you feel totally drained and you think you will never write again, you do not want to write again, you never want to hear the word "litera-ture" again. It is very strange. You are like an empty cistern; gradually the water, some kind of rain falls and the water seeps in and it begins to fill again. That side of writing is rather terrifying, the way it empties you psychologically.

Susana Onega: And the last question, if there is one?

Question from audience: The narrator appears twice in The French Lieutenant's Woman. *The first time he is described as a Victorian preacher and the second time as a modern person, I think you say "rather frenchified," with a touch of the modern impresario about him. Do you identify yourself with one of these descriptions?*

John Fowles: The answer to that is very simple. Yes, with both. I put myself in that book first of all as a hellfire preacher. You would not, well, I suppose you might, know them in Spain. They were a feature of Victorian England. They were the preachers who used to thunder at people and warned them of the terrible penalties of hell if they drank gin or if they even looked at a woman. It was really a specialty of the dissenting sects, the Protestant sects, not the Church of England, far more narrow and puritanical than that is. Then I put myself in as a kind of opera impresario because he has features of the novelist. One is always torn, whether the novel is a pulpit or not. It is very difficult in England because people hate being preached to. When I started in England I used to get this dreadful word, "didactic," used of me, always in an insulting way. I was "that dreadful didactic writer," trying to teach people how to behave in their morals, their politics and all the rest of it. That, I think, was really why I made myself into this parody of a hellfire preacher; and of course in another way novelists are, although our operas are for one person only, not unlike impresarios. We have these characters who are not quite flesh and blood but we hope to convince people by telling lies that they are real. When I say that all novelists are liars, of course you have to ask another question back at me, which is "Is the lie always a bad thing?" I think a lot of human pleasure has to do with lying, and so has a lot of human civilized behavior. We even have in English a nice expression for that . . . the "white lie"—the lie told by a good person to be kind to somebody else. "Have you read my latest novel?" You answer that you find it excellent, although you truly think it is absolutely awful. There are all sorts of situations where I think the word "lie" is much too clumsy-blanket a word to mean much. Fiction is the business of telling falsehoods about people who do not even exist. So, in that sense, you are lying.

Susana Onega: I am afraid we will have to put an end to this engaging discussion. We are all sorry, I know, but "that is life." We have to go. Thank you very much indeed.

[Transcription from the tape by Richard Pilcher]

Notes

Chapter 1

1. That is, we have the same story told twice from different perspectives. Thus *The Collector* may be described, in Genette's terminology *(Figures III)*, as a narrative with variable internal focalization where the second version functions as a homodiegetic internal analepsis.

2. Or hypodiscourse, in Mieke Bal's terminology *(Narratologie)*. On this point see also Genette's *Nouveau discours du récit*.

3. In Mieke Bal's terminology, coined for her English revised edition of *De theorie van vertellen en verhalen*, entitled *Narratology. Introduction to the Theory of Narrative* (p. 146).

4. Boris Eikhembaum greatly contributed to the classification of fiction by establishing the differences between the novel and the short story: "Le roman et la nouvelle ne sont pas des formes homogènes, mais au contraire des formes profondément étrangères l'une à l'autre . . . Le roman est une forme syncrétique . . . la nouvelle est une forme fondamentale, élémentaire (ce qui ne veut pas dire primitive). Le roman vient de l'histoire, du récit de voyages; la nouvelle vient du conte, de l'anecdote" ("Sur la théorie de la prose," in *Théorie de la littérature*, T. Todorov, ed., p. 202).

5. "Sexual prowess and sexual licence both tended to be linked with the aristocracy and the gentry in the middle-class belief. Defoe, for example, placed the responsibility for the immorality of the times squarely on the upper classes, and it is natural that dislike of the upper-class licence should extend to the literature which expressed middle-class opinions" (Watt, *The Rise . . .* , p. 163).

6. Robert Humphrey defines the soliloquy in the "stream-of consciousness" novel as "the technique of representing the psychic content and processes of a character directly from character to reader without the presence of an author, but with an audience tacitly assumed . . . the point of view is always the character's, and the level of consciousness is usually close to the surface" *(Stream-of-Consciousness . . .* , p. 36).

7. For a general view of the author's interpretation of Heraclitus's theory, see *The Aristos* (1964) 1980.

Chapter 2

1. Most existing criticism of the novel (mostly American) was published before the appearance of the 1977 revised edition. The present chapter, however, is based on the second, revised edition

of 1977, which no doubt Fowles himself considers to be an improvement on the first. On this see Fowles's foreword to the revised edition.

2. Joseph Campbell aptly synthesizes the threefold formula of the mythological adventure of the hero: "A hero ventures forth from the world of common day into a region of supernatural wonder; fabulous forces are there encountered and a decisive victory is won: the hero comes back from this mysterious adventure with the power to bestow boons on his fellow men" *(The Hero . . . ,* p. 30).

3. "Tout miroir interne réfléchissant l'ensemble du récit par reduplication simple, répétée, ou specieuse" (Dällenbach, *Le récit,* p. 52).

4. "L'éclatement consiste dans la dispersion des éléments de l'histoire-résumé à travers l'histoire principale. Chaque élément repéré ailleurs renvoie à la mise en abyme, qui, à son tour, renvoie au roman entier. Celui-ci perd ainsi son charactère linéaire parce que le dénouement vers lequel il évolue, se trouve révélé dès le début et resurgit partout" (Bal, *Narratologie,* p. 107).

5. In "John Fowles: Radical Romancer," Ronald Binns has stressed the links between *The Magus* and the traditional romance, establishing a series of parallelisms with Mrs. Radcliff's *The Mysteries of Udolpho,* which he takes to be *The Magus's* major source. "The gothic," Binn says, "is a deeply theatrical genre since, as Fiedler points out, many of its devices were borrowed from the stage. In *The Magus* the properties of suspense and sensation are brought out into the open, and almost from the beginning Nicholas is made aware that he is the voluntary leading-player in an elaborately arranged masque—or novel. His rationalist sensibility sustains a running commentary on the dramatic action together with an analytical forecast of what will happen next, but it is one of the meanings of the parable that his rationalism should prove always one step behind Conchis's godgame" (p. 326).

6. "L'icône diagrammatique *resemble* par analogie, à un signifié: si ce signifié est le récit entier dans lequel l'icône fonctionne, on peu parler d'une mise en abyme" (Bal, *Narratologie,* p. 108).

7. "Le plus troublant de la métalepse est bien dans cette hypothèse inacceptable et insistante, que l'extradiégetique est peut-être toujours déjà diégetique, et que le narrateur et ses narrataires, c'est-à-dire vous et moi, appartenons peut-être encore à quelque récit" (Genette, *Figures III,* p. 245).

Chapter 3

1. Fowles himself confirmed this interpretation in the A.E.D.E.A.N. interview (Onega, "Fowles," p. 75) when he answered the following question:

> *Question from the audience:* The narrator appears twice in *The French Lieutenant's Woman.* The first time he is described as a Victorian preacher, and the second time as a modern person, I think you say "rather frenchified," with a touch of the modern impresario about him. Do you identify yourself with one of these descriptions?
> *John Fowles:* The answer to that is very simple. Yes, with both. I put myself in that book first of all as a hellfire preacher. . . . Then I put myself in as a kind of opera impresario because he has features of the novelist.

2. Fowles explained in the A.E.D.E.A.N. interview (ibid., pp. 72–73) his real aim in prefacing every chapter of *The French Lieutenant's Woman* with quotations from Victorian writings:

> *Question from the audience:* Don't you think perhaps the literary allusions to the poetry

of the age are the key to the novel? I mean to the development of the characters, such as Charles, for instance?

John Fowles: No, the answer is "no" because the novel was already written when I fitted in the epigraphs. I picked them just as in the last novel I wrote, *A Maggot.* It was really to give the general feel of the period. . . . Certainly now and again, when I was reading generally, I would think, "that would be a good allusion," and I would note it down. But such allusions certainly did not affect the story at all.

Chapter 4

1. For example Peter Wolfe (*John Fowles, Magus and Moralist,* p. 182) and Peter Conradi (*John Fowles,* p. 95).

2. "et n'hésite pas à établir entre narrateur et personnage[s] une relation variable ou flotante, vertige pronominal accordé à une logique plus libre, et à une idée plus complexe de la 'personalité'" (*Figures III,* p. 253).

3. On this point, see also R. Alter (*"Daniel Martin* and the Mimetic Task," p. 70).

4. Andrea's death strongly echoes Alison's feigned suicide in *The Magus.*

5. Fowles has explained how *Daniel Martin* developed from this image: "In . . . one of my favourite novels in fact, *Daniel Martin,* I did have an image that in the novel is at the very end of the book. It was of a woman standing in a desert somewhere. I did not at that time even know where it was. She seemed to be weeping, to be lost, a moment of total desolation" (Onega, "Fowles," p. 61).

Chapter 5

1. Fowles has obliquely tried to cope with this anxiety by presenting novel writing as a visionary and compulsive activity, the product of genius, rather than of reason and logic. In the A.E.D.E.A.N. interview ("Fowles," p. 63) John Fowles made Nicholas Humphreys' theory his, that "playwrights, poets, novelists can all be associated with the notion of the shaman speaking both to and for the tribe," and said his novels are never written according to an elaborate, prepared plan, but on the contrary are made up of "ideas (that) flow in on you with such force that very often you cannot write them down, they come too fast" (ibid., p. 62). At the same time, Fowles rejected theory as a necessary part of the writing activity: "A novelist is truly very different from an expert on literature. We do not have to have ordered minds, we do not have to know Derrida and Barthes or the great theorists backwards" (ibid., p. 60), although he finally admitted that, in his case, the shamanistic inspiration only applies to "the writing of the first draft" (ibid., p. 63).

2. To my question (ibid., p. 67), "Would it be right to say that, for all their thematic and stylistic differences, all your novels are simply "variations" of the same novel?" John Fowles answered,

   Yes, in one sense. I have often said I have only written about one woman in my life. I mean, I feel that. I do not put it in the novels but I feel when writing that the heroine of one novel is the same woman as the heroine of another novel. They may be different enough in outward characteristics but they are for me a family—just one woman, basically. Novels, where they come from in your mind, whether they come from some prior unconscious text, I think I would really not like to say. I am not sure. I think also we are touching on an area where it is dangerous for the novelist to be too clever. . . . This is a job for the critics. They can say that I have certain characteristics of fictional literary behaviour and structure and so on. It is not for me to discover that I am a poor conditioned guinea pig or rabbit. It is safer that I keep that at a distance.

Chapter 6

1. As Elizabeth MacAndrew observes, "[In] the earliest Gothic romances . . . good and evil are starkly differentiated absolutes, but as succeeding works delved deeper into the idea of evil as psychological, evil quickly began to be seen as relative and in no time its pleasures were being explored" *(The Gothic Tradition in Fiction,* p. 4).

2. Here Fowles takes up and develops the same kind of symbolism he uses to express the archetypal complementarity of Alison/Lily/Rose when he makes Nicholas Urfe find the green pot of flowers on Conchis's tombstone "in which sat, rising from a cushion of inconspicuous white flowers (alisons) a white arum lily and a red rose" *(The Magus,* p. 559).

3. In private conversation John Fowles told me that his editors did not like the title of the novel, but this time they respected it, which hadn't been the case with *Variations.* The Spanish and French translators, however, have yielded to the temptation of avoiding the literal translation, in order to give more euphonic versions of it. The Spanish title, *Capricho* (1987), evokes the meaning of "maggot" as "whim or quirk" and also echoes Goya's "Caprichos," but, like the French title *La créature* (1987), fails to render the archetypal meaning of "maggot," thus unduly missing its most basic connotation.

Bibliography

Allen, Walter. 1970. "The Achievement of John Fowles," *Encounter* XXV 2 (August): 64–67.

Adam, Ian. 1972. *"The French Lieutenant's Woman:* A Discussion," *Victorian Studies* 15 (March): 344–47.

Alter, Robert. 1981. *"Daniel Martin* and the Mimetic Task," *Genre* (Spring) 15 (1): 65–78.

Amory, Mark. 1974. "Tales Out of School," London *Sunday Times Magazine* (22 September): 33–34, 36.

Bal, Mieke. 1977. *Narratologie (Essais sur la signification narrative dans quatre romans modernes).* Paris: Editions Klinksiek.

———. 1985. *Narratology. Introduction to the Theory of Narrative.* Toronto, Buffalo, London: Univ. Toronto Press. Translation revised and adapted for English-language readers by Christine van Boheemen, of the second revised edition of *De theorie van vertellen en verhalen* (1980, 1st. ed. 1978).

Baker, James R. 1986. "An Interview with John Fowles," *Michigan Quarterly Review* (Fall) 25 (4): 661–83.

Barnum, Carol. 1981. "John Fowles's *Daniel Martin:* A Vision of Whole Sight," *The Literary Review* Vol. 25, no. 1 (Fall): 64–79.

Barthes, Roland. 1968. "L'effet de réel," *Communications* No. 11. Paris: Editions du Seuil.

———. 1974. *S/Z.* New York: Hill & Wang. Transl. by Richard Miller from *S/Z* (1970).

———. 1975. *The Pleasure of the Text.* New York: Hill & Wang. Transl. by Richard Miller from *Le plaisir du texte* (1973).

———. 1977. "The Death of the Author," in *Image-Music-Text.* London: Fontana. This book contains thirteen essays published between 1961 and 1973, selected by Heath.

Bergonzi, Bernard. (1970) 1979. *The Situation of the Novel.* London and Basingstoke: Macmillan.

Binns, Ronald. 1973. "John Fowles: Radical Romancer," *Critical Quarterly* 15 (Winter) 1973: 317–34.

———. 1979. "Beckett, Lowry and the Anti-Novel," in *The Contemporary English Novel,* Malcolm Bradbury and David Palmer, eds. London: Edward Arnold, 89–112.

Bratlinger, Patrick. 1972. *"The French Lieutenant's Woman:* A Discussion," *Victorian Studies* 15 (March): 339–43.

Burden, Robert. 1979. "The Novel Interrogates Itself: Parody and Self-Consciousness in Contemporary English Fiction," in *The Contemporary English Novel,* Malcolm Bradbury and David Palmer, eds. London: Edward Arnold, 138–55.

Byron, Lord George Gordon, 6th. 1901. "First Letter on Bowles' *Strictures on Pope,"* in *The Works of Lord Byron: Letters and Journals* (six vols.) Rowland E. Prothero, ed. London, Vol. V, appendix 3, p. 554.

Campbell, Joseph. (1948) 1973. *The Hero with a Thousand Faces*. Princeton, N.J.: Princeton Univ. Press.

Campbell, Robert. 1983. "John Fowles. *Mantissa*," *Critical Quarterly* Vol. 25, no. 3 (Autumn): 84–86.

Chittick, K. A. 1985. "The Laboratory of Narrative and John Fowles's *Daniel Martin*," *English Studies in Canada* XI, I (March): 70–81.

Conradi, Peter. 1982. *John Fowles*. London: Methuen.

Dällenbach, Lucien. 1977. *Le récit spéculaire*. Paris: Editions du Seuil.

Defoe, Daniel. (1724) 1964. *Roxana or the Unfortunate Mistress*. London: Oxford Univ. Press.

Derrida, Jacques. 1976. *Of Grammatology*. Baltimore, Md.: John Hopkins Univ. Press. Transl. by Gayatri Chakravorty Spivak from *De la grammatologie* (1967).

———. 1985. *A Maggot*. London: Jonathan Cape.

Eliot, George. (1871–72) 1987. *Middlemarch*. Harmondsworth: Penguin.

Eliot, T. S. (1936) 1972. *Four Quartets*. London: Faber and Faber.

Eikhembaum, Boris. 1965. "Sur la théorie de la prose," in *Théorie de la litterature*. T. Todorov, ed. Paris: Editions du Seuil, pp. 192–212.

Evarts, Prescott, Jr. 1972. "Fowles' *The French Lieutenant's Woman* as Tragedy," *Critique* XIII, no. 3, 57–69.

Federman, Raymond. 1975. *Surfiction: Fiction Now . . . and Tomorrow*. Chicago, Ill.: Chicago Univ. Press.

Ferris, Ina. 1982. "Realist Intention and Mythic Impulse in *Daniel Martin*," *The Journal of Narrative Technique* Vol. 12, no. 2 (Spring): 146–53.

Fowles, John. 1963. *The Collector*. Tiptree, Essex: The Anchor Press.

———. (1964) 1980. *The Aristos*. Tiptree, Essex: The Anchor Press.

———. 1964. "On Being English but Not British," *The Texas Quarterly* 7 (Autumn): 154–62.

———. (1966) revised ed. 1977. *The Magus*. London: Jonathan Cape.

———. (1969) 1983. *The French Lieutenant's Woman*. Bungay, Suffolk: Triad/Granada.

———. 1974. *The Ebony Tower*. London: Jonathan Cape.

———. 1977. *Daniel Martin*. London: Jonathan Cape.

———. 1979. *The Tree*. New York: The Ecco Press.

———. 1982. *Mantissa*. London: Jonathan Cape.

Frias, Piedad. 1984. *Approximación al estudio de Lucky Jim: la obra en su entorno socio-cultural*. Unpublished M.A. Dissertation. Facultad de Filosofia y Letras: Universidad de Zaragoza.

Gardner, John. 1977. "In Defense of the Real," *Saturday Review* (1 October): 22–24.

Garret, Peter K. 1980. *The Victorian Multiplot Novel: Studies in Dialogical Form*. New Haven & London: Yale Univ. Press.

Gass, William H. 1970. *Fiction and the Figures of Life*. New York: New York Univ. Press.

Genette, Gérard. 1972. *Figures III*. Paris: Editions du Seuil.

———. 1980. *Narrative Discourse. An Essay in Method*. Transl. by Jane E. Lewin from "Discours du récit: essai de méthode," a portion of *Figures III*. New York: Cornell Univ. Press.

Gotts, Ian. 1985. "Fowles' *Mantissa*: Funfair in Another Village," *Critique* XXVI (Winter): 81–95.

Gussow, Mel. 1977. "Talk with John Fowles," *New York Times Book Review* (13 November): 3, 84–85.

Halpern, Daniel. 1971. "A Sort of Exile in Lyme Regis," *London Magazine* (March): 34–46.

Hardy, Thomas. (1888) 1976. *The Wessex Tales*. London: Macmillan.

Huffaker, Robert. 1980. *John Fowles*. Boston: Twayne Publishers.

Humphrey, Robert. 1954. *Stream-of-Consciousness in the Modern Novel*. Berkeley, Ca.: Univ. California Press.

James, Henry. (1934) 1984. "Preface to *The Tragic Muse*," in *The Art of the Novel*. New York: Northeastern Univ. Press.

Jung, Carl G. (1956) 1981. "Symbols of the Mother and of Rebirth," in *Symbols of Transformation. The Collected Works*. Vol. V, Sir Herbert Read et al., eds. London & Henley: Routledge & Kegan Paul, pp. 207–72. Transl. by R. F. C. Hull from *Wandlungen und Symbole der Libido* (1912).

––––––. (1956) 1981. "The Battle for Deliverance from the Mother," in *Symbols of Transformation. The Collected Works*. Vol. V, Sir Herbert Read et al., eds. London & Henley: Routledge & Kegan Paul, pp. 274–305. Transl. by R. F. C. Hull from *Wandlungen und Symbole der Libido* (1912).

––––––. (1959) 1980. "Concerning Rebirth," in *The Archetypes and the Collective Unconscious. The Collected Works*. Vol. IX (part I), Sir Herbert Read et al., eds. London & Henley: Routledge & Kegan Paul, pp. 113–47. Transl. by R. F. C. Hull from "Über Wiedergeburt," *Gestaltungen des Unbewussten* (1950).

––––––. (1958) 1981. "Psychology and Religion," in *Psychology and Religion: East and West. The Collected Works*. Vol. XI, Sir Herbert Read et al., eds. London & Henley: Routledge & Kegan Paul, pp. 3–105. Originally publ. in English as *The Terry Lectures* of 1937. Revised and augmented 1940.

––––––. (1958) 1981. "A Psychological Approach to the Dogma of the Trinity," in *Psychology and Religion: West and East. The Collected Works*. Vol. XI, Sir Herbert Read et al., eds. London & Henley: Routledge & Kegan Paul, pp. 107–200. Transl. by R. F. C. Hull from "Versuch zu einer psychologischen Deutung des Trinitätsdogmas," *Symbolick des Geistes* (1948).

Karl, Frederick R. 1959. *A Reader's Guide to the Contemporary English Novel*. London: Thames & Hudson.

Laughlin, Rosemary M. 1972. "Faces of Power in the Novels of John Fowles." *Critique* 13: 71–88.

Leitch, Vincent B. 1983. *Deconstructive Criticism: An Advanced Introduction*. London: Hutchinson Univ. Press.

Lodge, David. 1971. *The Novelist at the Crossroads*. London: Routledge & Kegan Paul.

––––––. 1981. "Ambiguous Ever After: Problematic Endings in English Fiction," in *Working with Structuralism*. London: Routledge & Kegan Paul, pp. 143–55.

Loveday, Simon. 1980. "The Style of John Fowles: Tense and Person in the First Chapter of *Daniel Martin*," *The Journal of Narrative Technique* Vol. 10, no. 3 (Fall): 198–204.

MacAndrew, Elizabeth. (1924) 1979. *The Gothic Tradition in Fiction*. New York: Columbia Univ. Press.

McSweeney, Kerry. 1987. "Withering into the Truth: John Fowles and *Daniel Martin*," *Critical Quarterly* Vol. 20, no. 4 (Winter): 31–38.

––––––. 1983. "John Fowles's Variations," in *Four Contemporary Writers: Angus Wilson, Brian Moore, John Fowles, V. S. Naipaul*. Québec: McGill-Queen's Univ. Press & London: Scolar Press.

Mellors, John. 1975. "Collectors and Creators: The Novels of John Fowles," *London Magazine* (February/March): 65–72.

Miller, Walter, Jr. 1985. "Chariots and Goddesses, or What?," *The New York Times Book Review* (8 September): 11.

Morrison, Blake. 1980. *The Movement: Poetry and Fiction of the 1950s*. Oxford and New York: Oxford Univ. Press.

Moynahan, Julian. 1985. "Fly Casting," *New Republic* 193 (7 October): 47–49.

Newquist, Roy (ed). 1964. "John Fowles," in *Counterpoint*. Chicago, Ill.: Rand MacNally, pp. 218–25.

Marlowe, Christopher. (1616) 1969. *Dr. Faustus*. Harmondsworth: Penguin.

Norris, Christopher. 1982. *Deconstruction: Theory and Practice*. London & New York: Methuen.

O'Brien, Flann. (1939) 1986. *At Swim-Two Birds*. Harmondsworth: Penguin.

Olshen, Barry N. 1978. *John Fowles*. New York: Frederick Ungar Publ. Co.

Onega, Susana. 1983. "Amor y muerte en *The Wessex Tales,* de Thomas Hardy," in *Cruz Ansata Ensayos.* Universidad Central de Bayamon Vol. 6 Almeria: Publigraph 181–94.

――――. 1987. "Form and Meaning in *The French Lieutenant's Woman,*" *Revista Canaria de Estudios Ingleses* No. 13/14 Abril, 77–107.

――――. 1988. "Fowles on Fowles," *Actas del X Congreso Nacional de A.E.D.E.A.N.* Zaragoza: Libreria General, pp. 57–76.

Pope, Alexander. 1939–1967. *The Poems of Alexander Pope.* John Butt, ed. 10 vols. London: Methuen.

Rankin, Elizabeth D. 1973. "Cryptic Coloration in *The French Lieutenant's Woman,*" *The Journal of Narrative Technique* 3 (September): 193–207.

Richardson, Samuel. (1740) 1969. *Pamela, or Virtue Rewarded.* Vols. I and II, London: Dent.

Ricks, Christopher. 1970. "The Unignorable Real," *New York Review of Books* 12 (February): 24.

Robinson, Robert. 1974. "Giving the Reader a Choice. A Conversation with John Fowles," *Listener* 92 (31 October): 584.

Sage, Lorna. 1974. "John Fowles," Profile 7, *The New Review,* London, Vol. 1, no. 7 (October): 31–37.

Scholes, Robert. 1967. *The Fabulators.* New York and Oxford: Oxford Univ. Press.

Shaw, Patricia. 1981. "The Role of the University in Modern English Fiction," *Atlantis* 3 no. 1, 44–68.

Spender, Stephen. (1933) 1978. *The Thirties and after: Poetry, Politics, People.* London: Macmillan.

Stolley, Richard B. 1970. *"The French Lieutenant's Woman*'s Man: Novelist John Fowles," *Life* 68 (29 May): 55–60.

Todorov, Tvetan, ed. 1965. *Théorie de la littérature.* Paris: Editions du Seuil.

Watt, Ian. (1957) 1974. *The Rise of the Novel: Studies in Defoe, Richardson and Fielding.* London: Chatto & Windus.

Waugh, Patricia. 1984. *Metafiction: The Theory and Practice of Self-Conscious Fiction.* London & New York: Methuen.

Wolfe, Peter. (1976) 1979. *John Fowles, Magus and Moralist.* London: Associated Univ. Press.

Woodcock, Bruce. 1984. *John Fowles and Masculinity.* Brighton: The Harvester Press Ltd.

Zöckler, Otto. 1877. *The Cross of Christ.* Transl. by Maurice Evans from *Das Kreuz Christus* (1875). London: Hodder and Stoughton.

Index

Note: John Fowles's books are individually listed. F. = John Fowles. Character names are followed by the abbreviations for the relevant book: